教育部人文社会科学研究青年基金项目

（19YJC740027）资助

浙大宁波理工学院外国语学院著作出版资助

汉语动名四字词语搭配在阅读加工中的眼动研究

李辉　著

中国宇航出版社
·北京·

图书在版编目（CIP）数据

汉语动名四字词语搭配在阅读加工中的眼动研究 / 李辉著. -- 北京 : 中国宇航出版社, 2023.9
ISBN 978-7-5159-2281-2

Ⅰ. ①汉… Ⅱ. ①李… Ⅲ. ①汉语－词语－研究 Ⅳ. ①H13

中国国家版本馆CIP数据核字(2023)第179515号

策划编辑 李琬琪　**封面设计** 李彦生
责任编辑 刘　杰　**责任校对** 李光燕

出　版
发　行 中国宇航出版社
社　址 北京市阜成路8号　**邮　编** 100830
（010）68768548
网　址 www.caphbook.com
经　销 新华书店
发行部 （010）68767386　（010）68371900
（010）68767382　（010）88100613（传真）
零售店 读者服务部
（010）68371105
承　印 北京厚诚则铭印刷科技有限公司
版　次 2023年9月第1版　2023年9月第1次印刷
规　格 880×1230　**开　本** 1/32
印　张 8.25　**字　数** 192千字
书　号 ISBN 978-7-5159-2281-2
定　价 68.00元

前　言

“搭配”（collocation）是指频繁共现的关联词对。搭配是程式语的一种，它比成语、词串更灵活，比自由词语组合更巩固。大量的言语产出研究发现，搭配的运用让语言表达更流畅，更准确。搭配知识是二语学习的重要内容，掌握搭配知识能有效促进学习者的阅读、写作等产出和接受技能。搭配分为语法搭配（e.g.，by chance）和词语搭配（e.g.，heavy rain）。

搭配是心理语言学、二语教学、语料库语言学等领域重要的研究课题。英语搭配的研究开始较早，并且已取得了丰硕的研究成果。汉语搭配，被广泛用于汉语书面和口语当中，然而，相关的研究却十分鲜见。众所周知，汉语与拼音文字的书写系统非常不同，汉语既不存在标记词边界的空格，也不存在任何其他标记词边界信息的语法特征，如英文中的词缀等等。汉语书写系统本身的特性导致汉语中的词具有模糊性以外，读者对词的概念也非常模糊，不同的人对词边界的划分不尽一致（Li et al. 2011），这无疑增加了汉语阅读中搭配加工的难度。由于英汉两种语言存在诸多差异，所以英语搭配的研究成果未必能完全解释汉语搭配加工机制。

本书聚焦汉语动名四字词语搭配（如“保护环境”），本书之所以选择汉语动名搭配为研究对象，是因为动名搭配是汉语中非常常用的搭配，具有代表性。基于以往的搭配研究成果，本书关注三个研究问题：（1）与汉语非搭配相比，汉语搭配是否具有加工优势？（2）如果汉语搭配具有加工优势，那么它是整体加工还是成分加工？（3）在句子阅读中，影响汉语搭配加工的因素有哪些？

为了回答以上三个问题，本书中包含三个研究，以及五个眼动实验。研究发现：在加工速度上，汉语词语搭配与非搭配相比更快，具有加工优势；搭配加工中既存在整体加工，又存在成分加工；语境预测性、搭配强度和联想强度影响阅读中汉语词语搭配的加工，其中搭配强度效应与语境预测性效应相互独立，而联想强度效应受语境预测性效应的影响。基于本研究的实验发现，我们提出了汉语动名搭配加工模型，该模型主要解释了汉语动名词语搭配的加工过程。

本研究的结论可以为汉语搭配和程式语的深入研究，为汉语词语搭配习得和运用提供参考，为汉语阅读眼动模型发展提供数据支持。当然，本研究也存在着一定的局限性，未来可利用事件相关电位技术对汉语词语搭配的大脑认知加工进行研究，对汉语词语搭配加工的其他影响因素开展进一步的实验研究。

本书得到了教育部人文社会科学研究青年基金项目（19YJC740027）和浙大宁波理工学院外国语学院著作出版资助。本书在撰写的过程中得到了我的导师浙江大学王小潞教授、曲阜师范大学李德高教授和英国莱斯特大学实验心理学与视觉科学学院凯文·B·佩特森（Kevin B. Paterson）教授的指导和帮助，在此表示诚挚的谢意。本书的出版还要特别感谢浙大宁波理工学院外国语学院领导和同事们的大力支持和帮助。

李辉

2023 年 6 月 6 日

Contents

Chapter 1 Introduction..1

1.1 Research background..1

1.2 Research objectives and questions..10

1.3 Research significance...12

1.4 Organization of the dissertation..14

Chapter 2 Literature Review..16

2.1 Working definition of collocations..16

2.2 Classification of collocations...20

2.3 Identification of collocations...21

2.4 Theoretical framework...23

2.4.1 Lexical priming theory..24

2.4.2 Usage-based theory and exemplar-based theory....................................26

2.4.3 Holistic processing theories...29

2.4.4 Analytic processing theory..31

2.4.5 Parallel processing theory..32

2.5 The processing of English collocation...33

2.5.1 The processing advantage of English collocation..................................33

2.5.2 Processing patterns of English collocation..38

2.5.3 Factors affecting the processing of English collocation.........................41

2.6 The processing of Chinese formulaic language..58

2.6.1 The processing of Chinese idioms..58

2.6.2 The processing of Chinese collocations..62

2.7 Conclusion........64

Chapter 3 Methodology........66

3.1 Introduction........66

3.2 Eye movements during reading........67

3.2.1 Background information of eye movements........67

3.2.2 Eye-tracking technology........72

3.2.3 Eye movement measures........73

3.2.4 Models of eye movement control during reading........75

3.2.5 Parafoveal processing during reading........81

3.3 Conclusion........88

Chapter 4 Study I: The Processing Advantages of Chinese Collocations........89

4.1 Introduction........89

4.2 Experiment 1: Comparison between Chinese collocations and non-collocations........90

4.2.1 Method........90

4.2.2 Results........96

4.2.3 Discussion........99

4.3 Conclusion........101

Chapter 5 Study II: Holistic or Analytic Processing........102

5.1 Introduction........102

5.2 Experiment 2: Manipulating the preview of the noun........108

5.2.1 Method........108

5.2.2 Results........113

5.2.3 Discussion........117

5.3 Experiment 3: Manipulating the preview of the last character......119
5.3.1 Method......119
5.3.2 Results......123
5.3.3 Discussion......127
5.4 Conclusion......128

Chapter 6 Study III: Influencing Factors......130
6.1 Introduction......130
6.2 Experiment 4: Effects of collocation strength and context......134
6.2.1 Methods......134
6.2.2 Results......138
6.2.3 Discussion......141
6.3 Experiment 5: Effects of association strength and context......143
6.3.1 Methods......143
6.3.2 Results......148
6.3.3 Discussion......152
6.4 Conclusion......153

Chapter 7 General Discussion......157
7.1 Introduction......157
7.2 The processing features of Chinese collocations......157
7.2.1 Quicker processing for collocations than non-collocations......157
7.2.2 Integration of both holistic and analytical processing......160
7.2.3 Linguistic factors influencing collocational processing......163
7.3 The processing model for Chinese verb-noun collocations......166
7.4 Conclusion......169

Chapter 8 Conclusion 170
8.1 Major findings 170
8.2 Implications 172
8.2.1 Theoretical implications 172
8.2.2 Practical implications 175
8.3 Limitations and suggestions for future studies 176
8.3.1 Limitations 176
8.3.2 Suggestions for future studies 177

Appendices 178
Appendix 1: Materials for Experiment 1 178
Appendix 2: Materials for Experiment 2 185
Appendix 3: Substitute Characters for Experiment 2 191
Appendix 4: Materials for Experiment 3 194
Appendix 5: Substitute Characters for Experiment 3 200
Appendix 6: Materials for Experiment 4 203
Appendix 7: Materials for Experiment 5 212

References 220

List of Abbreviations

2C	two-character
4C	rour-character
AoA	age of acquisition
CVCP model	Chinese verb-noun collocation processing model
CSL	Chinese as a second language
EER	emotional experience rating
FC	fixation count
FFD	first fixation duration
GD	gaze duration
L1	first language
L2	second language
M	mean
MCU	multi-constituent unit
MI	mutual information
ms	millisecond
NNSs	non-native speakers
NoS	number of strokes
NSs	native speakers
oFREQ	objective word frequency
oNOM	objective number of meanings
PoF	parafoveal-on-foveal

RPD	regression path duration
RRT	rereading time
RT	reaction time
SD	standard deviation
SFD	single fixation duration
sFREQ	subjective word frequency
SKIP	word-skipping
sNOM	subjective number of meanings
SER	sensory experience rating
ST	semantic transparency
TP	transitional probability
TRT	total reading time

Chapter 1 Introduction

1.1 Research background

Formulaic language has been studied in corpus linguistics and psycholinguistics. Formulaic language (frequently co-occurring sequences) include idioms (*black sheep, tie the knot*), collocations (*black coffee, shake hands*), binomials (*knife and fork, bride and groom*), lexical bundles (*as soon as, in the middle of the*), complex prepositions (*in front of, at the end of*), speech formulae (*how come? see you*), multi-word verbs (*take care of, rely on*) and so on (Siyanova-Chanturia 2015). Formulaic language differs in word length, literality, degree of lexical fixedness and so on. The length of formulaic sequences ranges from two to eight words, or even more. Idioms are figurative expressions, while other types of sequences are literal language. Some formulaic sequences such as idioms allow modification, while others like collocations do not. Formulaic sequences are widely used in English language. For instance, Erman & Warren (2000) found that the proportion of formulaic sequences was 58.6% in spoken language and 52.3% in written language. Conklin & Schmitt (2012) estimated that formulaic sequences make up one third to one half of English discourse. According to Hill (2000), collocations comprise more than two thirds of English discourse.

Extensive researches in applied and corpus linguistics have indicated that formulaic language played a very important role in language use and learning. For instance, a large number of speech production studies (e.g., Arnon & Priva 2013; Dechert 1983; Oppenheim 2000; Pawley & Syder 1983) found that when speakers used formulaic language, their outputs were smoother and more fluent and accurate. The fluent and accurate output was called "islands of reliability" by Dechert (1983). Pawley & Syder (1983) referred to formulaic sequences as "memorized sequences" and claimed that these strings are "recalled as whole or as automatically chained strings". Researchers after Pawley & Syder (1983) used similar expressions like "prepackaged" "prefabricated" "ready-made" "frozen" and "unanalysed" (for a review, see Jiang & Nekrasova 2007) to describe formulaic language. Wray (2002) claimed that formulaic sequences are "stored and retrieved whole from memory", and "processed like a morpheme" (Wray 2008: 12). In other words, formulaic sequences are believed to be processed as morpheme-like units without activating or analysing their individual components. This view of "holistic" nature of formulaic language was supported by other researchers (e.g., Dahlmann & Adolphs 2007; Jiang & Nekrasova 2007; Kim & Kim 2012; Underwood et al. 2004). The processing of formulaic sequences requires less cognitive capacity than that of the same length of novel language. It reduces the burden of working memory and increases processing efficiency. As Pawley & Syder (1983) pointed out, the storage of a large number of formulaic sequences in long-term memory will make up for the limitation of working memory and lead to the fluency of production. For instance, it was found that the longest novel word sequence native speakers can process is 8~10 words due to cognitive limitations. However, they can easily produce a sentence like "*You can lead a horse to water, but you can't make him drink*" (Conklin & Schmitt 2012). It has been noted that young children are capable of memorizing and producing formulaic sequences (e.g., *Lemme see, I wanna do it*) (e.g., Clark 1974; Cruttenden 1981; Lieven Nelson 1973; Peters 1983; Pine & Barnes 1992). Research has shown that formulaic language plays a crucial role in children's early linguistic development (e.g., Clark 1974; Peters 1977, 1983; Pine & Lieven 1993; Tomasello 2003; Tomasello & Brooks 1999). As Tomasello (2003) claimed, formulaic language is "of tremendous theoretical importance for theories of linguistic competence and performance" (p. 306).

As one class of formulaic language, collocations refer to frequently co-occurring associated word pairs (Biber et al. 1999). Collocations (e.g., *black coffee*) are in between free word combinations (e.g., *black cat*) and frozen idioms (e.g., *black sheep*) (van Lancker Sidtis 1975). Like other formulaic language, collocations are very frequent. Collocations comprise more than two thirds of English language in accordance with Hill (2000).

Recent years have seen a growing number of studies on collocations. One approach is to explore whether collocations enjoy processing advantage over non-collocations. This has been investigated using off-line measures such as a lexical decision task and on-line measures such as eye movements. For instance, in a lexical decision task, the participants were asked to judge whether a word string was composed of real words or not (Durrant & Doherty 2010; Ellis et al. 2009; Wolter & Yamashita 2015). The typical finding is that participants judge collocations (e.g., *parish church*) more quickly than novel phrases (e.g., *feature church*). Other researches have used eye movement measures to assess whether the processing advantage for collocations exists in reading. Eye movement studies have shown that collocations (e.g., *provide information*) are read faster than matched non-collocations (e.g., *compare information*) (Vilkaite 2016). There is strong evidence indicating that collocations are processed faster than matched novel language (Durrant & Doherty 2010; Ellis et al. 2008; Vilkaite 2016; Vilkaite & Schmitt 2017; Wolter & Gyllstad 2013; Wolter & Yamashita 2014). It is believed that the proper use of collocations is a prerequisite to be a proficient L2 learner (e.g., Cowie 1998; Granger & Bestgen 2014; Wray 2002). The proper use of collocations will reduce L2 learners' processing load and help them speak naturally and fluently like native speakers (Hill & Lewis 1997).

Other researchers have explored whether readers are sensitive to variation in the frequency of usage of collocations. This is commonly computed using measures of phrasal frequency (Gries & Ellis 2015) or mutual information (MI; Hunston 2002). Phrasal frequency provides a raw count of how often words are used together in a phrase, while MI provides a conditionalized count (i.e. a ratio) of how often they are used together in a phrase rather than separately. Sonbul (2015) examined eye movements for sentences containing synonymous adjective-noun pairs. These included strong collocations, such as *fatal mistake*, that have both high phrasal frequency and MI, weaker collocations, like *awful mistake*, that have lower phrasal frequency and MI, and phrases like *extreme mistake*, with very low phrasal frequency and MI. Reading times were shortest for strong collocations, longer for weak collocations, and longest for non-collocations; showing sensitivity to these frequency differences (i.e. differences in phrasal frequency and MI).

To date, previous studies have focused on English collocations. However, it is unclear whether the findings on collocations in alphabetic languages are sufficient to explain the processing mechanism of collocations in other (non-alphabetic) languages such as Chinese. It is well acknowledged that Chinese is distinct from English. Chinese is a logographic script. Written Chinese is made up of box-like characters instead of letters. Characters differ in complexity which is determined by the number of strokes, the number of radicals (combinations of strokes), and the structure of radicals per character. Each character occupies the same space and there is no space between the characters to mark the word boundaries. Thus, Chinese readers cannot separate words with low-level visual information and they have to use word knowledge to segment characters into words (Li et al. 2009).

A Chinese word can be made up of one to several characters. The character is the basic writing unit of Chinese. However, there has been a debate about whether the character or the word is the basic processing unit in Chinese sentences. Some studies provide evidence that the word is the basic processing unit in Chinese sentence reading which is similar to English writing systems (e.g., Rayner et al. 2007; Yan et al. 2010; Yang & McConkie 1999). For instance, it has been found that readers preferred a viewing location in reading which is the left within a word in English (Rayner & Fischer 1996; Rayner et al. 1998; Vitu et al. 1995), German (Radach & Kempe 1993), French (O'Regan 1981; Vitu et al. 1991) and many other alphabetic languages. The effect of the Preferred Viewing Location (PVL) was often used to prove that the word was the basic processing unit. Yan et al. (2010) found that there exists the effect of PVL in Chinese sentence reading, indicating that Chinese word is the processing unit.

The studies on the space between the words also support the findings that the word is the basic processing unit. Bai et al. (2008) investigated the processing difference among a normal unspaced text, a text with spaces between words, a text with spaces between characters, and a text with spaces between characters that yielded non-words. It turned out that the spaces between characters would interfere with the processing of sentence reading while the spaces between words would neither facilitate nor interfere with the processing of sentence reading. This result showed that the word was more likely to be the basic processing unit in Chinese sentence reading. However, according to Liu et al. (1974), the processing time under the word spacing condition was remarkably longer than the condition without word spacing. The spaces between words interfered with the participants' normal sentence reading. To some degree, there exist some problems in the studies of Bai et al. (2008) and Liu et al. (1974). The experimental materials collected by Liu et al. (1974) under the word spacing condition only included seven characters which made up six words. The monosyllabic words were the key components of their experimental materials. However, based on Zhang (2013), the monosyllabic words and the disyllabic words were almost equally distributed in the actual Chinese texts. Furthermore, according to Liu et al. (1974), the ecological characteristics of the experimental materials would affect the experiment results.

Among the commonly used 56,008 words (Lexicon of Common Words in Contemporary Chinese Research Team, 2008), 72% are two-character (2C) words. Many 2C words are used together as collocations. For instance, a 2C word 保护(*protect*) collocates with a 2C word 环境 (*environment*), making up a four-character (4C) collocation 保护环境 (*protect the environment*). According to a corpus based on film subtitles by Cai & Brysbaert (2010), 12% of words are four-character words based on word type frequency. Chinese collocations are widely used in Chinese language.

There are different types of Chinese collocations including verb-noun (e.g., 振兴经济: *revitalization of the economy*), noun-noun (e.g., 工业革命: *industrial revolution*) and adjective-adjective (e.g., 活泼可爱: *lively and lovely*) collocations and so on. The present study focuses on verb-noun collocations which are one of the most common collocations in Chinese. Verb-noun collocations play various grammatical roles in Chinese sentences. For instance, they can be used as subjects, predicates, objects and modifiers in sentences. Chinese linguist Lv (1942) claimed that a verb is the center of a sentence which was supported by French linguist Tesniere (1959). According to dependency grammar (Tesniere 1959), the verb connects other words in the sentence. In other words, verb-noun collocations play a central role in a sentence structure. However, verb-noun collocations have been found to be more difficult for learners to learn than other types of collocations (Bahns 1993; Nesselhauf 2003; Yamashita & Jiang 2010). Chinese verb-noun collocations are also very difficult for Chinese as foreign language (CFL) learners. For instance, Li (2016) found that verb-noun collocation errors CFL learners made accounted for 66% of the total collocation errors in CFL learners' essays.

Although Chinese collocations are widely used in written and spoken language, less attention has been paid to Chinese collocations. To the best of our knowledge, only two studies have explored the processing of Chinese 4C collocations. Lv & Shi (2016) explored the processing of verb-noun collocations (e.g., 采取措施: *take measures*) by using a lexical decision-making task. It was found that Chinese collocations were processed faster than non-collocations. Lv & Shi (2016)'s research is a pilot study on Chinese collocations. However, their research only explored the processing of Chinese collocations in isolation. Thus, their findings are not informative about the processing of collocations in context. Jiang et al. (2020) assessed the processing of verb-noun multi-word expressions by children and adults using an eye-tracking experiment. The results showed that adults and Grade 4 readers (9 years and 4 months to 10 years) processed collocations faster than control phrases in reading. Both Lv & Shi (2016) and Jiang et al. (2020) verified the processing advantage of Chinese collocations and the effect of phrase frequency. However, they did not consider other factors influencing the processing of Chinese collocations.

Clearly, to better understand the processing mechanism of Chinese collocations, more work is needed. The following three aspects are worthy of further investigation with reference to the previous research on English collocations. Firstly, more experimental evidence is needed to confirm the processing advantage of Chinese collocations over novel phrases. Secondly, whether Chinese collocations are processed holistically or analytically is a crucial question. Finally, other factors such as collocation strength and contextual predictability are needed to be focused on because they may affect the processing of Chinese collocations in reading. Accordingly, this dissertation focuses on the three aspects, namely, the processing advantage, the processing pattern and the influencing factors. This dissertation has vital theoretical and practical implications. This dissertation attempts to find out whether or not there are some differences in the processing of Chinese and English collocations, which may contribute to the understanding of language processing in different language systems. Moreover, the findings of the study may have some implications which can be of great assistance for the development of Chinese reading models for native Chinese as well as for Chinese as a second language (CSL) learners.

1.2 Research objectives and questions

This dissertation aims to explore the processing mechanism of Chinese 4C verb-noun collocations containing two 2C words (e.g., 保护环境: *protect the environment*) in reading. As mentioned above, verb-noun collocations play a central role in Chinese sentence structure. In addition, they are widely used in Chinese spoken and written language. Thus, this dissertation focuses on verb-noun collocations. Specifically, this dissertation attempts to assess whether Chinese verb-noun collocations have processing advantage over novel language in reading, whether they are processed holistically or analytically, and whether collocation strength, contextual predictability and association strength affect the processing of Chinese 4C collocations. The review of previous studies has shown that the three factors (collocation strength, contextual predictability and association strength) play an important role in the processing of English collocations. One may wonder what kind of roles they play in the processing of Chinese collocations.

Accordingly, the specific research questions are raised as follows:

(1) Are Chinese 4C collocations processed faster than control novel phrases in reading? (Chapter 3)

(2) Are Chinese 4C collocations processed holistically? (Chapter 4)

(3) How do collocation strength, contextual predictability and association strength influence the processing of Chinese 4C collocations in reading? (Chapter 5)

To answer the questions above, five eye-tracking experiments are conducted. Experiment 1 aims to answer the first question. The processing advantages of English collocations over novel phrases are well documented. Jiang et al. (2020) has demonstrated the processing advantage of Chinese collocations in reading. Thus, it is supposed that Experiment 1 will replicate the prior finding. There has been a debate about the holistic hypothesis, that is, formulaic language are holistically stored and processed. Studies to date have researched different types of formulaic sequences using various techniques and produced inconsistent results in this area. The present study attempts to explore this issue in Experiment 2 and 3 which will manipulate the preview of the constituent words of collocations. If the preview effects (longer fixations for the dissimilar constituent words) are found, we may infer that the constituent words are activated and processed. By contrast, if the preview effects are not observed, this might provide evidence that the collocations are processed holistically. Experiment 4 and 5 focuses on the factors influencing the processing of Chinese collocations, that is, contextual predictability, collocation strength and associative strength. There is a wealth of evidence demonstrating the effect of contextual predictability in the processing of words. The contextual effect has also been found in studies on English collocations. The present study may observe this effect as well. A few studies on English collocations have detected the effect of collocation strength which may be also found in the present study. There are inconsistent findings about whether the effect of collocation strength is independent of contextual effect. The present study will assess this issue. If there is no interaction between collocation strength and contextual predictability, we may conclude that the effect of collocation strength is independent of contextual effect. Otherwise, the result may provide further evidence that collocation strength is part of contextual constraint. Associative strength has been paid less attention. The present study will explore whether it occurs in the processing of Chinese collocations in reading.

1.3 Research significance

The research significance of this study is described as follows.

In terms of the theoretical significance, this dissertation contributes to the study on the cognitive processing unit during Chinese reading. The review of the literature has shown that words are regarded as the basic information processing units during Chinese reading (e.g., Rayner et al. 2007; Wang et al. 2010; Yan et al. 2010; Yang & McConkie 1999). However, there is no visual cue such as spaces to mark word boundaries. Therefore, it is hard to tell where a word starts and ends. Additionally, Chinese readers have no clear concept of words (e.g., Hoosain 1992; Li et al. 2015; Liu et al. 2013; Zang et al. 2011). This study attempts to explore how collocations are processed. If the processing advantage of Chinese collocations was found, it may imply that collocations are also likely to be regarded as processing units in Chinese reading.

On the other hand, the present study will provide evidence for the future research of computational models of eye movement control in Chinese reading. Previous research shows that the properties of characters and words affect eye movements in sentence reading (e.g.,

Li et al. 2013). In the existing Chinese eye-movement control models in reading (Li & Pollatsek 2020; Rayner et al. 2007), a core assumption is that lexical frequency is computed only across words instead of phrases. If the present study finds that collocations are lexicalized and processed holistically, it may imply that current models of eye movement control may need to be modified to include mechanisms that are sensitive to both the frequency of usage of multi-constituent units, as well as individual words.

Finally, the current study is helpful to better understand the processing mechanism of Chinese multi-word sequences. Collocations are widely used in Chinese language. However, compared with idioms, less attention has been paid to collocations. Collocations differ from idioms in fixedness and semantic transparency. Therefore, previous findings of idioms may not apply to the research of collocations. This dissertation provides readers with comprehensive research of Chinese collocations, which may fill an empirical gap of processing models of collocations and enrich the research of Chinese formulaic sequences. Meanwhile, the dissertation will test the existing hypothesis that formulaic sequences are processed holistically.

The current study will provide a psychological basis for the research in information science. Taking collocations as processing unions will increase efficiency of information search, classification and extraction. It will also improve people's work efficiency.

If Chinese collocations are found to be processed faster than novel language, the present findings may have some implications for Chinese as a second language (CSL) acquisition. The proper use of English collocations is a prerequisite to be a proficient L2 learner (e.g., Cowie 1998; Granger & Bestgen 2014; Wray 2002). The proper use of Chinese collocations will also reduce L2 learners' processing load and help them speak naturally and fluently like native speakers. The acquisition of Chinese collocations will be vital for CSL learners to increase the knowledge of Chinese collocations and develop the awareness of collocations.

1.4 Organization of the dissertation

This dissertation consists of eight chapters which are briefly introduced in this section.

Chapter 1 provides a brief introduction to research backgrounds and presents the research objectives and corresponding research questions of this dissertation. Then, the theoretical framework, the research methodology and significance are introduced. At the end of this chapter, the organization of this dissertation is presented.

Chapter 2 introduces the definition and classification of collocations, the way of identifying collocations, and the related theoretical frameworks. And then this chapter reviews the previous research on the processing of English collocations and Chinese formulaic language.

Chapter 3 introduces the research method, the technique of eye tracking, used in this dissertation. The introduction of eye-tracking technique includes the background information of eye movements, the eye-tracking technology, eye-movement measures, and the models of eye movement control during reading, and the parafoveal processing during reading.

This dissertation aims to explore three research questions. Accordingly, we conduct three studies. Chapter 4 illustrates Study I consisting of Experiment 1. Study I aims to assess whether Chinese collocations are processed faster than novel phrases in reading.

Chapter 5 presents Study II which contains Experiment 2 and 3. The two experiments explore whether Chinese collocations are processed holistically or analytically during natural reading.

Chapter 6 presents Study III consisting of Experiment 4 and 5. Study III examines the impacts of collocation strength, association strength and contextual predictability on the processing of Chinese collocations in reading. Specifically, Experiment 4 explores the effects of collocation strength and contextual predictability and Experiment 5 examines the effects of association strength and contextual predictability.

Chapter 7 is the general discussion based on the results and analyses from the above experiments. On the basis of the present findings, we propose a processing model for Chinese verb-noun collocations.

Chapter 8 is the conclusion of the study which reviews the main findings of the dissertation, summarizes the implications of these findings, points out the limitations of the present study, and then offers some directions for future research.

Chapter 2 Literature Review

2.1 Working definition of collocations

Firth (1957) put forward using the word collocation as a technical term. Firth (1968: 181) defined collocations as “habitual or customary” word combinations, which describes mutual expectancies of words. For example, in the collocation *heavy rain*, when readers encounter the word *heavy*, the collocate *rain* is expected, and vice versa. However, Benson (1989b) and Nation (2001) thought that collocations are unpredictable. Benson (1989b) regarded collocations as arbitrary recurrent word combinations. Nation (2001) also defined collocations as “items which frequently occur together and have some degree of semantic unpredictability”.

In the literature, other researchers have defined collocations from different perspectives. From a semantic perspective, Hausmann (1984) defined collocations as a combination of two lexical items with one of them is dominant semantically and the other is an addictive to the semantics of the base. For example, in the collocation *black coffee*, the base is *coffee*, and the collocate is *black* (Wanner 2004, p. 97). Similarly, Halliday (1976) described collocations as “semantically related lexical items”.

From a grammatical approach, collocations are defined as phrases with syntactic structures which are interrelated. Thus, the syntactic structure is also an important part of collocations. However, the item-oriented tradition ignores the syntactic restrictions on collocations (Greenbaum 1974). Kjellmer (1984, p. 48) defined collocations as "lexically determined and grammatically restricted sequences of words" and suggested to study collocations from the grammatical perspective.

From a text-oriented approach, Sinclair (1991: 170) defined collocations as "the occurrence of two or more words within a short space of each other in a text". In other words, a word and its collocate are within a set span. According to a study by Jones & Sinclair (1974), the collocate and the node are within a four-word span. This definition highlights the co-occurring of words in text which forms the precondition to study collocation in texts.

Although there is no agreement on the definition of collocations (for discussions, see Barfield & Gyllstad 2009; Nesselhauf 2003), there are two main traditions, that is, the phraseological tradition (see Cowie 1981, 1994; Howarth 1998; Nesselhauf 2003, 2005) and the statistical tradition or frequency-based tradition (Greenbaum 1974; Halliday 1966; Hoey 1991; Hunston 2002; McEnery & Wilson 2001; Partington 1998; Sinclair 1991; Stubbs 1995).

In the phraseological tradition, collocations are regarded as word combinations having some degrees of fixedness and occurring in grammatical constructions (Cowie 1981, 1988, 1991, 1994, 1998a). For instance, Cowie (1991) defined collocations as "word-combinations in which one element has a technical sense or a long-established figurative sense which has lost most of its analogical force". According to the phraseological approach, collocations are semantically transparent to some extent. In other words, at least one component word of a collocation has to be semantically nontransparent. This approach defines collocations from typological grounds and the frequency of occurrence is not regarded as a vital principle. For instance, although a phrase *red car* is frequent, it is not a collocation but a free word combination. It is because the phrase *red car* is fully transparent. Whereas a phrase *kill time* is regarded as a collocation because it is semi-transparent. There is no physical act of killing in this collocation. This phrase means "to make time pass quickly by doing something instead of waiting".

The frequency-based tradition which is from corpus linguistics defines collocations as "the relationship a lexical item has with items that appear with greater than random probability in its (textual) context" (e.g., Firth 1968; Greenbaum 1974; Hoey 1991: 7, 2005; cf. Greenbaum 1974; Moon 1998; Sinclair et al. 2004; Stubbs 2001). This tradition emphasizes the characteristics of co-occurrence of word combinations. For instance, Firth (1968) defined collocations as habitual and semantically related word combinations, which is from quantitative tradition (cf. Krishnamurthy 2000: 32). Greenbaum (1974) defined collocations as "a frequent co-occurrence of two lexical items in the language". Moon (1998) referred collocation as "frequently repeated or statistically significant co-occurrences, whether or not there are any special semantic bonds between collocating items". Hoey (1991) argued that “the relationship a lexical item has with items that appear with greater than random probability in its (textual) context”. Biber et al. (1999) defined collocations as “associations between lexical words, so that the words co-occur more frequently than expected by chance”. Geyken (2007) referred to collocations as lexical units which are composed of words with a strong relationship. Hill (2000) defined collocations as words which tend to habitually co-occur. Similarly, Nattinger & Decarrico (1992, p.36) also regarded collocations as word sequences that regularly co-occur. The frequency-based tradition highlights the mutual expectancy of collocations, and the mutual expectancy is greater than chance.

According to the frequency-based tradition, the co-occurrence of words is the crucial characteristic of collocations. However, the degree of the co-occurrence of a word and its collocate is different (Lewis 1993). For example, both *global warming* and *major problem* are considered collocations but *global* and *warming* are more likely to co-occur, whereas *major* and *problem* are less likely to occur together in a corpus. In addition, the strength of the connection between the two words in a collocation is not the same. For instance, *heavy* can be followed by *rain*, *frost*, *snow*, *schedule*, *traffic* and other words, while *traffic* tend to be preceded by *heavy*.

In the current study, collocations are defined as frequently co-occurring associated word pairs (Biber et al. 1999) based on the frequency-based tradition.

2.2 Classification of collocations

Collocations are classified into grammatical collocations (e.g., *by chance*) and lexical collocations (e.g., *heavy rain*) (e.g., Benson et al. 1997; Hill 2000). A grammatical collocation is a combination of a lexical word (noun, verb or adjective) and a grammatical word (preposition). A lexical collocation contains two lexical components. The structure of lexical collocations could be adjective + noun (*fast food*), verb + noun (*shake hands*), noun + verb (*car crash*), verb + adverb (*take it seriously*), or adverb + adjective (*seriously injured*).

According to the degree of idiomaticity, Howarth (1998) divided lexical collocation into four categories: free combination (*red car*), restricted collocation (*black coffee*), figurative idioms (*pay the price*), and pure idioms (*black sheep*).

Lewis (1997) classified collocations into strong and weak collocations based on fixedness and restrictedness. Strong collocations are more fixed and restricted than weak collocations. Sonbul (2015) also classified collocations into strong and weak collocations. According to Sonbul (2015), strong collocations are strongly associated and high frequent whereas weak collocations are weakly associated and less frequent function. For example, *golden opportunity* is a strong collocation and *nice sweater* is a weak collocation. In terms of phrasal frequency, collocations are divided into frequent and infrequent ones as well (Lewis 1997).

In studies of L2 acquisition, collocations are divided into congruent and incongruent collocations (e.g., Wolter & Gyllstad

2011, 2013; Wolter & Yamashita 2015; Yassami 2011). Congruent collocations refer to collocations in L2 that have translation equivalents in a first language (L1). Incongruent collocations are those that have no translation equivalents in L1. For example, *handsome man* is a congruent collocation across English and Chinese, because it has a Chinese translation equivalent "*帅男人*". Whereas *heavy rain* is considered an incongruent collocation across English and Chinese, because *heavy* would be literally translated as "*重*" in Chinese meaning weight. However, "*重雨*" is not a collocation and not even a phrase and it means differently from *heavy rain*.

2.3 Identification of collocations

The phraseological tradition focuses on the degree of semantic transparency and substitutability of the word elements of word combinations. According to the phraseological tradition, a word combination that can be regarded as a collocation must be semantically nontransparent. For instance, a phrase *heavy box* is a free word combination, while a phrase *heavy traffic* is considered a collocation because the meaning of *heavy traffic* is not semantically transparent. As we know, a box can be heavy in weight, while traffic can not be heavy. Actually, the phrase *heavy traffic* means busy traffic. With regards to substitutability, collocations must have certain degree of fixedness. In other words, there are not many words for the component.

Collocations can be extracted from corpora using the statistical approach (Gablasova et al. 2017). There are several criteria to identify collocations (for a review, see Matsuno 2017). The most frequently used measures are phrasal frequency and association strength between word combinations. Phrasal frequency describes the likelihood that certain word combinations emerge in a corpus. Frequent word combinations are normally regarded as collocations (Bartsch 2004; Clear 1993; Sinclair et al. 2004). Association strength was also used to identify collocations (Gregory et al.1999). Association strength is a statistical association indicating how likely two words co-occur. It can be used interchangeably with other terms such as "contingency" (the co-occurrence probability), "probability" or "predictability" (Yi et al. 2017). Association strength can be measured by various probabilistic measures such as transitional probability (TP), mutual information (MI), and t-score (for a review, see Durrant & Doherty 2010; Gablasova et al. 2017). The dominant measure is MI which has been verified to be a robust probabilistic measure (Ellis et al. 2008; Gregory et al. 1999), and has been used in many formulaic studies (e.g., Durrant & Schmitt 2009; Ellis et al. 2008; Siyanova-Chanturia 2015; Yi et al. 2017). MI proposed by Church and Hanks (1990) is computed as the "logarithmic ratio between the observed and expected occurrences of a word pair in a corpus" (Vilkaitem 2016). MI scores demonstrate the tendency of co-occurring of word combinations (Manning & Schütze 1999). The higher the MI value is, the more likely the words co-occur. Word combinations with MI scores of 3 or greater than 3 are viewed as collocations (Hunston 2002). Although MI scores are calculated based on frequency, MI is different from phrasal frequency. Phrasal frequency describes the likelihood that certain word combinations emerge in a corpus. But MI scores indicate the probability of the co-occurrence of constituent words in word combinations (Gries & Ellis 2015). Research showed that the correlation between MI scores and phrasal frequencies is weak (Yi et al. 2017).

Although frequent word combinations are normally regarded as collocations (Bartsch 2004; Clear 1993; Sinclair et al. 2004), research has shown that some frequent word combinations (e.g., *red car*) are not collocations. Thus, mere phrasal frequency is not a reliable criterion to identify collocations. MI scores indicate how often a word is used together with its collocate in a phrase. Word combinations with MI scores of 3 or greater than 3 are often viewed as collocations (Hunston 2002). However, MI tends to have high scores for low-frequency word combinations. Typically, a phrasal frequency threshold of 5 occurrences is used to offset the low frequency bias (Evert 2008). Thus, the present study used frequency threshold of 5 and MI scores threshold of 3 to identify collocations.

2.4 Theoretical framework

There are different theoretical suggestions to account for the processing advantages of collocations, such as lexical priming theory (Hoey 2005, 2012), usage-based (Langacker 1987; Goldberg 1995, 2006; Bybee 1998; Tomasello 2003), and exemplar-based (Bod 1998, 2006; Pierrehumbert 2001) theories which will be introduced in Section 2.4.1 and Section 2.4.2 respectively.

With regards to how formulaic sequences are processed and represented, researchers put forward various hypotheses. The holistic processing hypothesis (Wray 2002), the lexical representation hypothesis (Swinney & Cutler 1979), the idiom principle (Sinclair 1991), and the multi-constituent unit (MCU) hypothesis (Zang 2019) propose that formulaic sequences are processed holistically. The configuration hypothesis (Cacciari & Tabossi 1988) holds that idioms are represented and processed analytically. A dual-route processing model (Pollatsek et al. 2000) assumes that frequent phrases are processed holistically and less frequent phrases are processed analytically. A parallel language processing model (Matsuno 2017) claims that collocations are processed both holistically and analytically. Section 2.4.3, Section 2.4.4, and Section 2.4.5 will introduce these processing theories in detail.

2.4.1 Lexical priming theory

It is well-established that priming is common in language. Priming is a well-known effect which was first found by Meyer & Schvaneveldt (1971). It has been found that a word is recognized quickly when people have encountered another word which is related to it in some way. For instance, when the word *doctor* has been heard or seen, the word *nurse* is recognized faster compared to another unrelated word. Prior research has verified graphemic, associative, and syntactic priming effects in language (for a review, see Planck & Sereno 1991).

Hoey (2005) put forward the lexical priming theory. This theory holds that every word is lexically primed to occur together with other words and each word is acquired because it is "cumulatively loaded with the contexts and co-texts in which it is encountered" (Hoey 2005). Hoey refers to collocation as "a psychological association between words" which is "evidenced by their occurrence together in corpora more often than is explicable in terms of random distribution" (2005, pp.3-5). Thus, once a word in a collocation is encountered, it primes its collocate. In other words, collocates predict each other, that is, the presence of one constituent word of a collocation prompts the recognition or production of the other one. For instance, when a word *commit* is heard or seen, then the word *crime* or *suicide* will be brought to mind. And finally the collocation form *commit suicide* or *commit crime* will be produced.

The lexical priming theory is essentially compatible with spreading activation models (Collins & Loftus 1975): the activation of a word will spread to other related words (semantically, graphemically, phonologically related words, etc.) resulting in their activation. Thus, due to the priming relationships between two collocates, one collocate activates the other, which makes collocations predictable. Being predictable is one of the characteristics of collocations and is one of the reasons why collocations enjoy processing advantage over novel phrases.

According to the lexical priming theory (Hoey 2005), there is a priming association between the constituent words of collocations. The strength of the association may affect the processing of collocations.

This dissertation will explore how the strength of the association measured by MI scores affects the processing of Chinese collocations (Chapter 6).

2.4.2 Usage-based theory and exemplar-based theory

Usage-based theory (Bybee 1998, 2006; Goldberg 2006; Tomasello 2003) proposes that language acquisition, processing, use and representations are all influenced by the frequency of occurrence. When a word is encountered for the first time, it will "leave a trace in memory" (Langacker 2000) and each experience with it will activate nodes in the mental lexicon, and frequent activation of this unit will improve the memory (Barlow & Kemmer 2000; Bybee 2006; Croft & Cruse 2004; Tomasello 2005). Gradually, this word will be recognized and processed.

Exemplar-based theory (Bod 2006) assumes that every experience with a linguistic unit will be registered in memory, which results in a lot of exemplars (words, multi-word sequences, grammatical constructions) for language use (Bybee 2006; Ellis 2012; Goldberg 2006). An accumulation of various examples improves language acquisition and processing (Bod 2006).

Both usage-based theory (Bybee 1998, 2006; Goldberg 2006; Tomasello 2003) and exemplar-based theory (Bod 2006) claim that language is "a statistical accumulation of experiences" which changes with language use (Bod 2006; Ellis & O'Donnell 2012). Language acquisition is a dynamic and changing process in which every experience to a linguistic unit will affect the mental lexicon by reinforcing or modifying existing knowledge.

Additionally, the two theories assume that multi-word sequences are represented and processed in a way similar to words (Zang et al. 2021) and they are also influenced by the frequency of use. For example, Arnon & Snider (2010) assessed the response times to four-word phrases (e.g., *don't have to worry* vs. *don't have to wait*) differing in phrase frequency using a phrasal-decision task. The frequency of the final word was controlled. In this study, the effect of phrase frequency was found, due to shorter response times to frequent phrases compared to less frequent ones. This result indicates that frequency affects the processing of phrases. The possible reason is that frequently encountered multi-word sequences are lexicalized and represented as single units (Zang et al. 2021). Thus, words and phrases are processed in a similar way.

In contrast to the universal grammar theory which claims that language is a set of grammar rules and language acquisition is determined by an innate language system, the usage-based theory assumes that language is an inventory of linguistic units and language acquisition is an accumulation of experiences and shaped by language use (e.g., Ellis 2002). Frequent encounter with language will shape memory representations (Langacker 2000). MacWhinney (2001) claimed that when a form is encountered frequently, it becomes stronger. Wray (2002) and Kemmer & Barlow (2000) made a similar statement that "the more often a string is needed, the more likely it is to be stored in prefabricated form to save processing effort" (p. 25). Bybee & Hopper (2001) asserted that "high frequency phrases are stored in memory" (p. 17).

The usage-based theory is compatible with the connectionist approach (Christiansen & Chater 1999; Elman 1990) which claims that linguistic units do not exist in isolation but in networks. The units are connected with each other in the networks. The strength of the connections is affected by the frequency of occurrence (Bybee & McClelland 2005; McClennand & Rumelhart 1985; Rumelhart & McClelland 1986; Elman 1990). For instance, when the sequences *fish and* are encountered, the word *chips* will be activated. This is because the phrase *fish and chips* is frequently used. After reading *fish and*, readers will expect the following word *chips*. Thus, the predictability leads to the fast processing of this phrase.

The usage-based theory offers an explanation for the processing advantage of frequent sequences over less frequent ones (Bod et al. 2003; Bybee & Hopper 2001; Ellis 2002b, 2008b; Hoey 2005; Robinson & Ellis 2008). Additionally, this theory stresses the role of frequency and experience in shaping our mental representations (Bybee & Beckner 2009), that is, frequent exposure to a word or multiword sequences will help them to be stored and represented in the mental lexicon (Bybee & Scheibman 1999: 582). According to the usage-based theory, frequency is an important factor influencing the processing of formulaic sequences.

According to the usage-based theory, frequency is an important factor influencing the processing of words. The current study will explore the role of phrasal frequency (frequency at a phrasal level) on the processing of Chinese collocations (Chapter 6).

2.4.3 Holistic processing theories

Wray (2002) proposed the holistic processing hypothesis which claims that a formulaic sequence "appears to be prefabricated, that is, stored, retrieved whole from memory at the time of use". Erman & Warren (2000) stated that the holistic processing of formulaic language is common in corpus studies. Kjellmer (1991) demonstrated that "A large part of our mental lexicon consists of combinations of words that customarily co-occur" (p. 112). When speakers use nonformulas, it takes more time for them to consider individual words. In contrast, the holistic processing hypothesis holds that formulaic language is processed as single units without activating the constituents. Therefore, the processing of formulaic language is effortless with less processing load and fast (Peters 1983; Wray 1999; Wray & Perkins 2000).

A considerable amount of research (Conkin & Schmittm 2008, 2012; Dahlmann & Adolphs 2007; Jiang & Nekrasova 2007; Kim & Kim 2012; Siyanova-Chanturia et al. 2011; Underwood et al. 2004; Wray 2002) has provided evidence supporting the holistic processing hypothesis (Wray 2002). For instance, the research has shown that idioms are processed as single lexical units. Underwood et al. (2004) explored the processing of idioms using eye movements. The results showed that idioms are processed faster than novel phrases demonstrating the holistic processing of idioms. The lexical representation hypothesis (Swinney & Cutler 1979) proposed that idioms are stored and represented as long words in the mental lexicon. When the first word of an idiom is encountered, the whole lexical entry will be activated. Studies on phrasal verbs (e.g., Matlock & Heredia 2002) and compounds (e.g., Hillert & Swinney 2001) have also provided empirical evidence for the holistic processing. In an on-line grammaticality judgment task, Jiang & Nekrasova (2007) found that the reaction times were shorter for formulaic sequences compared to control phrases, which provided evidence supporting "the holistic nature of formulaic representation and processing".

The idiom principle (Sinclair 1991) suggests that "a language user has available to him or her a large number of semi-preconstructed phrases that constitute single choices, even though they might appear to be analyzable into segments" (p. 110). The idiom principle assumes that most of the language we produce is multi-word formulaic language or chunks instead of individual words. The fixed and semi-fixed chunks play an important role in language production. Chunking has been regarded as a crucial strategy in language processing. The use of chunks is the key to language fluency.

The MCU Hypothesis (Zang 2019) assumes that some multi-word units (e.g., idioms and spaced compounds) are likely to be lexicalized and represented as single linguistic units. The constituent words of MCUs may be identified in parallel and they are processed sequentially. The first constituent will activate the whole unit.

2.4.4 Analytic processing theory

Even though there is a wealth of evidence demonstrating the holistic processing of formulaic language, a growing number of studies have provided evidence against the holistic view. For example, Vilkaite (2016) found that non-adjacent collocations (e.g., *provide* some of the *information*) were processed faster than control phrases, which is against the holistic view. Matsuno (2017) found that collocations were both processed holistically and analytically.

Some studies showed that the processing of idioms has involved decompositional analyses as well (Sprenger et al. 2006), that is, the constituent words of idioms have been activated. Based on this finding, the configuration hypothesis (Cacciari & Tabossi 1988) was proposed. According to this hypothesis, idioms are a combination of their constituent words. The constituent words are identified one by one like novel phrases until enough information has activated to identify the figurative meaning of the idiom.

Research on compounds has produced different findings. Some support the analytical processing (Badecker 2001; Juhasz 2007; Libben 1998) and others claim that compounds are processed as a whole and at the same time the constituent is accessed and processed (Kuperman et al. 2008, 2009; Mondini et al. 2005; Pollatsek et al. 2000). To account for the findings on compounds, Pollatsek et al. (2000) proposed a dual-route processing model: a decompositional route and a direct processing route. The dual-route model suggests that the decompositional route is used in the processing of less frequent phrases, that is, the continent words of the phrase will be accessed, computed and analyzed. In contrast, the direct route is often taken in the processing of frequent phrases, that is, they will be processed holistically.

2.4.5 Parallel processing theory

Based on the research of Jiang (2000), Kintsch (1998), Levelt (1989, 1993), and McClelland (1987), Matsuno (2017) put forward the parallel language processing model (see Figure 2.1). We take a collocation *make decision* as an example. According to the parallel processing model (Matsuno 2017), when the word *make* is retrieved, the semantic, syntactic, morphemic, phonological, and orthographic information of this word will be fully or partially activated. For instance, the word *makes* and *made* will be activated. The grammar analysis may occur if necessary. The collocates of the word *make* may be activated as well in parallel with analytic processing. When the collocate *decision* is activated, the collocation *make decision* is recognized. Accordingly, the meaning of this collocation will be retrieved.

The parallel processing model (Matsuno 2017) is very valuable for accounting for the processing of collocations. However, it does not take other important factors such as phrasal frequency and predictability into consideration. These factors play an important role in the processing of collocations (Li et al. 2021). Moreover, this model describes the processing of collocations in alphabetic language. As reviewed in the Introduction, Chinese has unique characters. Therefore, this model cannot account for the processing pattern of Chinese collocations well.

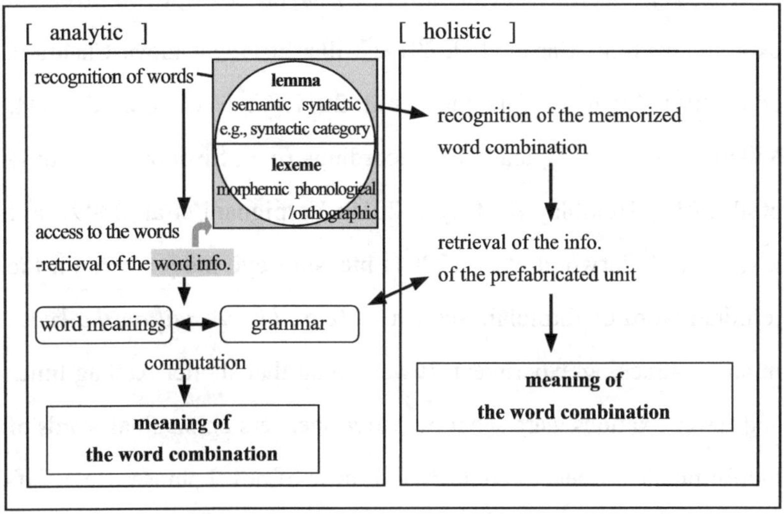

Figure 2.1 The parallel language processing model (Matsuno 2017)

Research to date has not assessed whether Chinese collocations are processed holistically, analytically, or in parallel. This issue is the key of understanding the representation and processing of Chinese collocations. This dissertation attempts to examine this issue in Chapter 5. In Chapter 7, we will propose a model to explain the processing of Chinese collocations.

2.5 The processing of English collocation

2.5.1 The processing advantage of English collocation

There is a wealth of evidence demonstrating that formulaic

sequences are processed faster than novel phrases in reaction time tasks (e.g., Conklin & Schmitt 2008; Jiang & Nekrasova 2007; Libben & Titone 2008; Tabossi et al. 2009), self-paced reading (e.g., Tremblay et al. 2011), recall tasks (Tremblay & Baayen 2010), eye-movement experiments (e.g., Carrol et al. 2016; Millar 2011; Siyanova-Chanturia et al. 2011; Siyanova-Chanturia et al. 2011; Underwood et al. 2004; Vilkaite 2016, 2017), and EEG recordings (e.g., Siyanova-Chanturia et al. 2017; Tremblay & Baayen 2010; Vespignani et al. 2009). For instance, Underwood et al. (2004) measure eye movements on the terminal word of formulaic sequences (e.g., *hit the nail on the head*) in an eye-tracking experiment. It was found that shorter reading times and fewer fixations were spent by native speakers on the final words of the formulaic sequences compared to those of novel phrases. In a self-paced reading task, Conklin & Schmitt (2008) use similar experimental materials. It was found that both native and non-native speakers spent less time reading the formulaic sequences compared to non-formulaic sequences. Thus, the authors conclude that "formulaic sequences are involved in more efficient language processing" (Conklin & Schmitt 2008: 86). Jiang & Nekrasova (2007) investigate the processing of formulaic and non-formulaic sequences by native and non-native speakers using an on-line grammaticality judgment task. Both groups have shorter reaction times and fewer errors when they judge the formulaic sequences.

Recent years have witnessed a growing interest in collocation processing. One of the research concerns is whether collocations are processed faster than control novel phrases. Previous research has examined this issue by employing off-line and on-line measures. Off-line measures consist of judgment tasks and lexical decision tasks. For example, Siyanova & Schmitt (2008) explored the processing of collocations by native and non-native English speakers using an acceptability judgment task. The participants were asked to rate each collocation in terms of its "commonness" using a six-point scale from very uncommon to very common. It was found that collocations were judged faster than non-collocations. Similarly, Wolter & Gyllstad (2013) asked participants to judge whether a string of words are commonly used in English or not. It was found that the response times and error rates for collocations were shorter than those for control phrases. In the lexical decision tasks (Durrant & Doherty 2010; Ellis et al. 2009; Wolter & Yamashita 2014), participants were instructed to judge whether a target string is composed of real words or not. The typical finding is that collocations are responded to quicker than novel phrases and therefore recognized more easily. For example, in the study by Durrant & Doherty (2010), participants were presented a list of word pairs which consisted of a prime word and a target word. The target word, either a real or a pseudoword, appeared swiftly after the prime word. The participants were asked to judge whether the target was a real word or not as quickly as possible. The finding was that participants spent less time making lexical decisions when the combination of the prime and target word was a collocation (e.g., *parish church*) rather than a novel phrase (e.g., *feature church*).

On-line measures such as self-paced reading tasks (e.g., Conklin & Schmitt 2008; Kim & Kim 2012; Schmitt & Underwood 2004) and eye-tracking experiments (e.g., Frisson et al. 2005; Li et al. 2021; McDonald & Shillcock 2003a, b; Sonbul 2015; Vilkaite 2016) have investigated whether this processing advantage for collocations is observed in reading. For instance, Vilkaite (2016) explored the processing of verb-noun collocations (e.g., *provide information*) using an eye-tracking experiment. The reading times of the nouns and the whole phrases were analysed respectively. The results indicated that collocations were processed faster than control phrases with shorter reading times. Moreover, the non-adjacent collocations (e.g., *provide some of the information*) enjoyed the processing advantage as well. Sonbul (2015) examined eye movements for sentences containing synonymous adjective-noun pairs. These included strong collocations, such as *fatal mistake*, that have both high phrasal frequency and MI, weaker collocations, like *awful mistake*, that have lower phrasal frequency and MI, and phrases like *extreme mistake*, with very low phrasal frequency and MI. Reading times were the shortest for strong collocations, longer for weak collocations, and the longest for non-collocations; showing sensitivity to these frequency differences (i.e., differences in phrasal frequency and MI).

It is worthy noticing that the same processing advantage has been found in various types of collocations. For instance, in a primed lexical decision task, Wolter & Gyllstad (2011) presented participants with adjective-noun collocations and control phrases and found that English native speakers spent less time with fewer errors when responding to collocations compared to novel phrases. Durrant & Doherty (2010) also found that adjective-noun collocations were processed faster than novel phrases using two priming tasks. Wolter & Gyllstad (2013) found the same processing advantage for verb-noun collocations in a grammaticality judgment task.

This processing advantage can be explained with usage-and exemplar-based models of language acquisition (e.g., Kemmer & Barlow 2000). According to these models, language acquisition, processing and use is regarded as an "experience-driven" process in which frequency plays an important role (e.g., Townsend & Bever 2001). Each experience with language will leave a trace in memory (Langacker 2000). The frequent use of language will accumulate lots of examples and shape the representation in the mental lexicon (Bybee 2006; Croft & Cruse 2004; Ellis 2012; Goldberg 2006), which facilitates its further use and processing. The frequency of language use influences the representation in our mental lexicon (Croft & Cruse 2004). The more frequently a string is experienced, the more likely it is stored in the mind (Wray 2002). Some researchers claimed that frequent collocations are stored and processed holistically (e.g., Conkin & Schmitt 2008, 2012; Siyanova-Chanturia et al. 2011; Underwood et al. 2004; Wray 2002). Thus, the use of collocations reduces the burden of working memory and increases processing efficiency (e.g., Millar 2011). While others (e.g., Siyanova-Chanturia 2015) argued that the processing advantage only evidences the effect of phrasal frequency.

In addition, language users are believed to store statistical information of words such as phrasal frequency and co-occurrence (McDonald & Shillcock 2003a, b), which facilitates the processing of collocations.

2.5.2 Processing patterns of English collocation

The last few decades have witnessed a large number of studies on the processing pattern of formulaic language. These studies focus on how formulaic sequences are presented and processed in the mental lexicon (e.g., Lukatela et al.1980). Specifically, their research concern is whether formulaic sequences are processed as an unanalysed whole or their constituents are accessed and processed as well (e.g., Taft & Forster 1975, 1976). It is generally acknowledged that formulaic sequences are stored and retrieved holistically. The evidence comes from the adjectives used to describe formulaic language. They are frozen (Hickey 1993; Lieven et al. 1992), ready-made (Raupach 1984; Weinert 1995), prepackaged (Clark 1974), unanalysed (Fillmore 1979; Hickey 1993; Lyons 1968), and prefabricated (Brown 1973; Hakuta 1974; Krashen & Scarcella 1978). Another evidence is from the definition of formulaic sequences. For example, formulaic sequences are referred to as word sequences that are "stored and retrieved whole from memory at the time of use" (Wray 2002). From this definition, we can see that formulas are believed to be stored and processed holistically.

A considerable amount of research has shown formulaic sequences are processed faster than novel language. For instance, Underwood et al. (2004) asked participants to read formulaic language of up to six words using the eye-tracking paradigm. The fixation times for the same word in a formulaic sequence (e.g., *as a matter of fact*) and in a novel phrase (e.g., *it's a well-known fact*) were compared. It was found that there were fewer fixations for words in formulaic sequences. Based on this finding, the authors concluded that the sequences were represented as a whole. However, this study has a limitation. The formulaic sequence and its corresponding control phrase differed in the substrings and the frequency of the substrings was not matched. Therefore, whether the processing advantage was due to the frequency of the substrings of that of the whole phrase was unknown.

Other studies have provided more evidence. For example, Sosa and MacFarlane (2002) asked participants to listen to two-word collocations (e.g., *sort of*) varying in frequency and monitor for *of*. It was found that the participants' reaction times were shorter when the word *of* was in high-frequency phrases (e.g., *kind of*) than in low-frequency ones (e.g., *each of*). This result suggested that high-frequency collocations were processed faster than novel phrases. Based on the processing advantage, some researchers claimed that formulaic sequences are lexicalized and so processed holistically during reading (Conkin & Schmitt 2008, 2012; Dahlmann & Adolphs 2007; Jiang & Nekrasova 2007; Kim & Kim 2012; Siyanova-Chanturia et al. 2011; Underwood et al. 2004; Wray 2002).

However, some researchers argued against the holistic processing hypothesis (e.g., Siyanova-Chanturia 2015; Vilkaite 2016). There is a considerable amount of empirical evidence from studies on compounds (Duñabeitia et al. 2007; Juhasz et al. 2003; Pollatsek et al. 2000). Compounds are words consisting of at least two morphemes (e.g., *supermarket, railway, keyboard*). One of the research concerns on compounds is whether or not the constituent of a compound is activated and processed during the on-line processing of compounds. Most studies on this issue used the frequency of constituent words as a variable and the constituent frequency effects, that is, the frequency of constituents influences the recognition time on a compound, provide evidence that constituents are activated. Using this method, Badecker (2001) found that a compositional approach was used in the processing of compounds. For instance, a compound "bluebird" is decomposed into two words "blue" and "bird". Juhasz (2007) and Libben (1998) claimed that compounds are decomposed into the constituent words during the processing. Pollatsek et al. (2000) argued that compounds are represented via the entire compound and the constituents. Mondini et al. (2005) believed that when a compound is accessed, its components and the whole form are activated (Kuperman et al. 2008, 2009).

Spaced compounds (e.g., *free style, car wash, front door*) are quite similar to collocations. Thus, the research findings on spaced compounds are valuable for the studies on collocations as a reference. Cutter et al. (2014) used an eye movement experiment to explore the processing of spaced compounds (e.g., *teddy bear*). The results showed that the constituents were processed in the processing of the compounds, which was against holistic processing of compounds.

Overall, researchers on compounds have drawn a consistent conclusion that compounds can be processed holistically, and meanwhile their constituents are activated and processed.

Overall, to test whether the holistic processing hypothesis is correct or wrong, we need more experimental researches.

2.5.3 Factors affecting the processing of English collocation

It is well established that frequency has strong effects on word processing. It is found that high-frequency words are processed faster than low-frequency words (Balota et al. 2004; Brysbaert et al. 2011). Eye-movements studies have found that high-frequency words are fixated for less time than low-frequency words (Inhoff & Rayner 1986; Rayner et al. 2004; Rayner & Duffy 1986; Rayner et al. 1996).

A wealth of studies have also examined effects of frequency at the phrase level and phrasal frequency effects. Phrasal frequency provides a raw count of how often words are used together in a phrase. Research has demonstrated that multi-word phrases such as idioms, binomials, collocations, phrasal verbs, and lexical bundles, are processed quickly than control phrases (Arnon & Snider 2010; Bannard & Matthews 2008; Janssen & Barber 2012; Janssen & Caramazza 2011; Matlock & Heredia 2002; Siyanova-Chanturia et al. 2011; Siyanova-Chanturia et al. 2011; Sosa & MacFarlane 2002; Tremblay et al. 2011; Tremblay & Tucker 2011).

For instance, Bannard & Matthews (2008) asked young children (two to three years old) to repeat sequences (e.g., *sit in your chair*) to assess their production ability using a sentence-repetition test. The sequences used in this test were chosen from British child-directed speech. The sequences differed in phrasal frequency but were matched on word frequency. For instance, a sequence *sit in your chair* is more frequent than a sequence *sit in your truck*, but *chair* is as frequent as *truck*. Bannard & Matthews found that children repeated high-frequency sequences (e.g., *sit in your chair*) faster than low-frequency sequences (e.g., *sit in your truck*). This shows that young children are sensitive to phrasal frequency.

Arnon & Snider (2010) explored the effect of phrasal frequency in the processing of four-word sequences (e.g., *don't have to worry*) by adults. In a phrasal decision task, participants were asked to decide whether a sequence was a phrase or not. The target sequences differed in phrasal frequency and the frequency of constituent words in the sequences were matched. The participants were instructed to make a decision as quickly as possible. It was found that the judge times were shorter for the higher-frequency phrases than for the lower-frequency ones. This finding suggested that frequency information of phrases is represented in the mental lexicon and it can be noticed, learned, and stored.

Similarly, Tremblay et al. (2011) investigated the role of phrasal frequency using a self-paced reading paradigm. Participants were asked to read sentences which contained lexical bundles (frequently co-occurring sequences of words, e.g., *in the middle of the*) and matched control phrases (e.g., *in the front of the*). It was found that the sentences with lexical bundles were read faster and the lexical bundles were recalled more correctly. These led Tremblay et al. to conclude that the frequent lexical bundles are more likely to be remembered in the brain.

Siyanova-Chanturia et al. (2011b) examined the processing of binomial phrases (a sequence of words in a specified order) by L1 and L2 learners using an eye tracking study. Binomial phrases (e.g., *bride and groom*) and their reversed forms (e.g., *groom and bride*) were contained in sentences. It was demonstrated that binomial phrases were read more quickly compared to their reversed forms. Since binomial phrases and their reversed forms have the same syntax and meaning but differ in phrasal frequency, this result indicated that the processing advantage of binomial phrases was due to the effect of phrasal frequency. In addition, both L1 and L2 learners were sensitive to the effect of phrasal frequency which was observed in both early and late eye-tracking measures.

A number of studies have detected the facilitation effect of phrasal frequency in the processing of collocations (e.g., Durrant & Doherty 2010; Siyanova & Schmitt 2008; Sonbul 2015). For instance, Siyanova & Schmitt (2008) used a judgment task to test the acceptability of adjective-noun collocations (e.g., *social services*) differing in phrasal frequency. The participants were asked to rate the targets by using a six-point scale from very uncommon to very common. The result showed that high-frequency collocations were judged faster than low-frequency collocations. In an eye-tracking experiment conducted by Sonbul (2015), the target words included two synonymous adjective-noun collocations and one novel phrase differing in frequency (e.g., *fatal mistake, awful mistake, extreme mistake*). The results showed that the frequency effect only occurred in early eye-movement measures, *first-pass reading time* (the sum of fixations on the target words in the first-pass reading), but not in late measures, fixation count (the total number of fixations on the target words), and total reading time (sum of all fixation duration on the nouns).

With regards to the effect of phrasal frequency in the L2 collocation processing, prior studies produced mixed results. In an acceptability judgment task, Wolter & Gyllstad (2013) found that non-native speakers (NNSs) responded significantly faster to collocations compared to novel language, indicating that NNSs are highly sensitive to the effect of phrasal frequency, while others indicate that NNSs are less sensitive to frequency information (e.g., Siyanova & Schmitt 2008; Wray 2002). Siyanova & Schmitt (2008) conducted two judgment tasks in which participants were asked to rate how common the collocations were. The results showed that NNSs did not judge the collocations as fast as native speakers (NSs) and they failed to separate high-frequency collocations from medium-frequency collocations. Thus, the authors argued that non-native speakers had "poorer intuition" of phrasal frequency. Wray (2002) argued that NNSs tend to be "more analytical" than NSs, and thus they are not good at obtaining frequency information.

In addition to the effect of phrasal frequency, contextual predictability also plays an important role in the processing of collocations. Contextual constraint allows readers to predict the upcoming word based on the preceding context, which facilitates word processing. Contextual predictability can be measured via a cloze task in which a group of participants are presented with sentence fragments up to the target word and are asked to write down the first word or words that come into their minds (Taylor 1953). A word's cloze probability is the proportion of participants who write the target word. Typically, the cloze probability is 60% or above for highly constrained words and 10% or less for neutral or unconstrained words (Rayner & Well 1996). A large number of researches have confirmed the effect of context in word processing (e.g., Rayner & Well 1996; Starr & Rayner 2001; Wang et al. 2019). It was found that the word embedded in a more predictable context was processed faster and skipped more often than the one in neutral context (e.g., Balota et al. 1985; Drieghe et al. 2005; Ehrlich & Rayner 1981; Fischler & Bloom 1979; McClelland & O'Regan 1981; Rayner & Well 1996; Rayner et al. 2004). Contextual effects on word processing were found on early eye-movement measures (e.g., Binder et al. 1999; Lavigne et al. 2000; Rayner et al. 2004), and late measures (e.g., Calvo & Meseguer 2002; Ehrlich & Rayner 1981; Rayner & Well 1996). The effect of contextual predictability was found in the collocational processing as well (Frisson et al. 2005; Li et al. 2021). For instance, Frisson et al. (2005) found the processing of verb-noun collocations received facilitation from the contextual predictability in eye-movement experiments.

McDonald & Shillcock (2003a, b) and Frisson et al. (2005) used a modified cloze test to assess the contextual predictability. They presented participants sentence fragments up to and including the verb of the verb-noun collocations. And then the participants were asked to write down the first word or words that came into their minds. In their cloze tests, the participants might use statistical information of the collocations to complete the test since the constituents of collocations were presented. As a result, the cloze value may be generated by transitional probability. Since TP was not separated from contextual predictability at the beginning, their conclusion that the effects of statistical information are part of contextual effects is doubtful (Vilkaite 2016). However, whether statistical information influences the processing of collocations or other formulaic language independently is a crucial question. If the independent role is verified, it will further confirm the psychological reality of collocations and support the usage-based models of language acquisition. In addition, the impact of statistical information will be taken into account by researchers when they study the processing of other formulaic language. The results show that collocations are processed faster than matched control phrases, which support McDonald & Shillcock's (2003a, b) finding that readers store the statistical information of collocations.

Electrophysiological research also provides evidence in support of the facilitative role of contextual constraint. Research has shown that the amplitude of N400 is increased when a word is semantically incongruous with the sentence context (Kutas & Hillyard 1980, 1983). N400 is a negative peak reflecting the integration with sentential context. When a word is quite surprising and unexpected in a sentence, the amplitude of N400 rises as well (Federmeier & Kutas 1999; Federmeier et al. 2007; Kutas & Hillyard 1984).

Another important factor that affects collocation processing is the co-occurrence probability which can be measured by transitional probabilities (TP) and mutual information (MI). Hoey (2005) suggested that there is a priming relationship between the constituent words in collocations. Thus, when a word (e.g., *fast*) is recognized, its collocate (e.g., *food*) will be primed and recognized quickly. TP refers to the probability of a word following another in a text. There is evidence indicating that TP influences language use and processing as well (e.g., Ellis et al. 2008; Ellis 2014; Frisson et al. 2005; Gregory et al. 1999; McDonald & Shillcock 2003a, b; Tremblay & Baayen 2010; Vilkaite 2016; Yi et al. 2017). For instance, Gregory et al. (1999) found that speakers used the probabilistic information of collocations in speech production in which collocations were expressed more fluently with shorter duration. Tremblay & Baayen (2010) found the effects of the whole-string contingency on the processing of four-word sequences (e.g., *becoming increasingly clear that*) in a recall task. McDonald & Shillcock (2003) explored the effect of TP using an eye-tracking experiment in which verb-noun phrases differing in TP (e.g., *accept defeat, accept losses*) were presented in neutral context. The length and frequency of the nouns were closely matched. TP effects were found in early eye-tracking measures (first-fixation duration, single-fixation duration and gaze duration) due to significantly shorter reading times for phrases with high TP than phrases with low TP. Thus, McDonald & Shillcock suggested that readers used the statistical co-occurrence of phrases to predict upcoming words, which facilitated the processing of the phrases in reading. Frisson el al. (2005) replicated McDonald & Shillcock's (2003a, b) experiments but manipulated contextual predictability. In Frisson el al.'s (2005) study, the target words were verb-noun collocations and contextual predictability (constrained context and neutral context) and TP (high-TP and low-TP) were manipulated. Experiment 1 found the early contextual effect and provided the evidence of TP effect, in line with McDonald & Shillcock (2003a). However, the authors thought that the TP effects might be caused by different predictability values of high- and the low-TP items. Experiment 2 showed that TP effects disappeared when the imbalance of contextual predictability was removed. Thus, the authors concluded that TP effects were part of contextual effects, and there was no clear evidence of independent TP effects.

Mutual information (MI) (Church et al. 1990) scores indicate the co-occurrence probability of the constituent words in word combinations (Manning & Schütze 1999; Vilkaitem 2016). Although both TP and MI indicate the statistical association between the constituent words in word pairs (Clear 1993), MI is distinct from TP. Forward or backward TP is unidirectional, whereas MI is bi-directional (Yi et al. 2017). MI is a better choice to measure mutual expectancy between constituent words in collocations. MI is computed as the "logarithmic ratio between the observed and expected occurrences of a word pair in a corpus" (Vilkaite 2016). Previous studies (Durrant & Doherty 2010; Ellis et al. 2008; Gregory et al. 1999; Sonbul 2015; Vilkaite 2016) have showed that English native speakers are sensitive to MI in the processing of multi-word sequences. For instance, in an eye-tracking experiment, Carrol & Conklin (2019) explored the influence of phrasal frequency, semantic association strength and MI scores on the processing of adjective-noun collocations. It was found that only MI scores did a good job of explaining the processing advantage of collocations in the final word analysis. The reaction times of the correct yes-responses were significantly shorter to the real phrases of high than to those of low MI scores. Moreover, the role of MI scores even seems important in the processing of other types of formulaic sequences. For instance, in a grammaticality judgment task, Elliset et al. (2008) asked participants to judge whether word strings such as "in the road" and "open your books to" were acceptable in English. Reaction times (RT) of correct yes-responses to the real phrases were analyzed with three variables, namely, word length, MI scores and frequency of the phrases. The results showed that MI scores were a predictor of RT, that is, the phrases with higher MI scores had shorter RT.

Phrasal frequency and the co-occurrence probabilities (e.g., TP, MI) are two statistical properties of collocations. McDonald & Shillcock (2003a) found that the effects of frequency and TP "have a similar locus in the time course the effects of lexical processing", and thus they argued that the two effects might influence the same stage of reading. Based on this finding, Sonbul (2015) employed collocation strength to combine the two types of statistical information (phrasal frequency and MI scores) as one variable to examine the processing of two *synonymous* adjective-noun collocations and one novel phrase (e.g., *fatal mistake, awful mistake, extreme mistake*) using the eye-movement tracking technique. The collocation strength which was determined based on phrasal frequency and MI scores which were obtained from the British National Corpus (Burnage & Dunlop 1992). In each stimulus pair, one word combination had both a higher phrasal frequency and a higher MI than the other. Based on these scores, Sonbul (2015) categorized the higher-scoring phrase as a strong collocation and the other as a weak collocation. The reading times were longer for the weak (e.g., *awful mistake*) than the strong (e.g., *fatal mistake*) collocations, but were the longest for the novel phrases. The results showed that the processing advantage for collocations was only detected in early eye-movement measure (first-pass reading time), but not in late measures, fixation count and total reading time.

Li et al. (2021) explored the effect of collocation strength and the effect of contextual predictability in the processing of adjective-noun collocations by native speakers using an eye-tracking experiment. Collocation strength was determined based on phrasal frequency and MI scores. Each pair of collocations was divided into strong and weaker collocations. Strong collocations (e.g., *black coffee*) had significantly higher phrasal frequency and MI scores than weaker collocations (e.g., *bitter coffee*). Both strong and weaker collocations were presented in predictable and neutral context. The effect of collocation strength was found due to shorter reading times for strong collocations compared to weaker ones. The effect of contextual predictability was also found due to shorter reading times for collocations presented in predictable context than in neutral context. The effects of collocation strength and contextual predictability were found in both early and late eye-movement measures. Additionally, there was no significant interaction between the two effects. This led the authors to conclude that the effect of collocation strength is independent from the effect of contextual predictability.

Researches to date have also explored the role of other statistical information such as mutual information (MI) in L2 collocation processing (e.g., Li et al. 2022; Sonbul 2015). It was found that non-native speakers were not sensitive to the effect of MI. The role of phrasal frequency and MI in the collocation processing was explored as well. In an eye-tracking experiment, Sonbul (2015) explored the processing of synonymous adjective-noun word pairs with the same noun in reading by native and non-native speakers. Each set of stimuli included two collocations which were categorized as strong (e.g., *fatal mistake*) and weaker collocations (e.g., *awful mistake*) based on phrasal frequency and MI scores, and one non-collocation (e.g., *extreme mistake*). The results showed that the first-pass reading time of both native and non-native speakers were significantly longer for weaker collocations with lower frequency and MI scores than strong collocations with high frequency and MI scores, but longest for non-collocations. This result indicated that both native and non-native speakers were sensitive to collocation strength in the early processing stage.

Vilkaite (2016) explored the processing of verb-noun collocations and novel phrases differing in phrasal frequency and MI using an eye-tracking experiment. It was found that native speakers read adjacent collocations (e.g., *provide information*) faster than control phrases (e.g., *compare information*) and this processing advantage extended to non-adjacent collocations (e.g., *provide some of the information*). In a follow-up experiment, Vilkaite & Schmitt (2017) explored NNSs' collocation processing by using the same material and design as Vilkaite (2016). It was found that advanced NNSs processed adjacent collocations faster than novel phrases as native speakers, but the processing advantage of non-adjacent collocations disappeared (Vilkaite & Schmitt 2017). Vilkaite & Schmitt (2017) suggested that compared with NSs, NNSs are less exposed to English, and a word and its collocate is not strongly associated. As a result, NNSs showed no facilitation effect for non-adjacent collocations.

Li et al. (2022) investigated the roles of contextual constraint and collocation strength on L2 collocational processing using an eye movement experiment. In this experiment, 40 English sentences including adjective-noun word pairs which consisted of strong (e.g., *black coffee*) and weak (e.g., *bitter coffee*) collocations were presented to 38 Chinese learners of English as a foreign language (EFL learners). The target words were embedded in highly predictable or neutral context. The results demonstrated the effects of collocation strength and contextual predictability. In addition, a late eye movement showed an interaction effect between the two factors, indicating that contextual predictability played a stronger influence on weak compared to strong collocations. The possible explanation is that EFL learners are less familiar with weak collocations and thus they rely more on contextual constraint during reading.

Semantic association is another factor influencing the processing of collocations. There is a considerable amount of empirical evidence from studies on binomials demonstrating the effect of semantic priming between words (e.g., Carroll & Slowiaczek 1986; Camblin et al. 2007). The effect of semantic priming is often present in word recognition. Research has shown that there were shorter reading times (first-pass reading time) for strongly associated words compared to weakly associated words. The priming between constitutent words of binomials can be explained with the spreading activation model (Collins & Loftus 1975). The automatic semantic priming occurs, due to common features or the association relationship between two words (e.g., Hutchison 2003; Lucas 2000). When two words are frequently used together, the relationship between them will be strengthened. Some fixed formulaic language such as idioms are processed as single units. The constituent words of such units are easily activated and processed quickly.

A growing number of studies have examined semantical priming between words (see McNamara 2004 for an overview). For instance, Peng et al. (1997) found that when a prime was a transposed word which was *semantically* related to a target word, the effect of semantic priming between the prime and target words appeared. Carroll & Slowiaczek (1986) found the priming effect when *semantically* related words appeared in the same sentential context. Similarly, Camblin et al. (2007) found that the associative priming effects only occurred in impoverished discourse context. It was found that both forward and backword priming effect existed in the processing of L1 collocations (Bonk 2003). Durrant (2009) found a similar priming effect in adjective-noun and noun-noun collocations among NSs. In a primed lexical decision, Wolter & Gyllstad (2011) found the effect of collocational priming for both native and non-native speakers.

Durrant & Doherty (2010) explored the collocational priming using two priming tasks. The experimental materials were adjective-noun word pairs which were divided into four types, namely, low-frequency novel phrases, moderate-frequency collocations, frequent collocations and *semantically* associated frequent collocations. Experiment 1 was an unmasked priming task in which the priming effect was observed between high frequency collocations with MI scores of 6 or greater, and this priming effect was found for both associated and non-associated collocations. This result indicated that collocational priming exists in frequent collocations whether they are associated or not. It is noticing that there is a limitation in Experiment 1. The participants might guess the upcoming word in the unmasked priming task, which can not reflect the organisation of mental lexicon (Lucas 2000). To make up the shortcoming of Experiment 1, Experiment 2 used a masked prime task in which primes were presented for a very short time and followed by masks. It has been acknowledged that this method can elicit automatic priming (de Groot & Nas 1991; Seren 1991; Perea & Rosa 2002). The result showed that the priming effect was only observed for the collocations which were both frequent collocations and semantic associates, indicating that both frequency of co-occurrence and semantic association affected the representation of collocations.

In the studies of second language (L2) collocation processing, research has examined the role of L1 collocational knowledge in the processing of collocations by L2 learners. It is well established that the influence of L1 knowledge on L2 collocational processing exists. There is a considerable amount of empirical evidence from studies conducted on congruency effects. For example, Carro et al. (2016) explored whether L1 (Swedish) idiom knowledge affects the comprehension of L2 (English) idiom comprehension using an eye-tracking paradigm. In the experiment, highly proficient L2 learners were asked to read sentences which contained idioms and control phrases. Three types of idioms were used, namely, English-only idioms which only exist in English (e.g., *pick your brains*), Swedish-only idioms which only exist in Swedish and are translated into English (e.g., *sit inside*), and congruent idioms which exist in both English and Swedish (e.g., *meet your match*). The results showed that the processing advantage of idioms over control phrases was found in all the three types of idioms. This advantage was due to shorter reading times and fewer fixations for idioms. Although L1-only idioms don't exist in L2, L1 knowledge facilitates the processing of L2 collocation. The analysis of the skipping rate on the final word of the idioms showed that higher skipping rates were observed for the final word of the Swedish-only and congruent idioms, but not English-only idioms. This result suggested that L2 idioms were not "as well entrenched in the mental lexicon" as the other two types of idioms. The authors concluded that L1 knowledge plays a facilitative role in the processing of L2 idioms.

In a phrase-acceptability judgment task, Yamashita & Jiang (2010) explored congruency on collocation processing. It was found that English for foreign language (EFL) learners made a faster judgment with less errors to collocations in L2 if there were equivalent collocations in L1 (congruent collocations), indicating that L1 influenced the processing of L2 collocation. Wolter & Gyllstad (2011, 2013) assessed congruency effects on L2 collocation processing as well. The results showed that congruent collocations are processed faster than incongruent collocations. In the follow-up studies, Wolter & Yamashita (2015) explored the processing of collocations which only exists in L1 (Japanese). The authors translated these L1-only collocations into L2 (English), and they failed to find the facilitation effect in the collocation processing.

Wolter & Gyllstad (2011) claimed that one explanation for the congruency effects in the collocation processing is due to the activation of L1 knowledge. When L2 collocations are encountered, L2 collocations will be translated into L1, and then the corresponding L1 knowledge of collocations is activated. As a result, the recognition of L2 collocations is accelerated.

There is now strong evidence suggesting that there is across-language lexical priming. However, the priming is asymmetrical, that is, the priming is mostly from L1 to L2 and less from L2 to L1 (e.g., Brysbaert & Duyck 2010; Schoonbaert et al. 2009).

Another important factor influencing the processing of collocations is adjacency. Although a majority of collocations are adjacent, non-adjacent sequences are also frequently used (Vilkaite 2016). However, relatively little empirical research has been done on the issue of adjacency. Vilkaite (2016) explored the processing of adjacent and non-adjacent collocations in reading using an eye-tracking paradigm. Four conditions were included in the experiment: (1) adjacent collocation (*provide information*), (2) adjacent control (*compare information*), (3) non-adjacent collocation (*provide some of the information*), (4) non-adjacent control (*compare some of the information*). Four measures were analysed: first fixation duration and first-pass reading time (early), total reading time, and total fixation count (late). The analysis of the phrase-final word suggested an overall stronger facilitative effect for adjacent items compared to non-adjacent ones. However, this effect varied across the eye-tracking measures. For example, no facilitation was found for non-adjacent collocation in the early measures, while total reading time and fixation count suggested faster processing for non-adjacent collocations than their controls. The author suggested that for the earliest stages of word access and retrieval, collocation status (i.e., frequent vs. novel phrase) did not affect processing, while it did in the later stages of processing. The analysis of the whole phrase showed consistently faster reading times for collocations than their controls, irrespective of adjacency.

2.6 The processing of Chinese formulaic language

With respect to the processing of Chinese formulaic language, the evidence is rather limited. Kong et al. (2016) found that frequent discontinuous correlative conjunctions (e.g., 因为……所以…… *because ... therefore ...* ; 虽然……也…… *although ... yet ...*) were processed more quickly compared to less frequent phrases in a grammaticality judgment task. More recently, Yi et al. (2017) assessed the impact of phrasal frequency and contingency (the co-occurring probability) on the processing of Chinese two-word adverbial sequences (e.g., 仍没: *have not yet*) in sentential context using the eye-tracking technique. The contingency of the adverbial sequences was measured by MI (mutual information, a measure that shows how likely the two words co-occur together). The results indicated that both phrasal frequency and contingency facilitated the processing of the multi-word sequences and both native and non-native Chinese speakers were sensitive to these two effects. Additionally, L2 learners were more sensitive to phrasal frequency compared to native speakers, which is different from earlier research (e.g., Siyanova-Chanturia, Conklin, & van Heuven, 2011).

2.6.1 The processing of Chinese idioms

Most Chinese multi-word studies focused on Chinese idioms.

Research has shown that Chinese idioms have processing advantage than novel phrases (e.g., Carrol & Conklin 2015; Gu & Liao 1995; Li et al. 2009; Yu 2014; Yu et al. 2016; Zang 2019). For instance, Gu & Liao (1995) asked participants to judge whether a linguistic unit was meaningful, and found that response times were faster for three-character idioms than for matched phrases. Similar results were observed in a naming task, such that idioms were named more quickly than matched phrases (Zhang & Shi 2009).

Carrol & Conklin (2015) examined native Chinese speakers' eye movements when they processed four-character Chinese idioms which were translated into English. The results showed that there were fewer fixations for the final word of the translated idioms compared to that of a control phrase. This study indicated the processing advantage of Chinese idioms.

Yu et al. (2016) assessed word *n+2* preview effects by comparing the eye movements on three-character Chinese idioms and those on control phrases using the boundary paradigm. The idioms (e.g., 揭疮疤, figuratively meaning expose others' secrets, and literally meaning pick a scab) and control phrases (e.g., 留疮疤: *have a scar*) are comprised of a verb (one character) and a noun (two characters). Yu et al. manipulated the preview of the noun. It was found that idioms were read faster than phrases with shorter reading times for idioms. However, the results did not show a processing advantage for the nouns when they were constituent words of idioms, indicating that this type of idioms was foveally processed, but not parafoveally processed.

Zang (2019) compared the processing of two-character words (multi-constituent units) and phrases using the boundary paradigm (Rayner 1975). The preview of the second constituent was manipulated with an identical character and a pseudocharacter. An invisible boundary was positioned before the targets. The results showed that a reliable preview effect was found on the first constituents of words. No preview effects were observed on the first constituents of phrases.

Zang (2019) proposed the multi-constituent unit (MCU) hypothesis based on the previous findings. The MCU Hypothesis assumes that some frequent linguistic units such as idioms and spaced compounds may be lexicalized and represented as single lexical units. Therefore, the constituents of MCUs are likely to be identified simultaneously, with the serial processing of the constituent words. According to the MCU Hypothesis, MCUs are represented as single words in the mental lexicon. The activation of one part of a MCU will lead to the activation of the other part, resulting in the parafoveal processing of the second part.

Zang et al. (2021) assessed whether idioms with "2 + 1" structure (e.g., 垫脚石: *stepping stones*) are processed as MCUs during natural reading using the boundary paradigm (Rayner, 1975). In Experiment 1, phrase type (idiom vs matched phrase) and preview of the noun (identical character, unrelated character or pseudocharacter) were manipulated with the same first constituent. It was found that there was a larger preview effect for idioms, due to fewer fixations for identical previews, indicating that idioms were parafoveally processed to a greater extent compared to control phrases. Experiment 2 orthogonally manipulated the preview of idioms and phrases. A greater preview effect of nouns in idioms compared to phrases was found. This result provided further evidence showing that idioms are lexicalised as MCUs and processed parafoveally as single units.

Different theories were proposed to account for the processing advantage of idioms. For instance, the lexical representation hypothesis (Swinney & Cutler 1979) claims that idioms are stored as long words in the mental lexicon. When the first constituent word of an idiom is encountered, the lexical entry of the whole unit will be activated. The configuration hypothesis (Cacciari & Tabossi 1988) assumes that idioms are stored as a configuration of their component words instead of single lexical units. When an idiom is heard or seen, each component word is activated, and the activation feeds up to the configuration. When the activation is enough, the idiomatic key will be reached, and then the figurative meaning of the idiom will be retrieved. The hybrid theories (Libben & Titone 2008; Titone & Connine 1999) propose that as idioms are encountered, the constituent words are identified simultaneously, and meanwhile the figurative meaning is retrieved. The processing of idioms is affected by many factors such as the frequency of the component word (Libben & Titone 2008). Although there are some differences in the three theories reviewed above, they all assume that idioms are processed as single units, which results in the processing advantage of the constituent words of idioms compared to novel phrases.

It has been acknowledged that there are boundary marks such as space in Chinese. In addition, a Chinese word may be composed of one character or more characters. Thus, it is difficult for Chinese readers to find word boundaries (e.g., Liu et al. 2013; Wang and Cheng 2021). Therefore, Chinese idioms may be processed as a single word due to their unique characteristics.

2.6.2 The processing of Chinese collocations

Lv & Shi (2016) is one of the two studies which have explored the processing of Chinese collocations. In a lexical decision-making task conducted by Lv & Shi (2016), stimuli were verb-noun word pairs consisting of two-character (2C) words (e.g., 采取措施 is made up of 采取 and 措施). Each pair combined a different verb with the same noun (e.g., 采取措施 and 采用措施, meaning take measures). The verbs in the same pair were synonyms with each other (e.g., 采取 and 采用). Each pair of verbs was matched in number of strokes and word frequency. One phrase from each pair was high-frequency collocation (e.g., 采取措施). The other was non-collocation (e.g., 采用措施). Each pair of phrases was put in two groups. The third group is novel phrases in which the same noun was used as in the former groups, but the verbs have nothing to do with those in the first and second groups. The experimental phrases were randomly presented to participants one by one. The participants were asked to judge as quickly as possible about whether the two words in each phrase were words or not. It was found that the reaction times were significantly shorter for collocations (e.g.,

采取措施) compared to non-collocations (e.g., 采用措施). This result indicated the processing advantage of Chinese collocations over novel phrases.

Jiang et al. (2020) extended the study of Bannard & Matthews (2008) who assessed young children's (two or three years old) sensitivity to the effect of frequency of phrases (e.g., *a drink of milk*) using a sentence-repeating task. Jiang et al. assessed whether Chinese 8 and 9-year-old children (third and fourth graders) and adults were sensitive to phrasal frequency or not during reading. In an eye-tracking experiment conducted by Jiang et al., stimuli were four-character verb-noun combinations chosen from BCC corpus (Xun et al. 2016), a 15-billion-character Chinese corpus. The phrase and lexical frequencies of the stimuli were extracted from BCC corpus. Each pair of the stimuli containing a different noun with the same verb was divided into a high-frequency phrase (collocation) (e.g., 参加会议: *attend the meeting*) and a low-frequency phrase (novel phrase) (e.g., 参加游戏: *attend the game*). The nouns in each pair were matched for frequency, the number of strokes and character structure. In addition, each pair was matched for association strength. Ten native Chinese adults who did not attend the eye-movement experiment were asked to provide the first word they thought of after seeing the verb in each pair (e.g., 参加: *attend*). The proportion of the nouns (e.g., 会议: *meeting*, or 游戏: *game*) was used as the score of association strength for the phrase. The collocation and novel phrase in each pair differed significantly in phrasal frequency. The collocation and the control phrase of each pair were embedded in the same sentence context. The naturalness of the experimental sentences was rated. Participants including children and adults were asked to read the sentences as quickly as possible for comprehension. The results showed that high-frequency collocations were read faster than low-frequency control phrases, indicating the effect of phrase frequency which was observed in the total reading time. Additionally, the reading time was the shortest for adults, longer for Grade 4 readers, and the longest for Grade 3 readers, indicating the role of age in reading times.

The present study focuses on verb-noun collocations which are one of the most common collocation subsets in Chinese. Chinese linguist Lv (1942) claimed that verb is the center of a sentence, which is supported by French linguist Tesniere (1959). According to dependency grammar (Tesniere 1959), the verb connects other words in the sentence. Verb-noun collocation plays the central role in a sentence structure. However, verb-noun collocations are very difficult for Chinese learners studying Chinese as a foreign language (CFL). For instance, Li (2016) found that verb-noun collocations errors CFL learners made accounted for 66% of the total collocation errors in CFL learners' essays. The present study is valuable for second language acquisition and teaching.

2.7 Conclusion

Chapter 2 introduces the definition, classification, identification of collocations and the theoretical framework consisting of five theories.

Previous studies on English collocations are reviewed from three aspects, that is, the processing advantage, the processing pattern and the influencing factors. The processing of Chinese formulaic sequences is summarized as well.

Chapter 3 Methodology

3.1 Introduction

In this dissertation, five eye-tracking experiments were conducted. The eye-tracking paradigm is believed to detect the on-line cognitive processing of lexical processing in natural reading (Just & Carpenter 1980; Rayner 1998, 2009; Rayner et al. 1989). Early and late eye-movement measures reflect early and late process of collocations respectively. The complete picture of the processing of collocations can be captured by analysing early and late eye-movement measures. In all the experiments, single sentences containing stimuli were presented to participants. In each experiment the stimuli were manipulated based on the experimental design. The properties of stimuli, such as frequency, number of strokes, were controlled. To make sure participants are engaged with the task, the stimuli sentences are followed by about 25% comprehension questions. Norming studies were carried out to rate naturalness and contextual predictability. To judge how natural the sentences sounded, a group of participants who did not attend eye-tracking experiments were asked to assess the sentences for naturalness by using a 5-point Likert scale (where 1 = very unnatural and 5 = very natural). Cloze test tasks were conducted to establish contextual predictability scores of the stimuli sentences. In the cloze test tasks, participants were presented with sentence fragments truncated immediately before the collocation phrase and participants were asked to provide a written continuation. The collocation is considered to be predictable if a continuation is the target collocation or phrases including its verb. For instance, the participants were presented with a sentence fragment "美国航天局明年将向金星____" (*NASA will ____ to Venus next year*). If the participants filled in the blank with the target collocation "发射火箭" (*launch a rocket*) or phrases like "发射卫星" (*launch a satellite*) or "发射飞船" (*launch a spacecraft*) which included the verb "发射" (*launch*), these continuation were taken to demonstrate predictability. Context was assessed as predictable if more than 50% of the responses were of this type.

3.2 Eye movements during reading

This section gives a brief introduction about eye movements which were used in this dissertation. Section 3.2.1 reviews the background information of eye movements. Section 3.2.2 introduces the eye-tracking technology used in this dissertation. Section 3.2.3 reports some eye movement measures used in this dissertation. Section 3.2.4 introduces some key models of eye movement control during reading. Section 3.2.5 examines the parafoveal processing during reading.

3.2.1 Background information of eye movements

When we read, we continually make rapid eye movements which

are called *saccades*. Between the saccades, there are pauses called *fixations*. During fixations, our eyes keep relatively still for around 225～250 ms (Rayner 2009). It was found that information of text is obtained during fixations (Rayner & Pollatsek 1989). Fixations can be first-pass (encountering the word for the first time) or rereading (refixating the word). In addition, not all words in text are fixated. Content words are fixated more often than function words. Specifically, content words and function words are fixated about 85% and 35% of the time respectively (Carpenter & Just 1983; Rayner & Duffy 1988). Research has shown that short words are more likely to be skipped (Rayner & McConkie 1976). Function words tend to be short and thus, they are less fixated. An example of eye movement record can be found in Figure 3.1.

Saccades range in length from 1 to over 15 letters. On average, the saccade length is 7～9 letter spaces in the text (Rayner 2009). During saccades, vision is suppressed (Matin 1974) and visual information is not acquired due to the fast movements of eyes (Uttal & Smith 1968) and the masking of the information before and after the saccade (Brooks et al. 1981; Campbell & Wurtz 1979; Chekaluk & Llewellyn 1990). Most of the time, we make progressive or forward saccades (left-to-right movements). Some time, we make regressive or backward saccades as well (right-to-left movements). The regressive saccades account for 10%～15% of all the saccades (Rayner, 2009). The reason why readers make regression may be because they have difficulty understanding the text.

Figure 3.1 A hypothetical eye movement record during reading

Note: Grey circles show fixations and arrows show direction of saccades including both progressive saccades (forward curves) and a regressive saccade (backward curve).

We make saccades frequently due to limitations in retinal acuity. Our visual field can be divided into three regions: the foveal region, the parafoveal region, and the peripheral region (Rayner 1998). Acuity is the best in the fovea (a 2° region of central vision). As the region extends out to 5° on either side of fixation (the *parafoveal*), visual acuity is reduced, but readers can still capture some visual information in the parafovea (Rayner 1998). The region beyond the parafovea is the *periphery* in which acuity gets even worse. Nothing can be obtained in this region. Thus, we have to make eye movements to put new words into the foveal region to see clearly.

Eye movements may be influenced by several factors such as textual difficulty, typographical variables, reading skill and characteristics of the writing system. Thus, as the text becomes more difficult, readers have longer fixations, shorter saccades and more regressions (Rayner 1998). Typographical variables such as print or display quality, font size and difficulty, letter spacing influence eye movements as well (Kolers et al. 1981; Morrison & Inhoff 1981). For instance, the increase in the difficulty to encode fonts leads to longer fixations, shorter saccades, and more regressions (Rayner et al. 2006d; Rayner et al. 2011). Skilled readers have shorter fixations, longer saccades, and less regressions than less skilled readers (Ashby, et al. 2005; Rayner 1998), as do less skilled readers. Additionally, eye movements differ in different writing systems. Different from English (alphabetic languages), written Chinese is logographic. The studies about the eye movements of Chinese readers have shown that first Chinese and English readers' average fixation durations are quite similar (about 225～250 msec) (Chen et al. 2003; Rayner, 1998; Sun & Feng 1999). Second, Chinese readers' perceptual span (the region of effective vision during an eye fixation) extends 1 character to the left of fixation to 2 to 3 characters to the right (Chen & Tang 1998; Inhoff & Liu 1997, 1998), whereas English readers' perceptual span extends 3 to 4 letters to the left of fixation to about 14 to 15 letters to the right of fixation (Rayner 1998). Third, Chinese readers' average saccades (about 2.6 characters) are much shorter than English readers' (about 7～8 letters) (Chen et al. 2003). Forth, Chinese readers have slightly higher regression rate (about 15%) than English readers (about 10%) (Chen et al. 2003; Rayner 1998). Fifth, the skipping rate of a word is quite similar in Chinese and English (Rayner et al. 2004). Recently, in the study of Liversedge et al. (2016), English native speakers were asked to read English text and Chinese native speakers were asked to read Chinese text which was translated from the English text. It was found that Chinese readers have longer fixation durations (245 ms vs. 207 ms), shorter saccade length (3.19 characters vs. 8.53 letters) and more skipping (47% vs. 36%) compared with English readers.

Eye-tracking has been widely used in reading research (e.g.,

Rayner 1998, 2009). Eye-tracking records readers' eye movement behavior in natural reading including when they look, where they look, and for how long. Rayner (1978) argued that eye-tracking provided an opportunity for researchers to "look into the mind" of subjects. In other words, eye-tracking helps researchers better understand the reading process of readers in real time (Liversedge & Findlay 2000; Rayner 2009). Eye tracking has been used based on two underlying assumptions. First, the text that is being fixated is what the reader is processing. Second, fixation durations and fixations reflect the cognitive effort needed in the processing of text, that is, longer durations and more fixations are reflective of greater effort that have been taken and shorter fixation durations, less fixations and higher skipping indicate less processing effort (Pickering et al. 2004, cited in Conklin & Pellicer-Sánchez 2016). Therefore, eye movements are believed to reflect the mechanisms of reading.

Eye-tracking has two main advantages compared with other techniques in reading research. First, unlike self-reading tasks, eye-tracking offers a way for participants to read text as naturally as they do in real life. In other commonly used reading research paradigms such as self-paced reading tasks, sentences are presented in a word-by-word manner, which may disrupt readers' processing and lead them to process words by words instead of phrases (Vilkaite 2016). However, a whole sentence or a passage can be presented in eye-tracking experiments. Moreover, while participants are reading, they do not have a secondary task such as pressing buttons or giving response.

Their reading proceeds smoothly without interruption. As a result, the eye-tracking is regarded as an ideal tool to explore the natural reading process (e.g., Duyck et al. 2007). Second, eye-tracking offers a very rich record of reading behaviour. The eye movements can be quantified with different measures which will be discussed in Section 3.3. More important, the measures are divided into early and late measures indicating different processing stages. In addition, this means that both early and late effects of the experimental manipulation can be detected and examined separately. In short, the eye-movement measures provide detailed data reflecting readers' moment-to-moment cognitive processing (Just & Carpenter 1980; Rayner 1998, 2009).

3.2.2 Eye-tracking technology

In the eye-tracking experiment, the participant is asked to read the text presented on a computer screen. The participant's eye movements will be recorded by using an eye-tracking tracker. In current experiments, we use EyeLink 1000 plus eye tracker (SR Research inc.) which involves a high-speed camera, capable of recording binocular eye movements at up to 2000 frames per second. We use this tracker to record right-eye gaze location every millisecond during binocular reading which is able to record fine details of eye movements. Sentences were displayed as black text on a light grey background on a monitor. The eye-tracker was calibrated to their eye movements using a three-point horizontal calibration procedure to ensure spatial accuracy less than 0.35° visual angle.

3.2.3 Eye movement measures

There are various eye movement measures. The measures used in the experiments in this dissertation are defined in Table 3.1.

Eye movement measures are divided into early and late measures reflecting early lexical access and later information integration respectively (e.g., Paterson et al. 1999; Rayner et al. 1989). Specifically, early measures include skipping rate, single fixation duration, first fixation duration, and gaze duration (or first-pass reading time for a phrase). Late measures contain rereading time, fixation count, regression-path duration, and total reading time.

Table 3.1 Eye movement measures reported in this dissertation

Measures	Definition
Skipping (SKIP) rate	The probability of not fixating a word during first-pass reading
Single fixation duration (SFD)	The duration of the fixation when only one fixation was made during first-pass reading
First fixation duration (FFD)	The first fixation on a word during the first-pass reading
Gaze duration (GD)	The sum of all first-pass fixations on a word
First-pass reading time (FPRT)	The sum of all first-pass fixations in a region
Rereading time (RRT)	The total reading time minus gaze duration
Regression-path duration (RPD)	The sum of all fixations from the first fixation in a region until a fixation to its right
Total reading time (TRT)	The sum of all fixations in a region
Fixation count (FC)	The total number of fixations on the target words
Regressions in (RI)	The probability of a regression back to a region
Regressions out (RO)	The probability of a regression out of a region

Eye movement measures are sensitive to experimental manipulations such as word frequency and contextual predictability. Early measures are sensitive to familiarity, lexical meaning (Reichle et al. 1998; Roberts & Siyanova-Chanturia 2013), frequency (e.g., Sonbul 2015) and contextual predictability (e.g., Rayner & Well 2014). Late measures are believed to indicate reanalysis and integration of information when the reader encounters processing difficulty, and recovery from processing difficulties (Paterson et al. 1999; Rayner et al. 1989). Late eye movement measures are also sensitive to frequency and contextual predictability (e.g., Li et al. 2021).

Early and late measures reflect different time courses of processing. The effect of a manipulation may be detected in early or late or both early and late measures. For instance, first fixation duration is an early measure sensitive to frequency. It was found that the first fixation durations of low-frequency words are longer than those of high-frequency words (e.g., Inhoff & Rayner 1986; Rayner & Duffy 1986), indicating that readers encounter early processing difficulty when reading low-frequency words. If late measures such as total reading time of a critical region in a condition are found significantly longer or shorter than those in another condition, this indicates that the manipulation has late effects in the processing of the critical region (Liversedge et al. 1998). Thus, it is vital to choose proper measures to examine the effect of the manipulation. Rayner (1998) argued that single eye movement measure is not enough to indicate cognitive processing. Therefore, it is suggested that researchers use a combination of early and late measures which captures the whole picture of readers' reading behavior, demonstrating the on-line cognitive processing of language in natural reading (e.g., Rayner 2009).

In this dissertation, eye movement measures are reported for two critical regions containing either the whole collocation or only the collocation noun (see Carrol & Conklin 2014; Vilkaite 2016). The noun analysis captures the collocational effect occurring in the noun (a predicted locus of facilitation). However, the noun analysis excludes the skipped nouns where may reflect the role of facilitation. The whole collocation analysis captures the effect occurring at the whole phrase including the skipped nouns (Vilkaite 2016). We reported eye movement measures that are sensitive to the early lexical access and the later integration processes. For the whole collocations and final nouns, we reported an early measure, first-pass reading time (FPRT, or gaze duration for a single word, GD), and three late measures: rereading time, fixation count and total reading time (Liversedge et al. 1998). For the nouns, we reported additional three early measures including word-skipping, single fixation duration, first fixation duration which are sensitive to the processing of single words.

3.2.4 Models of eye movement control during reading

Researchers have proposed various computational models of eye-movement control in reading to account for the behaviour of eye movements. The two primary models are the E-Z Reader model (Reichle & Drieghe 2013; Reichle et al. 1998; Reichle et al. 2006; Reichle et al.

2012; Reichle et al. 1999), and the SWIFT model (Engbert et al. 2002; Engbert et al. 2005).

The E-Z Reader (Reichle et al. 1998) claims that words are processed sequentially, that is, when the processing of one word is finished, the eyes move to next one.

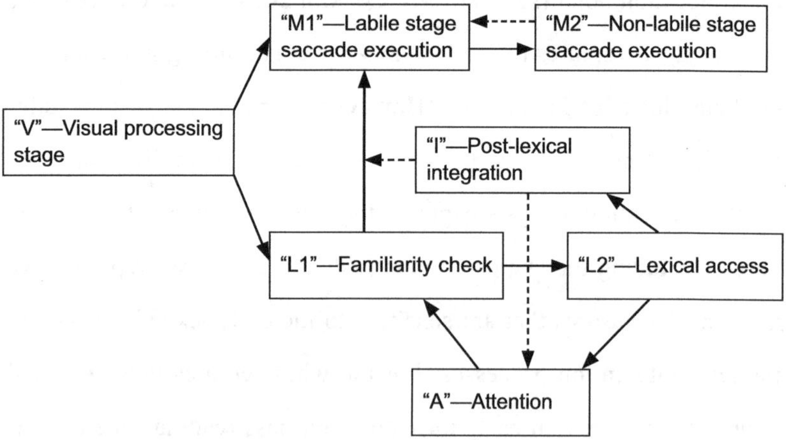

Figure 3.2 A simplified schematic of the E-Z reader model (Reichle et al. 2012)

As shown in Figure 3.2, E-Z Reader describes that visual information is first retrieved in the visal processing stage, and then feeds forward to the lexical processing stages. When a word is fixated, the lexical processing occurs in two stages. The first stage is the initial lexical processing in which the word familiarity is checked. Once the word is almost identified, an eye movement (saccade) may occur. Saccade programming consists of two stages which are a labile stage and the lexical access stage. When the two stages are completed, the saccade begins. In the labile stage, readers will identify a saccade target and calculate the distance to this target. In this process, saccade may be cancelled. In the lexical access stage, words are identified.

The first stage processing is affected several reasons such as word frequency, predictability and foveal eccentricity. Therefore, this model can account for effects of frequency and contextual constraint. It also can explain why some words may be skipped. If readers can get sufficient parafoveal processing, the saccade to this word can be cancelled and the eyes move to word *n+2*, resulting in word *n+1* being skipped.

The SWIFT model

SWIFT (Engbert et al. 2005) claims that words within the perceptual span are processed in parallel. SWIFT assumes that words with different activation levels compete for a winner. When the winner is produced, the target word is selected.

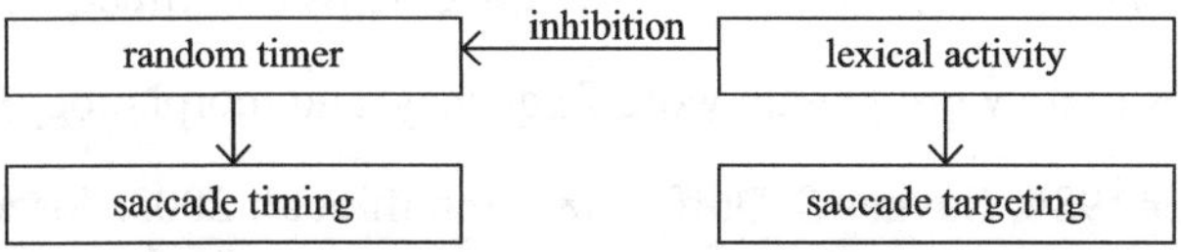

Figure 3.3 A simplified schematic of the SWIFT model (Engbert et al. 2005)

SWIFT also posits when the saccade occurs and what is the saccade target. The most active word is more likely to be the following saccade. When to move is dertermined by a random timer which is affected by lexical activation.

SWIFT also specifies that predictable, frequent and short words receive shorter fixations. Further, SWIFT posits that the fixation durations are influenced by the currently fixated words, the previous words and the next words. SWIFT also accounts for word skipping.

Words which have been sufficiently activated may be skipped.

The two models reviewed above can explain different eye movement behaviour during reading and they consider the influence of frequency and word predictability on reading times. However, these models differ in some aspects. The big difference is that E-Z Reader proposes that word processing is serial, whereas SWIFT assumes that processing is parallel.

Another obvious difference is about word skipping. SWIFT assumes that skipping can occur when the parafoveal word recognition is not finished, while E-Z Reader posits that skipping occurs when word $n+1$ is about to be processed.

Words are regarded as the basic processing units in the control model of eye movement in reading (Reichle et al. 1998; Pollatsek et al. 2001; Pollatsek et al. 2006). Eye movements are affected by word properties (e.g., word length, word frequency, and morphology) (Inhoff & Rayner 1986; Rayner & Duffy 1986; Inhoff et al. 2003; Joseph et al. 2009).

Rayner, Li & Pollatsek (2007) examined the reading behaviour of Chinese readers. It was found that the E-Z reading model can predict the behaviour of Chinese readers' eye movements. In the study, the character frequency was used as a variable. It was found that the eye movement behaviour can not be well predicted by characters as processing units.

Li et al. (2009) proposed a Chinese word recognition and segmentation model (see Figure 3.4). The model posits that Chinese characters are parally processed in parallel. The processing of characters is influenced by acuity and visual attention. Following the interactive activation framework (Mc-Clelland & Rumelhart 1981), the model assumes that when characters are recognized, information may feed up to words, resulting in the activation of words. In addition, the word information feeds back to the character level and facilitates the processing of characters. The activated words compete with each other until a winner is produced and then the word is recognized. In this model, Chinese recognition and word segmentation occur simultaneously. Further, the model claims that the processing of a character is affected by both words and other characters. When a character is a part of a word, it is processed faster than when it is not.

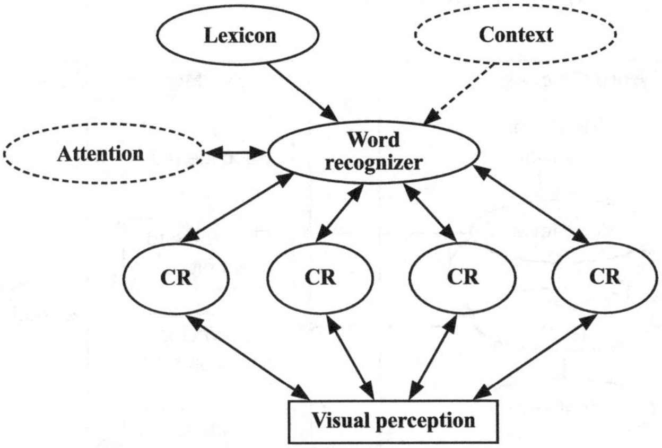

Figure 3.4 The framework of a word segmentation and recognition model (Li et al. 2009)

Note: CR refers to character recognizer.

Li & Pollatsek (2020) propose an integrated model of word processing and eye-movement control during Chinese reading (CRM) (see Figure 3.5). The model includes two modules. One is a word-processing module explaining the word processing. The other one is an eye-movement control module describing eye movements during reading. There are real communications between the two modules. The word-processing module provides the real-time processing information of characters and words for the eye-movement control module. The eye-movement control module makes decision about eye movements based on the information it has obtained. The eye-movement control module sends signals of eye movements to the word-processing module. The word-processing module changes its perceptual span after receiving the signal of eye movements.

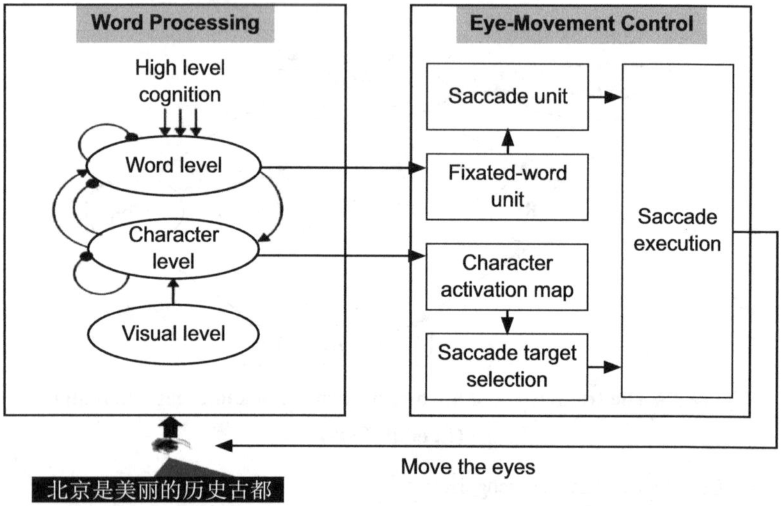

Figure 3.5 The architecture of the CRM model (Li & Pollatsek 2020)

According to the CRM, all characters within the perceptual span are processed in parallel. The activation of characters spreads to words and leads words to be activated. There are competitions between words. A word is identified and segmented when it wins the competitions. After it is recognized, the eyes move to another character. The CRM claims that word identification and segmentation is a unified process. Lexical identification drives eye movements.

3.2.5 Parafoveal processing during reading

Previous research has shown that readers process words in the foveal region which they are fixating (word *n*), and they also process words in the parafoveal region (e.g., word *n+1*) prior to their fixation (e.g., Hyönäet al. 2004; Juhasz et al. 2009; Rayner 1998; Rayner 2009; Schotter et al. 2012; White et al. 2008). For instance, when the first component word *sun* of a compound word *sunlight* is fixated, part of information of the second one *light* can be extracted as well. Numerous studies have revealed that before words are fixated, parafoveal information of the words can be extracted to be pre-processed (Rayner 2009; Schotter et al. 2012). Parafoveal information facilitates the processing of words during natural reading (Rayner et al. 1982).

A large number of studies have used the boundary paradigm (Rayner 1975) to explore the parafoveal processing. An invisible boundary is positioned before a target word which is embedded in a sentence in this paradigm. Before readers' fixation crosses the boundary, an identical or different parafoveal preview of the target word will be presented. As the eye crosses the boundary, the preview is replaced by the target word (see Figure 3.5). For example, for the target word *door*, the identical preview is word *door*, the different preview could be *more* or any other related or unrelated words. The word before the boundary is regarded as word *n* and the one directly after the boundary is word *n+1*. The preview effect (shorter fixations for identical than different previews) is often observed in the boundary paradigm. Previous research has demonstrated robust preview benefits for word *n+1* (see Cutter et al. 2015 for a review).

In the boundary paradigm (Rayner 1975), readers are not aware of the change of words. This is because the change occurs during a saccade in which the vision is suppressed. In normal reading, readers are able to process words parafoveally using valid previews, whereas invalid previews may disturb a readers' lexical processing. That is why identical or valide previews lead to shorter fixation times. The difference in fixation times made by different previews is referred to as the preview benefit (Schotter et al. 2012). This preview benefit means that readers benefit from parafoveal processing (Schotter & Leinenger 2016).

*

The newcomer is not used to the | xxxxx **traffic** in the big city during the rush hour.

*

The newcomer is not used to the | **heavy traffic** in the big city during the rush hour.

Figure 3.6 The architecture of the CRM model (Li & Pollatsek 2020)

Note: The vertical line represents the invisible boundary.

During natural reading, how much information is pre-processed is a key question. Research has shown that young readers' perceptual span is around 3～4 characters to the left of fixation and 14～15 letters to the right of fixation (Rayner & Bertera 1979; Rayner et al. 1982). The perceptual span is mainly affected by attentional factors. The growth of readers' reading skills may lead to the increase of their perceptual span (Häikiö et al. 2009; Rayner 1986). If the text is hard to read, readers' perceptual span may decrease (Henderson & Ferreira 1990). The Chinese readers have smaller perceptual span due to the greater visual complexity of Chinese characters (Inhoff & Liu 1998). Reading direction also influences the size of the perceptual span (Pollatsek et al. 1981).

There is evidence indicating that there are various semantic/ morphological preview effects in different writing systems (see Hohenstein & Kliegl 2014 for a review). Research shows that Chinese readers process semantic information parafoveally (Yan et al. 2009; Yang et al. 2012). One possibility is that no spaces exist between Chinese words and thus word *n+1* in Chinese will be closer to the fixation point than that in alphabetic language systems. Moreover, Chinese characters are composed of semantic radicals and *semantically* related words include orthographically similar radicals, which makes it easier for Chinese readers to obtain semantic information in the parafoveal processing.

There are two critical differences between the E-Z Reader model (Reichle et al. 2003) and the SWIFT model (Schad & Engbert 2012).

One is whether lexical processing is serial, one word at a time. The E-Z Reader model (Pollatsek et al. 2006; Reichle et al. 2003; Reichle et al. 1998) posits that words are processed serially, that is, the processing of word *n+1* will not begin until the processing of word *n* is finished. While the SWIFT model (Engbert et al. 2005; Engbert et al. 2002; Kliegl & Engbert 2003) and Glenmore (Reilly & Radach 2006) assume that words within the perceptual span are processed in parallel.

The other is whether the factors influencing the parafoveal processing are lexical or perceptual. Accordingly, examining parafoveal processing of formulaic sequences has theoretical implications. Specifically, if it was found that whether a word was a part of formulaic sequences affected the the processing of parafoveal information, this might imply that the formulaic sequence may be processed in parallel in the parafoveal region.

Another key difference between these two models is the parafoveal-on-foveal (PoF) effect. This effect refers to the influence the processing of word *n+1* brings on the processing of word *n*. According to the SWIFT model, word *n+1* can influence the processing of on word *n*. In the E-Z Reader model, however, there should be no evidence of PoF effects due to the serial processing of words.

Research has shown that the length of word *n+1* determines the spatial extent of parafoveal pre-processing. According to the SWIFT model, readers can obtain some type of preview benefits from word *n+1* and word *n+2* at the same time, whereas readers can only obtain preview benefits from word *n+1* based on the E-Z Reader model.

Pervious research has explored whether readers can obtain preview benefits from a word *n+2* (a word two words to the right of an invisible boundary). It was found that when word *n+1* is three-letter long, the preview effects of a word *n+2* can be observed (Angele & Rayner 2011; Kliegl et al. 2007; Radach et al. 2013; Risse & Kliegl 2011; 2012), but not when it is longer (Angele et al. 2008; Rayner et al. 2007). This is in line with both E-Z Reader and SWIFT models. In E-Z Reader, it is easier to identify a short rather than long word *n+1*. In SWIFT, both a short word *n+1* and word *n+2* can be processed in the perceptual span.

Cutter et al. (2014) found that when word *n+1* is a long word, word *n+2* can be parafoveally processed as well, only if these two words form a multi-word unit. In Cutter et al.'s (2014) study, word *n+1* and word *n+2* formed a spaced compound (e.g., *teddy bear*) and an invisible boundary was placed before word *n+1*. Word *n+1* was a long word with more than three letters. Nevertheless, a word *n+2* preview benefit was found in this study under the correct preview of word *n+1*. The author concluded that when word *n+2* is a constituent word of a multi-word unit, it can be parafoveally processed in alphabetic language.

Previous studies (Rayner et al. 2007; McDonald 2006; Kliegl et al. 2007; Angele et al. 2008) mainly explored PoF effects and preview benefits from word *n+2* using alphabetic languages. In recent years, several researchers explored this issue in Chinese language (e.g., Ma et al. 2015; Yang et al. 2009, 2012; Yu et al. 2016). For instance, Ma et al. (2015) investigated the PoF effect using two-character words as stimuli. The frequency of the first character and the phrasal frequency of the word were manipulated. It was found that the PoF effect was affected by the frequency of the first character, indicating that Chinese characters might be processed in parallel in the parafovea no matter whether they are part of words.

Yang et al. (2009) used two experiments to explore preview benefits from word *n+2* and the PoF effects. In Experiment 1, the target character was a one-character word. The results showed that when the boundary was placed at the end of character *n-1*, a preview effect was found on the target character. In Experiment 2, two-character words were used as the targets. It was found that there were preview benefits from word *n+1*. There was also some evidence for preview benefits for word *n+2*. When the boundary location was set at word *n-1*, the PoF effects were found on character *n-1* in the two experiments. However, these effects were only observed when character *n-1* was part of a two-character word. Overall, there is strong evidence suggesting that Chinese readers obtain preview benefits from character *n+2* and from word *n+1*. The preview benefits from word *n+2* were also found, which can be explained by both E-Z Reader and SWIFT models.

The review of the literature shows that there are no consistent findings about the processing patterns of formulaic language. Additionally, studies to date have not examined how Chinese collocations are processed and represented. Experiment 4 and 5 in this dissertation investigated this issue. Specifically, these two experiments examined whether collocations were processed holistically or the constituent words were activated and processed by employing the boundary paradigm (Rayner 1975). In Experiment 4, the previews of the nouns of collocations were manipulated. In Experiment 5, the last character of a collocation was manipulated, that is, in the dissimilar condition, the last character was replaced by another character. An invisible boundary was put in the middle of a collocation. The preview of word $n+1$ was manipulated. It was hypothesized that if spaced collocations are processed as lexical units then an interaction would be observed; if these idioms are parafoveally processed to a greater extent than phrases, that is, they are processed parafoveally as MCUs, then we should obtain a greater preview benefit effect from the second constituent for idioms than for matched phrases.

The preview of the word $n+1$ in strong collocations was compared with that of weak collocations. If a similar preview effect for word $n+1$ was found in the strong and weak collocations, the reader may process the collocations and control phrases in the similar way, indicating that the component word of collocations was activated and processed. If there is an advantage processing in collocations over matching phrases, the reader may regard the collocations as single lexical units during reading. This hypothesis was made on the basis that collocations may have multi-word unit representational status, that is, the first constituent of the collocations may activate the processing of the whole collocation, thus leading to the early extraction of information from word $n+1$ (the second constituent of the collocation). If this did occur, it would be strong evidence for the collocation being parafoveally processed as a multi-word unit.

3.3 Conclusion

This chapter introduces the methodology and the eye-tracking technology used in this dissertation. The introduction includes the background information of eye movements, the eye-tracking technology, eye-movement measures, and models of eye movement control during reading and parafoveal processing during reading.

Chapter 4 Study I: The Processing Advantages of Chinese Collocations

4.1 Introduction

Experiment 1 attempts to explore whether Chinese 4C collocations are processed faster than control phrases during natural reading. Different from Lv & Shi (2016) and Jiang et al. (2020) who chose collocations based on phrasal frequency, Experiment 1 chose the collocations based on phrasal frequency and MI scores. Although frequent word combinations are normally regarded as collocations (Bartsch 2004; Clear 1993; Sinclair et al. 2004), research has shown that some frequent word combinations (e.g., *red car*) are not collocations. Thus, mere phrasal frequency is not a reliable criterion to identify collocations. MI scores indicate how often a word is used together with its collocate in a phrase. Word combinations with MI scores of 3 or greater than 3 are often viewed as collocations (Hunston 2002). However, MI tends to have high scores for low-frequency word combinations. Typically, a phrasal frequency threshold of 5 occurrences is used to offset the low frequency bias (Evert 2008). Thus, the present study uses frequency threshold of 5 and MI scores threshold of 3 to identify collocations.

4.2 Experiment 1: Comparison between Chinese collocations and non-collocations

4.2.1 Method

Participants. Forty-four native Chinese speakers (30 female) aged 18～22 years (*M*= 19.8 years, *SD* = 1.1) from NingboTech University took part in the experiment. They all have normal or corrected-normal vision.

Materials & Design. Thirty-four pairs of verb-noun stimuli were selected from a database developed by Song & Li (2019). This database consists of 3783 commonly used 2C words and it provides thirteen types of feature scores for the 3783 words such as familiarity, age of acquisition and so on. Additionally, it provides the main response of each word out of 50 response words based on single word association tasks. Some of the prime words and their responses form 4C collocations which are the data source of our stimuli. Each pair consisted of a collocation (e.g., 修改文章, *revise the article*) and the corresponding control phrase (e.g., 修改结尾, *revise the ending*), and the two members shared the same verb (e.g., 修改, *revise*). As indicated in Table 4.1, the collocations and control phrases differed significantly in phrasal frequency ($t(66) = 3.299$, $p < .05$) and MI scores ($t(66) = 20.359$, $p < .001$). The phrasal frequency and lexical frequencies of collocations and control phrases were extracted from the BCC Corpus (Xun et al. 2016). MI scores were calculated based on a formula $\mathrm{MI}=\log_2\frac{O}{E}$ (Durrant & Doherty 2010) in which *O* and *E* are observed and expected occurrences of a word pair in a corpus. The nouns in two members were matched for the number of strokes ($t(66) = .089$, $p = .93$) and frequency ($t(66) = .184$, $p = .855$).

Each pair of the stimuli was presented in both predictable and neutral context. An example was shown in Table 4.2. The sentences were 15 to 22 characters in length ($M = 19.7$, $SD = 2.3$), with the collocations in the middle. A modified cloze test was used to assess contextual predictability of the sentences. Twenty participants (who did not take part in the experiment) were presented sentence fragments before the collocations. The participants were asked to write down the first word or words that came into their minds. The completions were assessed for the use of the collocation. The context predictability score was significantly higher in the predictable than in the neutral context (63.4% vs. 0.2%, $t(70) = 27.64$, $p < .001$), indicating that the predictable context is more predictable than neutral context.

Table 4.1 Stimulus characteristics in Experiment 1

Stimulus characteristic	Collocations	Non-collocations
Collocational frequency	703.79 (213.19)	.41 (.18) *
MI	9.68 (.39)	.40 (.23) *
Number of strokes	14.56 (.70)	14.47 (.71)
Noun frequency	24.42 (4.05)	23.37 (4.01)
Naturalness (Predictable Context)	4.17 (.46)	4.17 (.46)
Naturalness (Neutral Context)	4.00 (.42)	3.98 (.38)

Note: Standard Error of the Mean is shown in parentheses. Asterisks indicate statistically significant effects, $p < .05$.

Another group of 20 native speakers evaluated the sentences for naturalness (using a 5 point Likert scale where 1 = not natural and 5 = very natural; see Table 4.1). A two-way ANOVA showed no difference in naturalness across contexts, F (1, 19) = 1.341, p = .261, η^2 = .066, or between strong and weak collocations, F (1, 19) = 1.235, p = .280, η^2 = .061, with no interaction, F (1, 19) = .438, p = .516, η^2 = .023. The results showed sentences were rated as equally natural across conditions.

The length of the final sentences ranged from 15 to 22 characters (M = 19.7, SD = 2.3). The collocation always appeared near the middle of the sentence. Each pair of the targets was presented in four sentence frames as shown in Table 4.2. The experimental sentences were divided into two lists. Each list contained 36 pairs of strong and weak collocations in either neutral or predictable contexts. Each collocation was seen an equal number of times in each condition across the experiment. Additionally, each list contained 72 filler sentences and 8 practice sentences. Each participant read a total of 148 sentences. The practice sentences were presented at the beginning of the experiment and the other sentences were presented randomly.

Table 4.2 An example stimulus in Experiment 1

Context	Phrase type	Sample sentence
Predictable	collocation	编辑退回稿子希望他进一步**修改文章**并尽快提交。 The editor **returned the article** hoping that he could further revise it and submit it as soon as possible.

（revise the ending）

Context	Phrase type	Sample sentence
	Non-collocation	编辑退回稿子希望他进一步**修改结尾**并尽快提交。 The editor **returned the article** hoping that he could revise the ending and submit it as soon as possible.
Neutral	Collocation	吴丽的老师一直在办公室里**修改文章**很晚才回家。 Wu Li's teacher has been **revising the article** in the office and went home late.
	Non-collocation	吴丽的老师一直在办公室里**修改结尾**很晚才回家。 Wu Li's teacher has been **revising the ending** in the office and went home late.

Apparatus. An Eye Link 1000 Plus tower-mounted eye tracker was used to record gaze location every millisecond, recording right eye movements during binocular reading. Sentences were displayed in Song font on a 19 inch monitor with a 1024 × 768 pixel resolution. The stimuli were presented as black text on a light grey background. At 71 cm viewing distance, one Chinese character subtended about 0.8° of visual angle.

Procedure. Participants took part individually. On arrival, the participant had the procedure explained and was instructed to read normally and for comprehension. The participant was then seated at the eye-tracker and a chin and forehead rest used to minimize head movements. The eye-tracker was calibrated to their eye movements using a three-point horizontal calibration procedure to ensure spatial accuracy less than 0.35°. At the start of each trial, a fixation square appeared on the left side of the screen. Once the participant fixated this square, the square disappeared and the sentence was presented with the first letter in the sentence replacing the square. Once they finished reading, the participant pressed a response button and the sentence disappeared, replaced by a new trial or a comprehension question. They needed to answer the question by pressing one of two response buttons, and their answers were recorded by the computer. The yes/no comprehension questions accounted for 25% of all the sentences. Calibration accuracy was checked prior to each trial and the eye-tracker recalibrated as necessary to maintain high spatial accuracy. The experiment lasted approximately 30 minutes for each participant.

Analysis. Prior to data analysis, adjacent fixations were combined and short fixations (less than 80 ms) and long fixations (more than 1000 ms) were deleted following a standard procedure (affecting 3.7% of the data). In addition, fixations more than 2.5 standard deviations from the mean per condition for each participant were removed as an outlier. The remaining data were analysed using linear mixed effects models (LMEM; Baayen et al. 2008) conducted using R (R Core Team 2015) and the lme4 package (Bates et al. 2012). For all analyses, participants and stimuli were specified as crossed random effects and context type and phrase type were specified as fixed factors. Contrasts comparing levels of the fixed factors were specified using the "contr.sdif" function in the MASS package (Venables & Ripley 2002). The "emmeans" function in the emmeans package was used for the simple effect analysis (Lenth 2017). For all analyses, $t/z > 1.96$ were considered significant (e.g., Baayen 2008).

Eye movement measures are reported for two critical regions containing either the whole collocation or only the collocation noun (see Carrol & Conklin 2014; Vilkaite 2016). The noun analysis captures the collocational effect occurring in the noun (a predicted locus of facilitation). However, the noun analysis excludes the skipped nouns where may reflect the role of facilitation. The whole collocation analysis captures the effect occurring at the whole phrase including the skipped nouns (Vilkaite 2016).

We reported eye movement measures that are sensitive to the early lexical access and the later integration processes. For the whole collocations and final nouns, we reported an early measure, first-pass reading time (FPRT, or gaze duration for a single word, GD, i.e., the sum of all first-pass fixations in a region), and three late measures: rereading time (RRT, total reading time minus gaze duration), fixation count (FC, the total number of fixations on the target words) and total reading time (TRT, sum of all fixations in a region) (Liversedge et al. 1998). For the nouns, we reported additional three early measures including word-skipping (SKIP, probability of not fixating a word during first-pass reading), single fixation duration (SFD, the duration of the fixation when only one fixation was made during first-pass reading), first fixation duration (FFD, the first fixation on a word during the first-pass reading). The comprehension accuracy averaged 93% indicating that the participants understood the sentences well.

4.2.2 Results

Collocation Analysis. The descriptive results and the statistical results for the collocation analyses are summarized in Table 4.3 and Table 4.4, respectively. All measures showed that collocations were processed faster than control phrases, with shorter reading times and fewer fixations for collocations compared to control phrases. The main effect of contextual predictability was found in all measures, except for first-pass reading time, with shorter reading times and fewer fixations for collocations in predictable compared to neutral contexts. For all the measures, there were no significant interactions between collocational status and contextual predictability (all $t/z < 0.65$).

Table 4.3 Eye movements for the collocation phrases in Experiment 1

	Predictable Context		Neutral Context	
	Collocation	Non-collocation	Collocation	Non-collocation
FPRT (ms)	395 (9)	446 (10)	414 (9)	456 (10)
RRT (ms)	111 (8)	219 (14)	158 (10)	269 (15)
TRT (ms)	520 (11)	689 (17)	580 (13)	736 (17)
FC	2.16 (.04)	2.81 (.07)	2.42 (.06)	3.03 (.07)

Note: Standard Error of the Mean is shown in parentheses. FPRT = first-pass reading time, RRT = rereading time, TRT = total reading time, FC = fixation count.

Noun Analysis. The descriptive results and the statistical results for the noun analyses are summarized in Table 4.5 and Table 4.6, respectively. All measures showed a main effect of collocational status, with higher skipping rate, shorter reading times and fewer fixations for nouns in collocations than non-collocations. A significant effect of contextual predictability was found in rereading time, regression path duration, total reading time and fixation count. No other measures showed the effect of contextual predictability. This effect was due to shorter reading times and fewer fixations in predictable than neutral context. In line with the collocation analyses, no significant interactions were observed in any measures (all $t/z < 1.58$).

Table 4.4 Summary statistics for the collocation phrases in Experiment 1

Factor	Statistic	FPRT	RRT	TRT	FC
Intercept	β	425.74	187.16	628.46	2.60
	SE	20.19	23.74	36.66	0.13
	t/z	21.09	7.89	17.14	19.84
Context (neutral — predictable)	β	-14.02	-48.93	-53.32	-0.24
	SE	7.86	10.76	11.92	0.05
	t/z	-1.79	-4.55*	-4.47*	-4.57*
Collocation (collocation — non-collocation)	β	46.16	110.82	162.12	0.63
	SE	7.86	10.76	11.92	0.05
	t/z	5.88*	10.30*	13.60*	12.11*
Context × Collocation	β	10.04	0.81	13.70	0.05
	SE	15.71	21.52	23.85	0.10
	t/z	0.64	0.04	0.58	0.47

Note: Asterisks indicate statistically significant effects, $p < .05$. FPRT = first-pass reading time, RRT = rereading time, TRT = total reading time, FC = fixation count.

Table 4.5 Eye movements for the collocation nouns in Experiment 1

	Predictable Context		Neutral Context	
	Collocation	Non-collocation	Collocation	Non-collocation
SKIP (%)	22 (2)	14 (1)	19 (1)	13 (1)
FFD (ms)	243 (3)	251 (4)	244 (3)	254 (3)
GD (ms)	263 (5)	276 (5)	256 (4)	274 (5)
RRT (ms)	43 (4)	100 (7)	70 (6)	112 (7)
RPD (ms)	376 (10)	510 (16)	423 (12)	553 (15)
TRT (ms)	312 (7)	388 (9)	338 (8)	400 (9)
FC	1.03 (.03)	1.43 (.04)	1.17 (.03)	1.46 (.04)

Note: The Standard Error of the Mean is shown in parentheses. SKIP = word-skipping rate, FFD = first fixation duration, SFD = single fixation duration, GD = gaze duration, RRT = rereading time, TRT = total reading time, FC = fixation count.

Table 4.6 Summary statistics for the collocation nouns in Experiment 1

Factor	Statistic	SKIP	FFD	SFD	GD	RRT	RPD	TRT	FC
Intercept	β	-1.82	246.31	252.08	264.52	76.12	452.07	351.13	1.27
	SE	0.14	5.39	6.20	7.04	10.91	26.45	15.61	0.07
	t/z	-13.26	45.73	40.69	37.59	6.97	17.09	22.49	19.59
Context	β	0.13	-2.40	-1.95	3.76	-20.48	-45.59	-18.69	-0.08
	SE	0.10	3.18	4.21	5.08	5.97	11.85	7.35	0.03
	t/z	1.24	-0.76	-0.46	0.74	-3.43*	-3.85*	-2.54*	-2.51*
Collocation	β	-0.57	9.72	12.73	16.67	50.55	136.15	72.96	0.35
	SE	0.10	3.53	4.23	4.27	5.98	11.85	7.35	0.03
	t/z	-5.59*	2.75*	3.01*	3.90*	8.46*	11.49*	9.92*	10.71*
Context × Collocation	β	-0.11	-0.50	5.37	-2.27	18.20	12.99	19.24	0.10
	SE	0.21	6.34	8.43	8.55	11.96	23.71	14.71	0.06
	t/z	-0.53	0.08	0.64	-0.27	1.52	0.55	1.31	1.57

Note: The Standard Error of the Mean is shown in parentheses. SKIP = word-skipping rate, FFD = first fixation duration, SFD = single fixation duration, GD = gaze duration, RRT = rereading time, TRT = total reading time, FC = fixation coun.

4.2.3 Discussion

The results of this study show that collocations are read faster than novel phrases in reading, due to shorter reading times and fewer fixations for collocations than novel phrases. The results are in line with previous studies on English collocations (e.g., Durrant & Doherty 2010; Frisson et al. 2005; McDonald & Shillcock 2003a, b; Sonbul 2015; Vilkaite 2016; Wolter & Gyllstad 2011, 2013) and Chinese collocations (Jiang et al. 2020; Lv & Shi 2016). The effect of contextual predictability was also found, in line with previous studies (e.g., Frisson et al. 2005; Rayner 2009; Rayner & Well 1996).

The processing advantage of collocations over non-collocations was found in both early and late eye-movement measures, indicating that this advantage appeared in both lexical identification and meaning integration. This is consistent with Vilkaite's (2016) result. Sonbul (2015) also found the processing advantage of collocations using a similar methodology. However, only early eye-movement measures showed this effect. It is worth noting that the targets studied in Sonbul (2015) were adjective-noun collocations instead of verb-noun collocations used in Vilkaite's (2016) research and the current study. Prior research has suggested that the processing of adjective-noun and verb-noun collocations might be inherently different (Wolter & Yamashita 2015). This view is supported by the results of the current study. It is also valuable to compare the results found in the current study with Jiang et al.'s (2020) study which explored the processing of Chinese verb-noun collocations as well. In an eye-tracking experiment conducted by Jiang et al. (2020), collocations (参加会议，*attend the meeting*) differed from control phrases (参加游戏，*attend the game*) in phrasal frequency. The effect of collocation was only observed in the late measure (total reading time). Distinct from Jiang et al. (2020), the current study found the effect in both early and late measures. The different results of Jiang et al. (2020) and the current study may be due to the different experimental stimuli used in the two experiments. The current study compared the processing of collocations relative to non-collocations. However, Jiang et al. (2020) compared the eye movements of frequent collocations with those of less frequent collocations. Therefore, the results of Jiang et al. (2020) demonstrate the effect of phrasal frequency. In contrast, the present findings indicate the effect of collocation.

The present findings show that collocations are read more quickly than non-collocations. One possibility is that according to the usage-based theory (Bybee 1998, 2006; Goldberg 2006; Tomasello 2003), frequently used words or phrases may become lexicalized, so that they are processed and represented as single units (e.g., Conklin & Schmitt 2008, 2012; Siyanova-Chanturia et al. 2011; Underwood et al. 2004; Wray 2002; Zang 2019). Although the current study does not provide direct evidence about whether collocations are lexicalized, the present findings support the usage-based theory by showing that the frequency of usage of collocations facilitates the processing of collocations.

The other possibility is that the processing advantage occurs due to the priming effects between the collocates. According to the lexical priming theory (Hoey 2005), the priming association between the constituent words of collocations makes collocations predictable, which plays a facilitative role in the processing of collocations.

4.3 Conclusion

The present findings show that Chinese collocations, as defined using a combination of phrasal frequency and MI scores, enjoy the processing advantage over novel phrases.

The present findings are highly relevant to the future development of computational models of eye movement control in reading. As we noted in Chapter 3, a core assumption of current models (e.g., the E-Z Reader model; Reichle et al. 1998, 2003) is that lexical frequency is computed only across words and not phrases. Our findings sit alongside evidence from other studies showing that eye movements in reading are sensitive to the frequency of usage of various multi-constituent linguistic units, including idioms, spaced compounds, and collocations (e.g., Conklin & Schmitt 2008, 2012; Siyanova-Chanturia et al. 2011; Wray 2002; Zang 2019). These findings imply that current models of eye movement control may need to be modified to include mechanisms that are sensitive to both the frequency of usage of multi-constituent units, as well as individual words, if they are to fully account for the effects of lexical frequency in reading.

Chapter 5 Study II: Holistic or Analytic Processing

5.1 Introduction

There has been considerable debate about how formulaic sequences are represented and processed in language use. Some support the holistic view of formulaic sequences (Conkin & Schmitt 2008, 2012; Dahlmann & Adolphs, 2007; Jiang & Nekrasova 2007; Kim & Kim 2012; Pawley & Syder 1983; Siyanova-Chanturia et al. 2011; Sosa & MacFarlane 2002; Underwood et al. 2004; Wray 2002, 2008). They claimed that formulaic sequences are "stored and retrieved whole from memory" (Pawley & Syder 1983; Wray 2002), and "processed like a morpheme" (Wray 2008: 12) without processing or activated the individual parts of formulaic sequences.

However, others are against the holistic hypothesis. For instance, Siyanova-Chanturia (2015) pointed out most previous studies did not analyse the processing of individual components within the formulaic sequences. Therefore, they did not provide clear evidence to favour the holistic storage and processing hypothesis.

Using two decision tasks, Matsuno (2017) explored whether collocations were processed solely, that is, holistically or analytically, or parallelly, that is, holistically and analytically. The results demonstrated that collocations were parallelly processed in general and solely processed in some cases. Vilkaite (2016) found that non-adjacent collocations (e.g., *provide* some of the *information*) also enjoyed a similar but smaller processing advantage compared to adjacent collocations (e.g., *provide information*). Even though words were inserted in between collocates, collocations were still processed faster than novel phrases. This result argued against the "holistic" hypothesis and supported the usage-based theory which claimed that language is driven by frequency (Kemmer & Barlow 2000). Frequent use of words or phrases leaves trace in memory, which leads to their fast processing compared to novel phrases (Barlow & Kemmer 2000; Bybee 2006; Tomasello 2005).

With regards to the processing patterns of compounds, there are two different findings. One of them is that the decompositional route is used in the processing of compounds (Badecker 2001; Libben 1998). Specifically, a compound is decomposed into its constituent words when the compound is accessed. The other is that when a compound is retrieved, both the whole form and its components are activated (Kuperman et al. 2008, 2009; Mondini et al. 2005). For example, Pollatsek et al. (2000) found a significant whole-word frequency effect of compounds when the frequency of the first and second constituents was matched in an eye-tracking experiment. Crucially, both the whole-word frequency effect and the morpheme effect of the second constituent were found on gaze duration, indicating that the access to the whole-word the second morpheme happens at about the same time.

Based on the findings of research on compounds, Pollatsek et al. (2000) proposed a dual-route processing model, that is, a decompositional route and a direct processing route, during the processing of compounds. These two routes can be put in effect simultaneously. According to the dual-route model, frequent phrases are stored and processed holistically. They can be retrieved as a whole from the mental lexicon. The studies on idioms provide evidence for the direct processing route. Numerous studies have investigated the processing of idioms (e.g., Carrol & Conklin 2014; Swinney & Cutler 1979; Tabossi et al. 2009). These studies have revealed the processing advantage of idioms over matched novel sequences. For instance, Cieslicka (2006) found that idioms like "*bury the hatchet*" were processed faster than novel phrases like "*bury the axe*" in a priming study. In a self-paced reading experiment, Conklin & Schmitt (2008) asked participants to read a story containing idioms or novel phrases and found that the reading times were shorter for idioms compared to novel phrases. In an eye-movement experiment, Underwood et al. (2004) compared the eye movements on the final word of an idiomatic phrase (e.g., *honesty is the best policy*) and a novel phrase (e.g., *it seems that his policy*). The targets were embedded in a story context. It was found that readers had fewer fixations and shorter fixation durations in the idioms than the novel ones. Taken together, these studies provide evidence that familiar and frequent formulaic sequences like idioms can be accessed directly and processed faster than novel phrases.

In terms of the decompositional route which is also the computation or analysis route, the bottom-up, rule-based approach is used in language comprehension and processing (Wolter & Gyllstad 2016). This route is often carried out when less frequent novel phrases are encountered or when processing some formulaic sequences such as compounds which call for a compositional analysis. The empirical support can be found in previous research on compounds (Badecker 2001; Juhasz 2007; Libben 1998).

The debate regarding whether formulaic language is processed holistically mainly focuses on alphabetic languages. Recent years have witnessed a growing interest in lexical processing in non-alphabetic languages (e.g., Chinese) (see Li et al. 2015; Zang et al. 2011 for reviews). It is well acknowledged that Chinese is an unspaced language, which means that there are no word boundaries to discriminate words in text. Chinese words consist of one or more characters. Due to the unique characteristics of written Chinese, how Chinese words are lexically identified, serially or in parallel, has attracted a fair amount of interest. According to the model of Chinese word recognition and word segmentation (Li et al. 2009) and the model of Chinese word identification and eye movement control during Chinese reading (CRM) (Li & Pollatsek 2020), all the characters within the perceptual span are processed in parallel, and the activation of the characters results in the activation of words consisting of the characters. The activated words keep competing with each other until the winner is produced and the word is, therefore, recognized. These two models suggest that word identification and segmentation occur simultaneously. However, the models of Li et al. (2009) and Li & Pollatsek (2020) do not account for how Chinese multiple words are processed during reading. To address this issue, Zang (2019) put forward the multi-constituent unit (MCU) hypothesis. The MCU hypothesis assumes that some highly familiar multi-word sequences may be lexicalized and represented as single units. The constituent words are likely to be processed simultaneously and sequentially.

To understand the processing mechanism of formulaic sequences, the key issue is to find out how formulaic sequences are processed and represented. However, research to date has produced mixed results. The current study attempts to assess this issue. Inspired by previous research, the current study used the boundary paradigm (Rayner 1975) to explore the processing patterns of Chinese collocations. Research has shown that readers can process words in the fovea and they also can process information in the parafovea. In an alphabetic language such as English, readers extract up to 3～4 characters to the left of fixation, and 14～15 characters to the right of fixation (McConkie & Rayner 1975, 1976). In a logographic, character-based language such as Chinese readers extract up to 1 character to the left of fixation, and 3 characters to the right of fixation (Inhoff & Liu 1998). In the current study, an invisible boundary was put in the middle of a four-character collocation. When the verb is fixated, readers can process the noun parafoveally.

The preview of word $n+1$ was manipulated. We compared the

preview of word *n+1* in strong collocations relative weak collocations. According to the MCU hypothesis (Zang 2019), frequent formulaic sequences may be lexicalized and represented as single linguistic units. The first constituent of multi-consitutent units will activate the whole unit, and then this activation will extend to the parafoveal processing, resulting in the pre-processing of the second constituent. Therefore, if there is an advantage processing for word *n+1* in strong collocations compared to weak collocations in Study II, the reader may process the collocations as single lexical units during reading. If a similar preview effect for word *n+1* was found in strong collocations and weak collocations, the reader may process the two types of collocations in a similar way, indicating that the constituent words are activated and processed. If a parafoveal-on-foveal (PoF) effect (the influence of the parafoveal processing of word *n+1* on word *n*) is observed, we also can conclude that the constituent words are accessed, indicating that the collocations are processed analytically. This is because the presence of the PoF effect means that word *n+1* is activated before word *n* finishes its processing, demonstrating the parallel processing of the constituent words.

Experiment 2 and 3 manipulated the previews of the nouns in collocations. Specifically, in Experiment 2, the noun was replaced with two characters which cannot form a word in the dissimilar preview condition. In Experiment 3, the last character of the noun was substituted with another character.

5.2 Experiment 2: Manipulating the preview of the noun

5.2.1 Method

Participants. Fifty young adults (*M*= 20.4, range= 18～23 years, 42 female) from NingboTech University took part in the experiment. All of them are native Chinese speakers with normal or corrected-to-normal vision.

Materials & Design. Thirty two pairs of Chinese 4-character collocations were chosen from the database developed by Song & Li (2019). Each pair consisted of a strong collocation and a weak collocation. Each pair of collocations had the same verb with a different noun. Strong and weaker collocations significantly differed in collocation frequency, associative strength and MI scores. Other feature scores of the stimuli were closely matched (see Table 5.1). An independent-samples *t*-test demonstrated the significant differences between strong and weaker collocations in MI scores ($t(62) = 4.411$, $p < .001$), phrasal frequency ($t(62) = 3.988$, $p < .001$), and association strength ($t(62) = 7.039$, $p < .001$). An independent-samples *t*-test confirmed that, across the stimulus set, strong and weaker collocations were closely matched in number of meanings ($t(62) = .022$, $p = .190$), subjective number of meanings ($t(62) = .170$, $p = .866$), noun frequency ($t(62) = 1.139$, $p = .259$), subjective frequency ($t(62) = -.079$, $p = .937$), number of strokes ($t(62) = .740$, $p = .462$), age of acquisition ($t(62) = .569$, $p = .572$), compositionality ($t(62) = 1.768$, $p = .904$), semantic transparency($t(62) = .743$, $p = .461$), concreteness ($t(62) =$

.252, $p = .802$), emotional experience rating ($t(62) = -1.392$, $p = .169$), imageability ($t(62) = -1.671$, $p = .100$), familiarity ($t(62) = -.340$, $p = .735$) and sensory experience rating ($t(62) = .843$, $p = .402$).

Table 5.1 Summary of stimulus characteristics in Experiment 2

Stimulus characteristic	Strong collocations	Weaker collocations
Collocational frequency	1579.28 (364.66)	121.81 (24.09)
MI	10.89 (.53)	7.84 (.45)
Association strength	.26 (.03)	.06 (.00)
Number of meanings	2.2 (.23)	1.75 (.13)
Subjective number of meanings	1.62 (.04)	1.61 (.04)
Noun frequency	25.48 (4.06)	19.70 (3.04)
Subjective frequency	4.55 (.19)	4.57 (.16)
Number of strokes	16.00 (.81)	15.16 (.81)
Age of acquisition	2.45 (.11)	2.39 (.10)
Compositionality	4.38 (.12)	4.03 (.15)
Semantical transparency	5.51 (.09)	5.41 (.08)
Concreteness	4.74 (.18)	4.67 (.19)
Emotional experience rating	3.93 (.12)	4.19 (.15)
Imageability	4.34 (.13)	4.77 (.20)
Familiarity	5.99 (.12)	6.04 (.09)
Sensory experience rating	3.93 (.12)	3.77 (.15)

The boundary paradigm (Rayner, 1975) was used. The invisible boundary was located in the middle of the collocations. The preview of the nouns of verb-noun collocations was manipulated. When the reader moved his or her eyes across an invisible boundary, the preview was replaced by the noun of target collocations. There were two types of previews: (a) identical preview, that is, the preview was identical to the noun of the target collocations (e.g., 规定as the preview of规定); (b) dissimilar preview, namely, the preview was two characters which was a non-word (e.g., 和拉as the preview of 规定). For instance, in the example (see Table 5.2), the target strings are the strong collocation (违反规定: *violate the regulations*) and the weaker collocation (违反纪律: *violate the law*) in bold, but presented normally in the experiment. The two types of previews for the target word 规定 are the identical preview (规定) and the dissimilar preview (和拉).

Prior studies have shown evidence of character frequency within words influencing word recognition in Chinese. Zhang & Peng (1992) found effects in a lexical decision task, by varying character frequency while controlling word frequency. Words with high-frequency characters were identified more quickly and accurately than words with low-frequency characters. Yan et al. (2006) independently varied the frequency of a target word and the characters composing it during a sentence reading task. Results showed that both word frequency and character frequency influenced the processing of the fixated word in first-pass reading times. Crucially, fixations were longer on words with low-frequency characters than words with high-frequency characters. In a similar manner, character frequency might also influence the processing of words located in the parafovea (Ma et al. 2015).

Thus, the dissimilar previews (e.g., 和拉) were closely matched with the target words (e.g., 规定) in number of strokes (dissimilar previews: M = 8.06, SD = .46; target words: M = 8.06, SD = .46) and character frequency (dissimilar previews: M = 3.62, SD = .03; target words: $M = 3.61$, $SD = .03$) based on SUBTLEX-CH (Cai & Brysbaert, 2010). An independent-samples *t*-test demonstrated that there were no significant differences between dissimilar preview and target words in number of strokes ($t(126) = .000$, $p = 1.000$) and character frequency ($t(126) = .196$, $p = .845$). Additionally, the substituted characters did not share the same radical with the characters in target words, meaning that they were not similar orthographically.

Each pair of collocations were presented into sentences in four conditions as shown in Table 5.2 and the targets were embedded in the same neutral context sentence ranging from 13 to 18 characters long ($M = 15.7$, $SD = 1.2$). The targets were in the middle of the sentence, namely, the distance was at least four characters away from both the beginning and the end of the sentence. The same procedures for obtaining predictability and naturalness were performed as in Experiment 1.

Table 5.2 An example of the Chinese sentences used in Experiment 2

Phrase type	Preview type	Sample sentence
Strong collocation	Identical	周小平因为**违反**|**规定**被单位处罚了。
	Dissimilar	周小平因为**违反**|**和拉**被单位处罚了。
Weak collocation	Identical	周小平因为**违反**|**纪律**被单位处罚了。
	Dissimilar	周小平因为**违反**|**刚说**被单位处罚了。

Note: The vertical line represents the position of the invisible boundary. The English translation for the sentence is "Zhou Xiaoping was punished by the unit for violating the regulations. / Zhou Xiaoping was punished by the unit for violating the law."

Each participant randomly read one sentence from the four conditions in each pair of collocations. In Experiment 3, the same experimental design was used as in Experiment 2, that is, one set of targets was embedded into sentences from four conditions. The experimental sentences of Experiment 2 and 3 were counter-balanced and divided into two lists. Each list had 64 sentences which contained equal number of sentences from eight conditions. Each participant read 64 target sentences, 64 filler and 8 practice sentences.

Apparatus. Eye movements were recorded with an SR Research Eye Link 1000 Plus tower-mounted eye tracker with a sampling rate of 1000 Hz. Sentences were displayed on an 24-inch DELL monitor with a resolution of 1920×1080 and a refresh rate of 165 Hz. Viewing was binocular, but only movements of the right eye were recorded. The sentences were presented in Song font in black on a light grey background. At 71 cm viewing distance, each Chinese character subtended about 1.1° of visual angle.

Procedure. For sentences presented with the boundary paradigm (Rayner 1975), before participants' eyes crossed the boundary, either an identical or dissimilar word *n+1* was displayed as a preview, and as soon as participants' eyes crossed the boundary, the preview word was replaced by the correct target in the text. The boundary change was programmed using SR Research Experiment Builder. Participants were instructed to read for comprehension. After reading each sentence, the participant pressed a button to move on. One fourth of the sentences were followed by a yes/no comprehension question. The experiment took approximately 30 minutes.

5.2.2 Results

The comprehension accuracy averaged 95% indicating that participants understood the sentences well. Trials in which an eyeblink occurred when crossing the boundary or fixating a target word were deleted (affecting 3.8% of trials). 3.8% of trials were discarded due to the late display change, that is, the display changes completed more than 10 ms after the onset of the subsequent fixation based on previous studies (Slattery et al. 2011). Fixations less than 80 ms or greater than 1000 ms were eliminated from the analyses following a standard procedure (affecting 7.1% of the data). In addition, fixations more than 2.5 standard deviations from the mean per condition for each participant were removed as an outlier. The remaining data were analyzed using linear mixed effects models (LMEM; Baayen et al. 2008) conducted using R (R Core Team 2015) and the lme4 package (Bates et al. 2012). For all analyses, participants and stimuli were specified as crossed random effects and preview type and collocation strength were specified as fixed factors. Contrasts comparing levels of the fixed factors were specified using the "contr.sdif" function in the MASS package (Venables & Ripley 2002). A full random effects model was used where possible (Barr et al. 2013). If this failed to converge, we increased iterations using the "bobyqa" optimiser (Powell 2009), before trimming the random structure until it converged, first for random effects for stimuli, then participants. For all analyses, *t/z* values greater than 1.96 were considered statistically significant (see, e.g., Baayen 2008).

In the current study, the boundary was positioned in the middle of a collocation. Analyses were carried out for the first constituent (word *n*) and the second constituent (word *n+1*). The measures reported were FFD, GD, SKIP, RPD, and TRT on the verbs (word *n*) and the nouns (word *n+1*). The means and standard deviations are shown in Table 5.3. The beta values from the models are displayed in Table 5.4.

Table 5.3 Eye movement measures for all regions in Experiment 2

Analysis	Collocation	Preview	FFD	GD	RPD	TRT	SKIP
Word *n*	Strong	Identical	227 (5)	252 (6)	301 (10)	372 (14)	0.22 (.02)
		Dissimilar	241 (5)	283 (8)	321 (10)	434 (16)	0.21 (.02)
	Weak	Identical	240 (6)	275 (8)	302 (10)	407 (17)	0.23 (.02)
		Dissimilar	237 (5)	278 (9)	310 (9)	427 (17)	0.27 (.02)
Word *n+1*	Strong	Identical	227 (5)	249 (6)	424 (19)	317 (11)	0.19 (.02)
		Dissimilar	245 (5)	287 (8)	515 (20)	382 (12)	0.14 (.02)
	Weak	Identical	231 (5)	264 (8)	520 (24)	378 (15)	0.17 (.02)
		Dissimilar	255 (6)	296 (7)	548 (22)	01 (13)	0.13 (.02)

Table 5.4 Summary statistics for all measures in Experiment 2

Factor	Statistic	FFD	GD	RPD	TRT	SKIP
			Word *n*			
Intercept	*β*	232.62	264.3	304.27	397.49	-1.59
	SE	6.05	9.34	10.62	21.86	0.2
	t/z	38.44	28.29	28.65	18.18	-7.85
Preview	*β*	3.74	18.21	11.33	47.35	0.09
	SE	5.14	8.46	10.66	16.58	0.16
	t/z	0.73	2.15	1.06	2.86	0.6
Collocation	*β*	3.11	7.37	-6.03	16.06	0.25
	SE	4.72	7.15	9.23	13.72	0.14
	t/z	0.66	1.03	-0.65	1.17	1.8
Context × Collocation	*β*	-20.54	-39.48	-25.98	-57.4	0.49
	SE	10.23	16.8	21.37	33.26	0.32
	t/z	-2.01	-2.35	-1.22	-1.73	1.55
			Word *n+1*			
Intercept	*β*	237.44	268.56	484.16	357.76	
	SE	5.5	8.56	31.75	17.86	
	t/z	43.2	31.38	15.25	20.03	
Preview	*β*	21.25	35.58	73.05	49.86	
	SE	6.1	7.38	21.19	12.77	
	t/z	3.48	4.82	3.45	3.9	
Collocation	*β*	9.14	14.02	67.75	44.02	
	SE	4.88	7	17.71	12.29	
	t/z	1.88	2	3.82	3.58	
Context × Collocation	*β*	8.01	-5.6	-50.63	-39.76	
	SE	10.07	14.72	42.09	25.38	
	t/z	0.8	-0.38	-1.2	-1.57	

Note: Asterisks indicate statistically significant effects. Marginally significant effects are underlined ($p < .05$). FFD = first fixation duration, GD = gaze duration, RPD = regression path duration, TRT = total reading time.

Word *n*

The effect of the preview of the noun (word *n+1*) on the verb (word *n*) was found in gaze duration and total reading time due to shorter reading times for the identical preview compared to dissimilar preview, providing evidence for PoF effects (the influence of parafoveal text characteristics on reading behaviour for preceding words) (see Kennedy & Pynte 2005). In addition, there was an interaction between preview type and collocation strength in first fixation duration and gaze duration (see Figure 5.1). The planned contrasts showed that the interaction was due to increased times on the verb (word *n*) in dissimilar preview condition than in identical preview condition for strong collocations, whereas this preview effect did not appear for weaker collocations. For first fixation durations, this effect was 14 ms for strong collocations with a difference of −3 ms for weaker collocations; the respective differences for gaze durations were 31 ms and 3 ms.

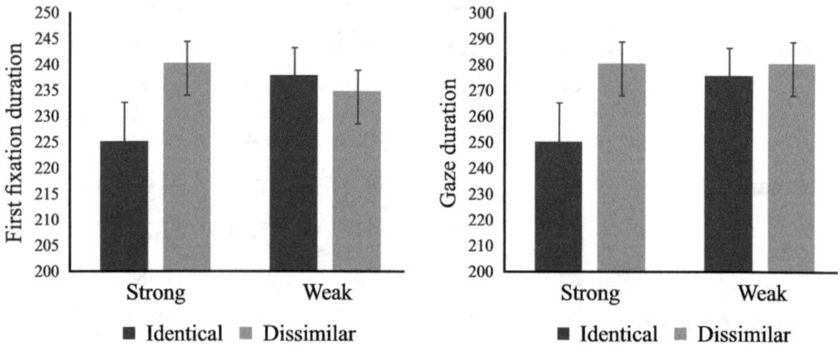

Figure 5.1 Interactions between collocation strength and preview type in first fixation duration and gaze duration for word *n*

Note: Error bars correspond to the Standard Error of the Mean.

Word *n +1*

All fixation time measures showed the preview effect, with shorter reading times in identical preview condition than in dissimilar preview condition, in line with preview effects in previous studies (Liversedge & Findlay 2000; Rayner 2009; Zang 2021). The effect of collocation strength was observed in GD, RPD and TRT with shorter reading times for strong compared to weaker collocations. A marginally significant difference between strong and weaker collocations was found in FFD as well. No significant interaction between collocation strength and preview type was detected ($t/z < 1.6$).

5.2.3 Discussion

The present findings demonstrate the PoF effects which reflect the processing of word *n+1* affecting fixation times on the currently fixated word (word *n*). The PoF effects were found in GD and TRT, due to shorter reading times for the word *n* in the identical preview condition compared to dissimilar preview condition. Further, FFD and GD showed a significant interaction between the preview type and collocation strength in word *n*. The further analysis showed that the interaction was due to larger preview benefit effects in word *n* for strong compared to weak collocations, indicating that strong collocations are parafoveally processed to a greater extent than weak collocations. As mentioned in Introduction of this chapter, the emergence of PoF effects indicates that word *n+1* is activated before the processing of word *n* is finished. Therefore, the present findings indicate that the constitutent words of collocations are processed in parallel, in other words, the collocations are processed analytically.

The PoF effect is a critical difference between the SWIFT model and E-Z Reader model. The E-Z Reader model claims that lexical processing is serial, and therefore there should be no evidence of PoF effects of a lexical origin. The SWIFT model assumes that attention is distributed among the currently fixated word and all words within the perceptual span and therefore several words can be processed in parallel. In the SWIFT model, the properties of the word to the right of fixation (word *n+1*) can influence the duration of the fixation on word *n*. Therefore, the present findings suggest that the constituent words in collocations are processed in parallel, which supports the SWIFT model. Further, the PoF effects appeared in gaze duration and the interaction emerged in first fixation duration and gaze duration, indicating that the PoF effects occurred in the early processing stage. This result, therefore, showed that the constituent words were activated in lexical recognition. In addition, the PoF effects were also observed in TRT, indicating that the PoF effects played a role in later processing stage.

Reliable preview benefits for word *n+1* have been found in the current study. All fixation time measures showed significant preview effects on word *n+1*, due to less reading times for word *n+1* in identical compared to dissimilar preview condition, in line with previous studies (see Cutter et al. 2015 for a review). The effect of collocation strength was also found in all the measures. There were significantly shorter times in GD, RPD and TRT for strong compared to weak collocations, with a marginally significant difference in FFD, indicating the facilitative role of collocation strength in the processing of collocations, in line with previous studies (Li et al. 2021; Sonbul 2015). As noted in Section 5.1, the processing advantage of strong collocations over weak collocations in word *n+1* indicates the holistic processing of collocations.

5.3 Experiment 3: Manipulating the preview of the last character

5.3.1 Method

Participants. Forty-six young adults (*M*= 20.2, range= 19～24 years, 35 females) from NingboTech University took part in the experiment. All of them are native Chinese speakers with normal or corrected-to-normal vision.

Materials & Design. Thirty-two pairs of Chinese 4-character collocations were chosen from the database developed by Song & Li (2019). Each pair of collocations had the same verb with a different noun. Each pair consisted of a strong collocation (e.g., 出席会议, *attend the meeting*) and a weak collocation (e.g., 出席活动, *attend the activities*). Strong and weaker collocations significantly differed in collocation frequency, associative strength and MI scores. Other feature scores of the stimuli were closely matched (see Table 5.5). An independent-samples *t*-test demonstrated the significant differences between strong and weaker collocations in MI scores ($t(62) = 3.835$,

$p < .001$), phrasal frequency ($t(62) = 3.350$, $p = .001$), and association strength ($t(62) = 8.386$, $p < .001$). An independent-sample t-test showed that there were no significant differences between strong and weaker collocations in number of meanings ($t(62) = 1.005$, $p = .319$), subjective number of meanings ($t(62) = -1.136$, $p = .260$), noun frequency ($t(62) = 1.413$, $p = .163$), subjective frequency ($t(62) = -.091$, $p = .928$), number of strokes ($t(62) = .379$, $p = .706$), age of acquisition ($t(62) = -.616$, $p = .540$), compositionality ($t(62) = 1.879$, $p = .065$), semantic transparency($t(62) = 1.639$, $p = .106$), concreteness ($t(62) = .541$, $p = .590$), emotional experience rating ($t(62) = -.148$, $p = .883$), imageability ($t(62) = -1.335$, $p = .187$), familiarity ($t(62) = .195$, $p = .846$) and sensory experience rating ($t(62) = -.729$, $p = .469$).

In Experiment 3, the invisible boundaries were placed in the middle of the collocations. The preview of the nouns of verb-noun collocations was manipulated. When the reader moved his or her eyes across an invisible boundary, the preview was replaced by the noun of target collocations. There were two types of previews: (a) identical preview, that is, the preview was identical to the noun of the target collocations (e.g., 出席会议 as the preview of 出席会议); (b) dissimilar preview, namely, the last character of the preview was substituted by another character (e.g., 出席会目as the preview of 出席会议). In addition, the last two characters of the dissimilar preview were a non-word and the last characters of the dissimilar previews were closely matched with the ones of the target collocations in number of strokes and character frequency based on SUBTLEX-CH-CHR (Cai &

Brysbaert 2010). An independent-samples *t*-test demonstrated that there were no significant differences between dissimilar preview and target words in number of strokes ($t(126) = .119$, $p = .906$) and character frequency ($t(126) = -.432$, $p = .667$). In addition, the substituted character and the target character did not have the same radical, indicating that they were different orthographically.

Each pair of collocations were presented into sentences in four conditions as shown in Table 5.6 and the targets were embedded in the same neutral context sentence ranging from 13 to 18 characters long (M = 15.7 characters). The targets were in the middle of the sentence, namely, the distance was at least four characters away from both the beginning and the end of the sentence. The same procedures for obtaining predictability and naturalness were performed as in Experiment 1. Results showed that the sentences were rated very high on a scale from 1 (not natural) to 6 (very natural): M =5.79, SD =0.20, Min 1 (not natural) to 6 (very natural): M =5.79, SD =0.20, Min =5.37, Max =6.00.

Table 5.5 Summary of stimulus characteristics in Experiment 3

Stimulus characteristics	Strong collocations	Weaker collocations
Collocation frequency	1742.16 (452.96)	214.56 (52.83)
MI	10.09 (0.33)	7.79 (0.50)
Association strength	0.27 (0.02)	0.06 (0.00)
Number of meanings	2.34 (0.28)	1.97 (0.25)
Subjective number of meanings	1.55 (0.04)	1.62 (0.04)
Objective noun frequency	27.83 (4.22)	19.99 (3.60)
Subjective noun frequency	4.58 (0.17)	4.60 (0.19)

(revise the ending)

Stimulus characteristics	Strong collocations	Weaker collocations
Number of strokes	16.31 (0.78)	15.91 (0.74)
Age of acquisition	2.23 (0.10)	2.32 (0.10)
Compositionality	4.66 (0.15)	4.25 (0.16)
Semantic transparency	5.68 (0.11)	5.44 (0.10)
Concreteness	4.92 (0.13)	4.81 (0.17)
Emotional experience rating	4.07 (0.17)	4.10 (0.12)
Imageability	4.52 (0.17)	4.86 (0.19)
Familiarity	6.05 (0.09)	6.03 (0.10)
Sensory experience rating	3.96 (0.12)	4.09 (0.13)

Each participant randomly read one sentence from the four conditions in each pair of collocations. Each participant read 32 target sentences and he or she read equal number of sentences from all the conditions. In Experiment 3, the same experimental design was used as in Experiment 2, that is, one set of targets was embedded into sentences from four conditions. The experimental sentences from Experiment 2 and 3 were divided into four lists. Each list had 64 sentences which contained equal number of sentences from eight conditions. Each participant read 64 target sentences, 64 filler and 8 practice sentences.

Apparatus. Eye movements were recorded with an SR Research Eye Link 1000 Plus tower-mounted eye tracker with a sampling rate of 1000 Hz. Sentences were displayed on an 24-inch DELL monitor with a resolution of 1920×1080 and a refresh rate of 165 Hz. Viewing was binocular, but only movements of the right eye were recorded. The stimuli were presented as black text on a light grey background. At 71 cm viewing distance, each Chinese character subtended about 1.1° of visual angle.

Table 5.6 An example of Chinese sentences used in Experiment 3

Phrase type	Preview type	Sample sentence
Strong collocation	Identical	王教授今天会出席**会议**并发表讲话。
	Dissimilar	王教授今天会出席**会目**并发表讲话。
Weak collocation	Identical	王教授今天会出席**活动**并发表讲话。
	Dissimilar	王教授今天会出席**活光**并发表讲话。

Note: Target words are in bold. The vertical line represents the position of the invisible boundary. The English translation for the sentence is "Professor Wang will **attend the meeting** and deliver a speech today. / Professor Wang will **attend the event** and deliver a speech today."

Procedure. The same apparatus was used as in Experiment 2.

5.3.2 Results

The comprehension accuracy averaged 94% indicating that participants understood the sentences well. Five participants were replaced because they realized over 10% display change. Fixations less than 80 ms or greater than 1000 ms were eliminated from the analyses following a standard procedure (affecting 6.09% of the data). 4.5% of trials were discarded due to the late display change, that is, the display changes completed more than 10 ms after the onset of the subsequent fixation based on previous studies (Slattery et al. 2011). Trials in which an eyeblink occurred when crossing the boundary or fixating a target word were deleted (affecting 0.7% of trials). In addition, fixations more than 2.5 standard deviations from the mean per condition for each participant was removed as an outlier. The remaining data were analyzed using linear mixed effects models (LMEM; Baayen et al. 2008) conducted using R (R Core Team 2015) and the lme4 package (Bates et al. 2012). For all analyses, participants and stimuli were specified as crossed random effects and context, preview and collocational strength were specified as fixed factors. Contrasts comparing levels of the fixed factors were specified using the "contr.sdif" function in the MASS package (Venables & Ripley 2002). For all analyses, $t/z > 1.96$ were considered significant. A number of eye movement measures including first fixation duration (FFD), gaze duration (GD), skipping probability (SKIP), regression-path duration (RPD), total reading time (TRT), were reported on the word *n* (the verbs) and the word *n+1* (the nouns). The means and standard deviations are shown in Table 5.7. The beta values from the models are displayed in Table 5.8.

Table 5.7 Eye movement measures for all regions in Experiment 3

Analysis	Collocation	Preview	FFD	GD	RPD	TRT	SKIP
Word *n*	Strong collocation	Identical	235 (5)	268 (7)	296 (8)	363 (12)	.20 (.02)
		Dissimilar	230 (5)	275 (9)	311 (10)	389 (14)	.22 (.02)
	Weak collocation	Identical	230 (5)	270 (8)	300 (9)	366 (14)	.22 (.02)
		Dissimilar	240 (5)	277 (8)	323 (11)	401 (15)	.22 (.02)
Word *n+1*	Strong collocation	Identical	231 (5)	259 (7)	461 (19)	359 (15)	.20 (.02)
		Dissimilar	247 (6)	286 (8)	522 (23)	404 (17)	.13 (.02)
	Weak collocation	Identical	236 (5)	269 (8)	472 (25)	366 (14)	.17 (.02)
		Dissimilar	255 (6)	301 (10)	519 (25)	408 (16)	.12 (.02)

Note: Asterisks indicate statistically significant effects. FFD = first fixation duration, GD = gaze duration, RPD = regression path duration, TRT = total reading time.

Word *n*

The main PoF effects were observed in RPD, and TRT, indicating that fixation times on the pre-target word were shorter in the identical condition compared to the dissimilar condition. Additionally, no main effects of collocation strength were found in all the measures, indicating that previewing either strong or weaker collocation failed to facilitate the processing of the verbs in collocations (word *n*). There was no interaction with preview type and collocation strength.

Word *n+1*

The main effect of preview was found in FFD, GD, RPD, TRT, and SKIP, due to less skipping and shorter processing times in the identical condition than in the dissimilar condition (first fixation duration, β= 16.69, *SE*= 4.95, t=3.38; gaze duration, β= 29.62, *SE*= 7.7, t=3.85; regression path duration, β= 57.13, *SE*= 20.27, t=2.82; total reading time, β= 45.89, *SE*= 13.65, t=3.36; skipping, β= 0.55, *SE*= 0.16, z =3.41). There was no significant effect of collocation strength in all measures. No significant interaction between preview type and collocation strength was found ($t/z < 1.1$).

Table 5.8 LMM statistics for all measures in Experiment 3

Factor	Statistic	FFD	GD	RPD	TRT	SKIP
			Word *n*			
Intercept	*β*	232.28	268.58	304.42	374.26	
	SE	4.76	7.82	8.88	15	
	t/z	48.76	34.34	34.28	24.95	
Preview	*β*	1.87	6.97	19.05	30.38	
	SE	4.69	7.55	8.82	12.22	
	t/z	0.4	0.92	2.16*	2.49	
Collocation strength	*β*	3.15	0.77	9.41	2.19	
	SE	5.17	8.53	10.1	14.37	
	t/z	0.61	0.09	0.93	0.15	
Preview×Collocation	*β*	10.53	-5.89	0.09	-6.44	
strength	*SE*	10.5	17.4	20.75	29.66	
	t/z	1	-0.34	0	-0.22	
			Word *n+1*			
Intercept	*β*	241.68	277.22	480.6	376.96	2.13
	SE	6.67	9.53	33.97	20.81	0.21
	t/z	36.24	29.08	14.15	18.12	10.4
Preview	*β*	16.69	29.62	57.13	45.89	0.55
	SE	4.95	7.7	20.27	13.65	0.16
	t/z	3.38*	3.85*	2.82*	3.36*	3.41*
Collocation strength	*β*	6.72	9.1	14.66	5.26	0.09
	SE	5.38	8.97	26.06	17.3	0.19
	t/z	1.25	1.02	0.56	0.3	0.5
Preview×Collocation	*β*	1.79	6.99	14.62	12.11	0.42
strength	*SE*	10.76	17.97	52.33	34.72	0.39
	t/z	0.17	0.39	0.28	0.35	1.07

Note: Asterisks indicate statistically significant effects. FFD = first fixation duration, GD = gaze duration, RPD = regression path duration, TRT = total reading time.

5.3.3 Discussion

RPD and TRT showed significant PoF effects with shorter reading times in word *n* under the identical preview condition compared to the dissimilar preview condition, indicating the analytical processing of collocations. No significant main effects of collocation strength were observed. There was no interaction between collocation strength and preview type. The PoF effects occurred in the late measures (RPD and TRT), indicating the constituent words were activated in the later stage of the processing of word *n*. However, the constituent words were first activated in the early stage in Experiment 2. This inconsistence may be due to different previews. In Experiment 2, the preview of the noun was manipulated. However, Experiment 3 manipulated the last character of the collocation. It may be harder for readers to notice the difference in one character compared to a word consisting of two characters.

The analysis of word *n+1* indicated that all measures showed significant effects of *n+1* preview type, with shorter fixation times and more skipping in the identical compared to dissimilar previews. This finding is in consistent with the result of Experiment 2. There was no main effect of collocation strength, indicating that strong and weak collocations had similar preview on word *n+1*. This is different from the finding of Experiment 2. The possible reason is the difference in previews. No interaction between collocation strength and preview types was observed.

5.4 Conclusion

Experiment 2 and 3 attempted to explore whether Chinese collocations are processed holistically or analytically. The boundary paradigm was used in the two experiments in which different preview types were manipulated. In Experiment 2, the noun was replaced with two characters (a non-word) in the dissimilar preview condition. In Experiment 3, the last character of the noun was replaced with another character.

The significant PoF effect was found in both Experiment 2 and 3. The PoF effect refers to the influence of the parafoveal processing of word $n+1$ on the currently fixated word n. The occurrence of the PoF effect means that word $n+1$ is activated before word n finishes its processing, demonstrating the parallel processing of the constituent words. The finding supports the SWIFT model (Engbert et al. 2005) which assumes that attention is distributed among all words within the perceptual span and therefore several words can be processed in parallel. The present finding provides novel evidencing supporting the Matsuno's (2017) view that collocations are processed in parallel.

According to the MCU hypothesis (Zang 2019) and the Lexical Representation hypothesis (Swinney & Cutler 1979), collocations may have multi-word unit representational status, that is, the first constituent of the collocations may activate the processing of the whole collocation, thus leading to the early extraction of information from word $n+1$ (the second constituent of the collocation). In Experiment 2, the main effect of collocation strength was found in word $n+1$, which shows the processing advantage of the nouns in strong collocations over weak collocation. This finding provides strong evidence for the collocation being processed as a multi-word unit. Therefore, this finding suggests that collocations are processed holistically as well, in line with the findings of English spaced compounds (Cutter et al. 2014) and idioms (e.g., Yu et al. 2016; Zang 2019).

Chapter 6 Study III: Influencing Factors

6.1 Introduction

It has been adequately demonstrated words that appear frequently in written text are read more quickly (i.e., shorter eye fixations) than are low-frequency words (Hyönä & Olson 1995; Inhoff & Rayner 1986; Rayner & Duffy 1986; Rayner & Fischer 1996; Vitu 1991). Frequency has been shown to affect language processing at all levels of representation (Ellis 2002). Phrasal frequency (the frequency of usage of words as a phrase) has been found to have a strong effect on collocation processing. In a L1 context, Ellis et al. (2009), adopting a frequency-based definition of collocation, investigated whether the word recognition of L1 speakers of English would be sensitive to collocation frequency. They found that there was a clear tendency whereby the higher the collocational frequency in the language, the faster the participants recognized letter strings as real English words. Also adopting a frequency-based definition of collocation, Siyanova-Chanturia et al. (2011) made similar observations for both L1 and L2 in an eye-tracking study using binomials (e.g., *bride and groom, heart and soul*) as target items embedded in sentence contexts. Furthermore, Wolter & Gyllstad (2013) observed clear frequency effects in L1 and

L2 using a phrasal judgment task where participants were asked to judge whether adjective-noun combinations (e.g., *good news, mutual trust*) were commonly used in English or not.

Words that are predictable from prior context are read more quickly and are less likely to be directly fixated than are unpredictable words (Ehrlich & Rayner 1981; Rayner & Well 1996). There is also some evidence suggesting that predictability and frequency affect different reading processes, since several experiments using various techniques have found additive effects of the two variables (Rayner et al. 2004; Forster 1981; Stanovich & West 1983).

Similar effects of contextual predictability are known to influence word processing. Reaction times are faster to predictable versus unpredictable words in a variety of behavioral tasks, such as lexical or phrasal decision (Arnon & Snider 2010; Fischler & Bloom 1979; Forster 1981; Stanovich & West 1983), naming (Forster 1981; McClelland & O'Regan 1981), and speech monitoring (Cole & Perfetti 1980). Moreover, eye-tracking studies show that readers fixate less on predictable than unpredictable words (Ehrlich & Rayner 1981; Rayner & Well 1996). And, as early as 1980, Kutas & Hillyard reported evidence for a reduced neural signal — the N400 event-related potential (ERP) — to *semantically* predictable versus unpredictable words in sentence contexts (Kutas & Hillyard 1980, 1984).

Associative strength is another influencing factor. The definition of collocations such as "habitual and *semantically* related word combinations" (Firth 1968) implies that there exists associative relationship between collocates. Hoey (2005) claimed that there is a priming association between a word and its collocate, which makes collocations predictable. Schmitt (1998) claimed that word associations reflect the strongest mental connections between words in the mind. Associative strength between word combinations determines how likely the existence of one word predicts the other word. For the strongly associated collocations, the appearance of one component word can predict the other one. Associative strength can be obtained by a word association test in which participants are presented a prime word and then they are asked to write down the first word or words that come to their minds. For word pairs, the associative strength is the probability of participants who generate Word 2 in response to Word 1. Association strength can come from word association norms such as the Edinburgh Associative Thesaurus (Luka & Petten 2014).

A large number of studies have affirmed collocational priming (Durrant & Doherty 2010; McDonald & Shillcock 2003a, b; Wolter & Gyllstad 2011). The association facilitates the processing of collocations (Durrant & Doherty 2010). For instance, in a lexical decision task (Durrant & Doherty 2010), a prime word was presented briefly followed by a target string. Participants were asked to judge whether the target string was a real word or not. The prime word and the target was either a collocation (e.g., *parish church*) or a novel phrase. The results showed that compared with novel phrases, collocations were processed faster with shorter reaction times and lower error rates.

In addition to collocational frequency, contextual predictability and associative strength, a few studies have explored semantic transparency in word combinations. Semantic transparency has been investigated extensively in compound processing. Studies on compound processing frequently modify semantic transparency in terms of how elements directly contribute to the compound's meaning. According to A-Bialy ET AL. (2013) and Frisson et al. (2008), there are four different types of items that are typically used: fully transparent items (TT), like eyesight; partially opaque items (OT), like eyetooth, where the opaque constituent comes first; or (TO), like sugarcane, where the opaque component comes last; and fully opaque items (OO), like catwalk. Frisson et al. (2008) discovered that when compounds were provided with a gap between them, like honey moon (OO), dish washer (TT), god child (OT), and stair case (TO), participants read transparent items faster than fully or partially opaque items.

Gyllstad & Wolter (2016) take semantic transparency into account on collocational studies. Gyllstad & Wolter (2016) investigates whether two types of word combinations (free combinations and collocations) differ in terms of processing using a visual semantic judgment task. It was found that collocations were processed slower than free combinations due to the *semantically* semi-transparent nature of collocations. The results suggested that degree of semantic transparency together with phrasal frequency played an important role in collocational processing.

Study III attempted to assess the factors influencing the processing of Chinese collocations. Inspired by the previous studies on formulaic language in alphabetic language, the current study focuses on three factors: contextual predictability, collocation strength and association strength. It has been acknowledged that Chinese is from a different writing system. Therefore, the influencing factors reviewed above may play a different role in the processing of Chinese formulaic language such as collocations. For instance, the lack of spacing between Chinese words might lead Chinese readers to rely more heavily on contextual information than do readers of English to process words. In this case, we would expect contextual constraint/predictability to have stronger effects in Chinese than is the case in English. Experiment 4 and 5 will explore the role of the three factors in the processing of Chinese collocations during reading.

6.2 Experiment 4: Effects of collocation strength and context

This experiment attempted to find out the influence of collocation strength and contextual predictability on the processing of Chinese collocations. Specifically, strong and weaker Chinese collocations were embedded in either predictable or neutral sentential context. The stimuli used in Experiment 4 and 5 came from the same data source.

6.2.1 Methods

Participants. Thirty-six young adults (32 females) aged 18～23 years (*M* = 20.6 years, *SD* = 1.2) were recruited in the same way as in Experiment 1. None of them participated the previous experiments.

Materials & Design. The experiment was a 2 (context: predictable, neutral) × 2 (collocation strength: strong, weak) mixed design. Stimuli were 36 pairs of verb-noun collocations. Following Sonbul (2015) and Li et al. (2021), each pair of the stimuli with the same verb and a different noun was categorized as strong (e.g., 布置作业, *assign homework*) and weaker collocations (布置任务, *assign tasks*) based on phrasal frequency and MI scores. Compared with weaker collocations, strong collocations had both higher phrasal frequency and MI scores. An independent-sample *t*-test demonstrated significant differences between the strong and weaker collocations in phrasal frequency ($t(70) = 3.076, p < .05$) and MI ($t(70) = 3.072, p < .05$).

According to the research of Song & Li (2019), word recognition is influenced by thirteen word features including number of strokes (NOS), objective word frequency (oFREQ), subjective word frequency (sFREQ), age of acquisition (AOA), compositionality, concreteness, emotional experience rating (EER), imageability, familiarity, subjective number of meanings (sNOM), objective number of meanings (oNOM), sensory experience rating (SER), and semantic transparency (ST). For instance, research has shown that NOS influences the efficiency of recognition of Chinese characters (e.g., Liversedge et al., 2014), and oFREQ predicts Chinese word recognition (e.g., Liversedge et al. 2014). Compositionality is a valuable variable in studying the contribution of constituents to the meaning of the whole issue (e.g., Li et al., 2016). It has shown that both EER (Newcombe et al. 2012) and SER (Juhasz et al. 2011) play an important role in word recognition

(Barsalou 2008; Goldman & de Vignemont 2009).

Table 6.1 Summary of stimulus characteristics in Experiment 4

Stimulus characteristic	Strong collocations	Weak collocations
Collocational frequency	837.42 (192.10)	222.72 (55.07) *
MI	9.74 (.40)	8.03 (.39) *
Association strength	.11 (.01)	.11 (.01)
Number of meanings	2.11 (.23)	1.86 (.19)
Subjective number of meanings	1.59 (.04)	1.51 (.04)
Noun frequency	26.01 (3.93)	20.61 (2.84)
Subjective frequency	4.74 (.14)	4.77 (.17)
Number of strokes	14.89 (.78)	14.42 (.56)
Age of acquisition	2.16 (.09)	2.19 (.11)
Compositionality	4.28 (.14)	4.13 (.16)
Transparency	5.47 (.09)	5.43 (.11)
Concreteness	5.07 (.15)	5.11 (.16)
Emotional experience rating	3.98 (.13)	3.88 (.13)
Imageability	4.45 (.21)	4.89 (.13)
Familiarity	6.03 (.10)	6.07 (.10)
Sensory experience rating	4.20 (.14)	3.92 (.15)
Naturalness (Predictable Context)	4.30 (.4)	4.20 (.5)
Naturalness (Neutral Context)	4.1 (.4)	4.1 (.4)

Note: Standard Error of the Mean is shown in parentheses. Asterisks indicate statistically significant effects, $p < .05$.

The length of the final sentences ranged from 15 to 22 characters ($M = 19.7$, $SD = 2.3$). The collocation always appeared near the middle of the sentence. Each pair of the targets was presented in four sentence frames as shown in Table 6.2. The experimental sentences were divided into two lists. Each list contained 36 pairs of strong and weak collocations in either neutral or predictable contexts. Each collocation was seen an equal number of times in each condition across the experiment. Additionally, each list contained 72 filler sentences and 8 practice sentences. Each participant read a total of 152 sentences. The practice sentences were presented at the beginning of the experiment and the other sentences were presented randomly.

Apparatus. The apparatus was the same as in Experiment 1.

Procedure & Analyses. The general procedure, measures and analyses were the same as for Experiment 1. The comprehension accuracy averaged 95% indicating that participants understood the sentences well. Short fixations (less than 80 ms) and long fixations (more than 1000 ms) were deleted following a standard procedure (affecting 5% of the data). For all analyses, participants and stimuli were specified as crossed random effects and collocation strength and contextual predictability were specified as fixed factors.

Table 6.2 An example of Chinese sentences used in Experiment 4

Context	Collocation strength	Sentence
Predictable	Strong	老师讲完课之后给学生**布置作业**巩固知识点。 The teacher **assigned homework** to the students to consolidate the knowledge points after the class.
	Weak	老师讲完课之后给学生**布置任务**巩固知识点。 The teacher **assigned tasks** to the students to consolidate the knowledge points after the class.

（revise the ending）

Context	Collocation strength	Sentence
Neutral	Strong	该系统会自动地在课后**布置作业**并进行检查。 The system will automatically **assign homework** and check after class.
	Weak	该系统会自动地在课后**布置任务**并进行检查。 The system will automatically **assign tasks** and check after class.

6.2.2 Results

Collocation Analyses. Means for the collocation are shown in Table 6.3 and statistical results reported in Table 6.4. All measures showed a significant effect of collocation strength, with shorter reading times and fewer fixations for strong compared to weak collocations. The main effect of contextual predictability was found in all measures, with shorter reading times and fewer fixations for collocations in predictable compared to neutral contexts. For all the measures, there were no significant interactions between collocation strength and contextual predictability (all $t/z < 1.64$).

Table 6.3 Eye movements for the collocation in Experiment 4

	Predictable Context		Neutral Context	
	Strong Collocation	Weak Collocation	Strong Collocation	Weak Collocation
FPRT (ms)	345 (8)	344 (8)	369 (8)	397 (9)
RRT (ms)	126 (9)	171 (12)	167 (11)	199 (12)
TRT (ms)	486 (12)	533 (14)	549 (13)	605 (14)
FC	2.1 (.1)	2.3 (.1)	2.4 (.1)	2.6 (.1)

Note: The Standard Error of the Mean is shown in parentheses. FPRT = first-pass reading time, RRT = rereading time, TRT = total reading time, FC = fixation count.

Table 6.4 Summary statistics for the collocation phrase in Experiment 4

Factor	Statistic	FPRT	RRT	TRT	FC
	β	362.06	164.58	542.36	2.38
Intercept	*SE*	17.47	25.63	34.73	0.14
	t/z	20.72	6.42	15.62	16.71
Context	*β*	-40.00	-33.68	-70.79	-0.27
(neutral — predictable)	*SE*	6.81	9.20	12.08	0.05
	t/z	-5.87*	3.66 *	-5.89*	-5.72*
Collocation	*β*	14.43	39.89	55.50	0.20
(strong — weak)	*SE*	6.81	9.20	10.72	0.05
	t/z	2.12*	4.34*	5.18*	4.32*
	β	-22.26	15.83	-4.96	0.04
Context × Collocation	*SE*	13.62	18.39	21.45	0.09
	t/z	-1.63	0.86	-0.23	0.48

Note: Asterisks indicate statistically significant effects, $p < .05$. FPRT = first-pass reading time, RRT = rereading time, TRT = total reading time, FC = fixation count.

Noun Analysis. Means for the noun analyses are shown in Table 6.5 and statistical effects reported in Table 6.6. All measures, except for first fixation duration and single fixation duration, showed a main effect of association strength, with higher skipping rate, shorter reading times and fewer fixations for strong compared to weak collocations. There was a significant effect of contextual predictability for skipping, single fixation duration and fixation count. This effect was due to more skips, shorter reading times and fewer fixations for collocations presented in predictable than neutral context. In line with the collocation analyses, no significant interactions were observed in any measures (all *t/z* < 0.66).

Table 6.5 Eye movements for the collocation noun in Experiment 4

	Predictable Context		Neutral Context	
	Strong Collocation	Weak Collocation	Strong Collocation	Weak Collocation
SKIP (%)	24 (2)	20 (2)	18 (2)	14 (1)
FFD (ms)	225 (3)	229 (3)	230 (3)	232 (3)
SFD (ms)	221 (4)	227 (4)	230 (5)	234 (5)
GD (ms)	244 (5)	254 (5)	244 (4)	255 (5)
RRT (ms)	55 (6)	85 (8)	70 (7)	94 (7)
TRT (ms)	316 (8)	350 (10)	322 (8)	360 (9)
FC	1.1 (.0)	1.3 (.0)	1.2 (.0)	1.4 (.0)

Note: The Standard Error of the Mean is shown in parentheses. SKIP = word-skipping rate, FFD = first fixation duration, SFD = single fixation duration, GD = gaze duration, RRT = rereading time, TRT = total reading time, FC = fixation count.

Table 6.6 Summary statistics for the collocation noun in Experiment 4

Factor	Statistic	SKIP	FFD	SFD	GD	RRT	TRT	FC
Intercept	β	-1.63	227.99	228.84	246.67	70.85	328.36	1.23
	SE	0.15	4.62	4.66	6.08	12.05	16.03	0.08
	t/z	-11.18	49.36	49.10	40.59	5.88	20.49	16.22
Context	β	0.44	-5.46	-8.87	-2.47	-12.84	-12.48	-0.11
	SE	0.10	3.07	4.17	5.78	8.83	8.80	0.03
	t/z	4.17*	-1.78	-2.13*	-0.43	-1.45	-1.42	-3.33*

(revise the ending)

Factor	Statistic	SKIP	FFD	SFD	GD	RRT	TRT	FC
Collocation	*β*	-0.27	3.10	4.96	10.52	26.98	36.38	0.16
	SE	0.10	3.07	4.16	4.29	6.10	7.78	0.03
	t/z	2.58*	1.01	1.19	2.46*	4.42*	4.67*	4.67*
Context × Collocation	*β*	0.02	4.02	4.17	1.44	7.17	-0.12	0.02
	SE	0.21	6.14	8.34	8.57	12.20	15.57	0.07
	t/z	0.08	0.65	0.50	0.17	0.59	-0.01	0.34

Note: The Standard Error of the Mean is shown in parentheses. SKIP = word-skipping rate, FFD = first fixation duration, SFD = single fixation duration, GD = gaze duration, RRT = rereading time, TRT = total reading time, FC = fixation count.

6.2.3 Discussion

The results of Experiment 4 showed that strong collocations were processed faster than weaker collocations, due to significantly shorter reading times and fewer fixations for strong compared to weaker collocations. The effect of collocation strength was found in both early and late eye movement measures, indicating that collocation strength facilitated the early identification and late integration of collocation processing. This is consistent with the findings from English collocations (Li et al., 2021).

The main effect of contextual predictability was detected as well. It was found that the reading times for collocations were shorter in predictable than neutral contexts, which is in line with previous researches (e.g., Frisson et al. 2005; Li et al. 2021; Rayner 2009; Rayner & Well 1996). Crucially, the effect of contextual predictability and the effect of collocation strength were both found in the early measures, that is, first-pass reading in the collocation analysis and skipping rate in the noun analysis. This indicated that the two effects played a role in the same time course of collocation processing. Additionally, no interaction was found between the two effects. This result supported the suggestions of Li et al. (2021) that the effect of collocation strength was independent of the effect of contextual predictability. Meanwhile, this contrasted with the view of Frisson et al. (2005) that the co-occurrence measures such as transitional probability was not a separate measure but part of contextual constraints.

Experiment 4 provided novel evidence that the effect of collocation strength and the effect of contextual predictability facilitated the processing of Chinese collocations. Additionally, there was no interaction between the effect of collocation strength and the effect of contextual predictability. The two effects were found in both early and late measures in the two studies. In Experiment 4, the same experimental design was adopted as Li et al. (2021) who studied English collocations. Specifically, the present study determined the collocation strength based on phrasal frequency and MI scores, following previous studies (Li et al. 2021; Sonbul 2015). Strong collocations had significantly higher phrasal frequency and MI scores than weaker collocations. Strong and weaker collocations were embedded in both predictable and neutral sentence contexts. The present results are consistent with those of Li et al. (2021), indicating that the collocations have similar processing patterns in both alphabetic and non-alphabetic languages.

The effect of contextual predictability found in present study was in line with previous studies (e.g., Frisson et al. 2005; Li et al. 2021; Rayner 2009; Rayner & Well 1996). The effect of contextual predictability appeared in both early and late processing stages of collocations. It is worthy noticing that the effects of collocation strength and contextual predictability were found in the same eye movements (first-pass reading in the collocation analysis and skipping rate in the noun analysis) with no interaction. This result indicates that the effect of collocation strength was independent of the effect of contextual predictability, which is in contrast with the view that the co-occurrence measure was part of contextual constraints (Frisson et al. 2005).

6.3 Experiment 5: Effects of association strength and context

Experiment 5 aimed to explore the role of association strength and contextual predictability on the processing of Chinese collocations. Specifically, Chinese collocations which were divided into strong-and weak-associated collocations were embedded in different context. The stimuli used in Experiment 3 came from the same data source as in Experiment 1.

6.3.1 Methods

Participants. Thirty-eight Chinese adults (26 females) aged 18～22 years (M= 19.5 years, SD = 1.1) from NingboTech University took part in the experiment. All have normal or corrected-normal vision. None participated in the previous Experiments.

Materials & Design. Stimuli were 38 pairs of verb-noun collocations chosen from the same data source as in Experiment 1, the database developed by Song & Li (2019). As in Experiment 1, the phrasal frequency of the stimuli was obtained from the BCC Corpus (Xun et al. 2016). MI scores were calculated based on a formula MI= $\log_2\frac{O}{E}$ (Durrant & Doherty 2010) in which O and E are observed and expected occurrences of a word pair in a corpus. MI is typically used as a measure to indicate how likely a word combination will co-occur. A phrase with MI score of 3 or above is often regarded as a collocation (Hunston, 2002). All phrases had an MI above 3 (see Table 6.7), indicating that all the stimuli were collocations.

The association strength between the verb and noun of the collocation and the other feature scores of the stimuli were obtained from the database (Song & Li 2019). A word that is frequently used as a response in a word-association task should be more common in use than a word that is not often used as a response in such a task. Thus, as a second step to determine the target words, we subsequently conducted a task of single-word association with the initially selected words as the stimuli. Each pair of the stimuli was categorized as a strongly and a weakly-associated collocation based on association strength scores. An independent-samples t-test demonstrated the significant differences between strongly and weakly-associated collocations in association strength ($t(74) = 8.519$, $p < .001$). An independent-samples t-test confirmed that, across the stimulus set, strongly and weakly-associated collocations were closely matched in MI scores ($t(74) = .926$, $p =$

.357), phrasal frequency ($t(74) = .159$, $p = .874$), objective number of meanings ($t(74) = -.574$, $p = .590$), subjective number of meanings ($t(74) = .874$, $p = .385$), objective noun frequency ($t(74) = .050$, $p = .960$), subjective noun frequency ($t(74) = 1.658$, $p = .101$), number of strokes ($t(74) = .072$, $p = .943$), age of acquisition ($t(74) = .327$, $p = .744$), compositionality ($t(74) = -.095$, $p = .924$), semantic transparency($t(74) = .599$, $p = .551$), concreteness ($t(74) = 1.058$, $p = .293$), emotional experience rating ($t(74) = .721$, $p = .473$), imageability ($t(74) = -.357$, $p = .722$), familiarity ($t(74) = 1.094$, $p = .277$) and sensory experience rating ($t(74) = .412$, $p = .682$).

Table 6.7 Summary of stimulus characteristics in Experiment 5

Stimulus characteristic	Strongly-associated collocations	Weakly-associated collocations
Collocational frequency	564.61(126.21)	535.55 (131.76)
Association strength	.23 (.02)	.07 (.00) *
MI	9.51 (.33)	9.02 (.41)
Number of meanings	1.89 (.21)	2.05 (.20)
Subjective number of meanings	1.59 (.03)	1.54 (.04)
Noun frequency	21.52 (3.60)	21.24 (4.19)
Subjective frequency	4.91 (.13)	4.54 (.18)
Number of strokes	16.34 (.76)	16.26 (.79)
Age of acquisition	2.25 (.11)	2.21 (.10)
Compositionality	4.38 (.15)	4.40 (.16)
Transparency	5.64 (.09)	5.57 (.09)
Concreteness	5.27 (.16)	5.05 (.13)
Emotional experience rating	3.99 (.16)	3.83 (.15)
Imageability	4.65 (.14)	4.72 (.13)

(revise the ending)

Stimulus characteristic	Strongly-associated collocations	Weakly-associated collocations
Familiarity	6.14 (.09)	6.00 (.08)
Sensory experience rating	4.14 (.13)	4.07 (.14)
Naturalness (predictable context)	4.23 (.16)	4.16 (.22)
Naturalness (neutral context)	4.18 (.27)	4.10 (.27)

Note: Standard Error of the Mean is shown in parentheses. Asterisks indicate statistically significant effects, $p < .05$.

38 pairs of sentence frames were created in which strongly and weakly-associated collocations were inserted interchangeably (see Table 6.8). The sentences were 14 to 22 characters long (M = 19.89, SD = 2.41). The collocation always appeared near the middle of the sentences were presented as a single line of text. To examine effects of contextual predictability, a modified cloze test was used. In the test, twenty participants who did not participate in the eye-tracking experiment were presented with sentence fragments before collocations and asked to write down the first word or words that came into their minds. As indicated in Table 6.6, the context predictability score was significantly higher in the predictable than in the neutral context (66% vs. 1%, $t_{(74)} = 27.135, p < .001$).

An example stimulus set is shown in Table 6.8. Another group of 20 native speakers evaluated the final stimulus set for naturalness (using a 5 point Likert scale where 1 = not natural and 5 = very natural). An analysis of these data using a two-way ANOVA showed no difference in naturalness ratings across neutral and predictable contexts, F (1, 19) = 1.341, p = .261, η^2 = .066, or between sentences containing strongly and weakly-associated collocations, F (1, 19) = 1.235, p = .280, η^2 = .061, with no interaction, F (1, 19) = .438, p = .516, η^2 = .023. The results indicated that strongly and weakly-associated collocations appeared equally acceptable in predictable and neutral contexts.

Table 6.8 An example of Chinese sentences used in Experiment 5

Context	Association strength	Sample sentence
Predictable	Strong	在练习钢琴时老师会及时给她**指出错误**让她改正。 When she is practicing the piano, her teacher will **point out her mistakes** in time and ask her to correct them.
	Weak	在练习钢琴时老师会及时给她**指出缺点**让她改正。 When she is practicing the piano, the teacher will **point out her shortcomings** in time and ask her to correct them.
Neutral	Strong	陈乐乐非常希望吴敏能够给她**指出错误**帮她过关。 Chen Lele really hopes that Wu Min can **point out her mistakes** and help her pass the exam.
	Weak	陈乐乐非常希望吴敏能够给她**指出缺点**帮她过关。 Chen Lele really hopes that Wu Min can **point out her shortcomings** and help her pass the exam.

Each pair of the targets was presented in four sentence frames as shown in Table 6.8. The stimuli were divided into two lists. Each included half the predictable sentence frames and half the neutral sentence frames. Half of the sentences of each list came from Group 1 and the other half came from Group 2. For each pair of targets, two of the four sentence frames with the different collocation or context appeared in the same list. This ensured an equal number of high- and low-frequency collocations in neutral and predictable frames were viewed. In addition, each list contained 72 filler sentences and 8 practice sentences. The practice sentences were presented at the beginning of the experiment. The other sentences were presented randomly. Each participant read a total of 156 sentences.

Apparatus, Procedure & Analyses. Apparatus, Procedure & Analyses were the same as in Experiment 1. As in Experiment 1, fixations shorter than 80 ms or longer than 1000 ms were deleted (affecting 5.22% of the data). The average comprehension accuracy was 91.3%.

6.3.2 Results

Collocation Analyses. Means for the collocation are shown in Table 6.9 and statistical results reported in Table 6.10. All measures, except for first-pass reading time, showed a significant effect of association strength, with shorter reading times and fewer fixations for strongly compared to weakly-associated collocations. In addition, all measures, except for first-pass reading time, showed an effect of contextual predictability, with shorter reading times and fewer fixations for collocations in predictable compared to neutral contexts. No significant interactions were observed in eye movement measures (all $t/z < 1.25$).

Table 6.9 Eye movements for the collocation phrase in Experiment 5

	Predictable Context		Neutral Context	
	Strong Association	Weak Association	Strong Association	Weak Association
FPRT (ms)	375 (9)	379 (10)	381 (8)	387 (8)
RRT (ms)	143 (9)	151 (9)	172 (10)	200 (11)
TRT (ms)	538 (12)	557 (13)	572 (13)	613 (14)
FC	2.06 (.05)	2.15 (.06)	2.28 (.06)	2.35 (.06)

Note: The Standard Error of the Mean is shown in parentheses. FPRT = first-pass reading time, RRT = rereading time, TRT = total reading time.

Table 6.10 Summary statistics for the collocation phrase in Experiment 5

Factor	Statistic	FPRT	RRT	TRT	FC
Intercept	β	378.79	164.16	566.45	2.21
	SE	19.98	19.77	30.67	0.16
	t/z	18.96	8.30	18.47	14.05
Context (neutral — predictable)	β	-7.32	-40.72	-49.44	-0.21
	SE	7.43	8.71	13.83	0.05
	t/z	-0.99	-4.67 *	-3.58*	-3.95*
Association Strength (strong — weak)	β	4.41	17.23	29.05	0.08
	SE	7.43	8.71	10.73	0.04
	t/z	0.59	1.98*	2.71*	1.96*
Context × Association Strength	β	-2.08	-21.40	-26.64	0.01
	SE	14.92	17.49	21.53	0.09
	t/z	-0.14	-1.22	-1.24	0.06

Note: Asterisks indicate statistically significant effects, $p < .05$. FPRT = first-pass reading time, RRT = rereading time, TRT = total reading time.

Noun Analyses. Means for the noun analyses are shown in Table 6.11 and statistical effects reported in Table 6.12. The effect of contextual predictability was found in skipping and fixation count, with higher skipping rates and fewer fixations in predictable compared to neutral context. There was a significant main effect of association strength in total reading time and fixation count. This was due to less total reading times and fewer fixations for nouns in strongly compared to weakly-associated collocations. An interaction between contextual predictability and association strength were observed in first fixation duration (see Figure 6.1). Follow-up contrasts showed the interaction was due to larger increases in reading times for strongly associated collocations in predictable compared to neutral contexts (β = -9.07, *SE* = 4.68, t = -1.94). In addition, the first fixation duration was shorter for strongly compared to weakly associated collocations in neutral context (β = -8.51, *SE* = 4.48, t = -1.90).

Table 6.11 Eye movement measures for the collocation noun in Experiment 5

	Predictable Context		Neutral Context	
	Strong Association	Weak Association	Strong Association	Weak Association
SKIP (%)	24 (2)	21 (2)	16 (1)	18 (1)
FFD (ms)	245 (4)	238 (4)	236 (3)	244 (3)
SFD (ms)	247 (5)	248 (6)	234 (4)	243 (4)
GD (ms)	264 (5)	267 (6)	253 (4)	267 (5)
RRT (ms)	66 (6)	72 (6)	65 (6)	78 (6)
TRT (ms)	346 (8)	362 (9)	332 (8)	356 (8)
FC	1.11 (.03)	1.23 (.04)	1.22 (.03)	1.26 (.03)

Note: The Standard Error of the Mean is shown in parentheses. SKIP = word-skipping rate, FFD = first fixation duration, SFD = single fixation duration, GD = gaze duration, RRT = rereading time, TRT = total reading time, FC = fixation count.

Table 6.12 Summary statistics for the collocation noun in Experiment 5

Factor	Statistic	SKIP	FFD	SFD	GD	RRT	TRT	FC
Intercept	*β*	-1.63	240.11	243.30	259.48	65.94	339.77	1.21
	SE	0.15	5.27	5.92	8.19	8.23	14.28	0.07
	t/z	-10.53	44.29	41.10	31.68	8.01	23.79	17.57
Context	*β*	0.38	1.27	6.88	2.98	-4.79	4.13	-0.07
	SE	0.10	3.32	4.43	5.93	5.58	10.84	0.03
	t/z	3.73*	0.38	1.55	0.50	-0.86	0.38	-2.18*
Association Strength	*β*	0.01	0.71	6.60	8.23	9.64	20.08	0.08
	SE	0.10	3.30	4.39	4.43	5.55	7.43	0.03
	t/z	0.06	0.21	1.50	1.86	1.74	2.70*	2.60*
Context × Association Strength	*β*	-0.28	-15.61	-6.80	-11.16	-6.64	-9.71	0.06
	SE	0.20	6.59	8.78	8.85	11.11	14.87	0.06
	t/z	-1.39	-2.37*	-0.78	-1.26	-0.60	-0.65	1.03

Note: Asterisks indicate statistically significant effects, $p < .05$. SKIP = word-skipping rate, FFD = first fixation duration, SFD = single fixation duration, GD = gaze duration, RRT = rereading time, TRT = total reading time, FC = fixation count.

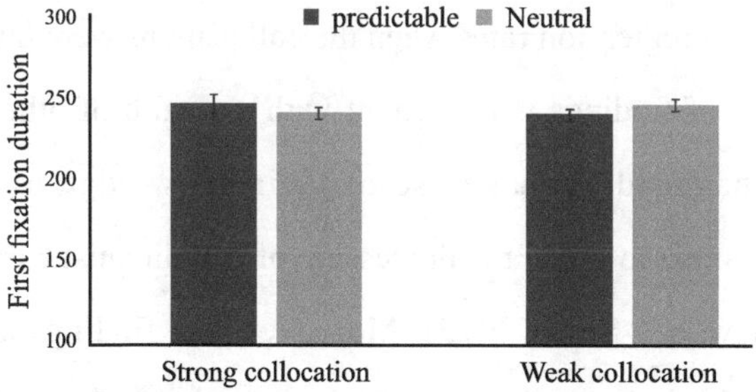

Figure 6.1 Interactions between association strength and contextual predictability in first fixation duration for the collocation

Note: Error bars correspond to the Standard Error of the Mean.

6.3.3 Discussion

The present experiment was conducted to assess the role that association strength plays in the processing of Chinese collocations in reading. Based on association strength, each pair of collocations was divided into strong and weak collocations. Phrasal frequency, MI scores and other linguistic features of collocations were matched between strong and weak collocations. The present findings provide evidence that eye movements are sensitive to association strength of collocations. It was found that readers spent shorter reading times for strongly-associated collocations compared to weakly-associated collocations, indicating the facilitative role of association strength which is in line with the previous findings (e.g., Durrant & Doherty 2010). These effects were observed in the late eye movement measures, TRT, RRT and FC, indicating that association strength influenced the late processing stage of collocations.

Strong and weak collocations were embedded in either a predictive or neutral sentence context. The results showed that readers spent less time at the collocations when they were predicted by the context and with increased regression rates when the collocations were unpredicted. This pattern of findings is consistent with a wealth of other research showing that readers make use of their knowledge of the prior linguistic context to guide the processing of new linguistic information (for a review, see Staub 2015). Moreover, our findings are in line with the findings from other studies showing that eye movements are affected by contextual predictability of words (e.g., Whitford & Titone

2014). The predictability effects were obtained in both early measures of skipping rates and later measures of total reading time and fixation counts. It, therefore, appears that Chinese readers can make rapid use of their knowledge of the prior context to guide the recognition of collocative phrases.

There has been a debate about whether or not semantic association is independent from contextual effect. Some studies argue that semantic association is part of contextual predictability (e.g., Luka & Petten 2014; Frisson et al. 2005). While others think that it is independent from contextual effect (e.g., McDonald & Shillcock 2003a, b). The current study explored this issue as well. The results show that the association strength and contextual predictability interactively influence the processing of the collocations. This interaction effect was emerged in early eye movement measure, in first fixation duration for the collocation noun. This effect (see Figure 6.1) was due to larger predictability effects (i.e., longer reading times in neutral vs. predictive contexts) for the weak when compared to strong collocations. As this effect was emerged relatively early in processing, it seems likely that it reflects an influence on word recognition processes. This interaction between predictability and association strength stands in contrast with evidence showing that these two factors independently influence readers' eye movements (McDonald & Shillcock 2003a, b).

6.4 Conclusion

Experiment 4 and 5 explored the factors influencing the processing of Chinese collocations in natural reading. Inspired by previous research on English formulaic language, the current study focused on three factors: contextual predictability, association strength and collocation strength by using two eye-tracking experiments. The same experimental design was employed in these two experiments. Specifically, native Chinese speakers were presented single sentences in which target collocations were embedded in either predictable or neutral context. The two experiments used different materials and were finished by different participants.

The present findings provide novel evidence that contextual predictability, association strength and collocation strength facilitate the processing of Chinese collocation in natural reading. Specifically, the effects of contextual predictability were found in both Experiment 4 and 5.The results indicate that when the collocations are more predictable by the context, readers will spend less time in the collocations and with fewer fixations and less skipping rates. The present findings are in line with a wealth of previous researches showing that readers are sensitive to contextual predictability which can help them process words or phrases faster (for a review, see Staub 2015). Both the early and later eye movement measures showed the effect of contextual predictability, indicating that contextual predictability facilitated the word recognition in the early stage and the integration of the collocation with the sentence context in the later stage.

Experiment 4 assessed the effects of collocation frequency by examining eye movements for collocations that were categorized as either strong or weak, depending on their frequency of written usage (as defined using phrasal frequency and MI). It was found that readers spent less time reading strong collocations compared to weak collocations. The effects of collocation strength were observed in both early eye movements measures (first-pass reading time) and later measures (total reading time and fixation count). This finding indicated that collocation strength influenced both the early stage of word recognition and the later stage of processing integration. Crucially, no interaction between contextual predictability and collocation strength was found in Experiment 4, indicating that the effects of collocation frequency are independent of contextual effects. These findings contribute to the debate concerning this issue by demonstrating that the frequency of usage of such phrases can influence eye movements during reading, and that this effect cannot be simply explained in terms of a specific form of contextual constraint, in line with previous research (McDonald & Shillcock, 2003a, b; Li et al. 2021).

As mentioned in the introduction, collocations are semantically related word combinations (Firth 1968) and there is a priming association between constituent words in collocations (Hoey 2005). Due to the priming relationship, one word can predict its collocate. The predictability is determined by the strength of the association been constituent words. Experiment 5 explored the influence of association strength on Chinese collocations in reading. It was found that strongly-associated collocations were processed faster than weakly-associated ones, due to less total reading time and fewer fixations. Crucially, an interaction between association strength and contextual predictability was detected in first fixation duration, which is against the view that association strength is independent of contextual predictability (e.g., Luka & Petten 2014). This result suggests that in the absence of a constraining context, readers experienced greater difficulty in the word recognition in the early stage of processing.

The current study contributes to the development of Chinese computational models of eye movement control in reading. As noted in Chapter 3, the current models (e.g., the E-Z Reader model; Reichle et al. 1998, 2003) are based on words but not phrases. The present findings provide valuable evidence showing that eye movements in reading are sensitive to the frequency of usage of collocations. Similar findings are also found in other formulaic language including idioms, and spaced compounds (e.g., Conklin & Schmitt 2008, 2012; Siyanova-Chanturia et al. 2011; Wray 2002; Zang 2019). Taken together, these findings suggest that the future models of eye movement control should include mechanisms that are sensitive to the frequency of usage both at phrasal level and lexical level.

Chapter 7 General Discussion

7.1 Introduction

This dissertation aims to explore the processing mechanism of Chinese verb-noun collocations during reading using the eye-tracking paradigm. Specifically, this dissertation examined three topics: the processing advantage of Chinese collocations, the processing patterns of Chinese collocations, and the factors influencing the processing of Chinese collocations. Accordingly, three studies were conducted to examine these topics. Chapter 7 reviews and discusses the findings of this dissertation. Section 7.2 discusses the first finding, that is, Chinese collocations are processed faster than novel phrases. Section 7.3 discusses the second finding, that is, Chinese collocations are processed both holistically and analytically. Section 7.4 discusses the third finding, that is, contextual predictability, collocation strength, and association strength affect the processing of Chinese collocations. Section 7.5 describes the processing model for Chinese collocations during reading we proposed. Section 7.6 is a summary of Chapter 7.

7.2 The processing features of Chinese collocations

7.2.1 Quicker processing for collocations than non-collocations

Study I attempted to find out whether Chinese collocations

(defined using phrasal frequency and MI scores) enjoy processing advantage over novel phrases during reading. To address this issue, Experiment 1 compared the processing of collocations and novel phrases using measures of eye movements. It was found that there were shorter reading times for collocations compared to non-collocations. In addition, the nouns of collocations were skipped more often than those of non-collocations. These results demonstrate that Chinese collocations are processed faster than non-collocations. The processing advantage of collocations was observed in both early and late eye-movement measures.

Research has shown that Chinese readers are sensitive to the frequency of characters and words (e.g., Rayner et al. 2005; Yan et al. 2006). Results of Experiment 1 demonstrate that phrasal frequency facilitates the processing of Chinese collocations, in line with previous research (Jiang et al. 2020; Lv and Shi 2016). The present findings provide further evidence indicating that Chinese readers are sensitive to phrasal frequency. The findings of the previous research and the current study imply that Chinese readers are sensitive to the frequency of various linguistic units, characters, words, and multi-word sequences.

A large number of studies have showed that phrasal frequency facilitated the processing of English collocations (e.g., Durrant & Doherty 2010; Frisson et al. 2005; McDonald & Shillcock 2003a, b; Sonbul 2015; Vilkaite 2016). The present findings sit alongside the findings from previous studies indicate that phrasal frequency plays a similar role in the processing of collocations in different languages.

The effect of phrasal frequency was found in both early and late eye-movement measures, indicating the facilitation appeared in both lexical identification and meaning integration. This finding is in line with the previous studies on binominals (Siyanova-Chanturia et al. 2011b), and collocations (Vilkaite 2016).

The results provide evidence supporting the usage-based theory (Bybee 1998; Goldberg 2006; Tomasello 2003), exemplar-based theory (Bod 2006) and the lexical priming theory (Hoey 2005). Both the usage-based theory and the exemplar-based theory claim that language acquisition, processing, use and representations are determined by the frequency of occurrence and language is "a statistical accumulation of experiences" (Bod 2006; Ellis & O'Donnell 2012). Frequent use of multi-word sequences may lead them to be lexicalized, stored in prefabricated form and processed and represented as single units (Kemmer & Barlow 2000; Zang et al. 2020), which is one possible reason for the processing advantage of collocations. The other possibility is that collocations are highly predictable. According to Hoey's (2005) lexical priming theory, there is a priming relationship between the constituent words of collocations. When one part of a collocation is present, the other one will be predicted and activated.

Overall, the present findings show that the processing advantage of Chinese collocations is due to their frequency and predictability, which is in line with the previous studies on multi-word sequences (Conklin & Schmitt 2008; Jiang & Nekrasova 2007; Siyanova & Schmitt 2008; Sosa & MacFarlane 2002).

7.2.2 Integration of both holistic and analytical processing

Whether formulaic language is processed holistically has been a topic of debate in the field of psycholinguistics and psychology. One view is that formulaic sequences are processed as single units without activating the constituents (Conkin & Schmitt 2008, 2012; Dahlmann & Adolphs 2007; Jiang & Nekrasova 2007; Kim & Kim 2012; Pawley & Syder 1983; Siyanova-Chanturia et al. 2011; Sosa &MacFarlane 2002; Underwood et al. 2004; Wray 2002, 2008). Another view claims that formulaic language is processed analytically (Badecker 2001; Juhasz 2007; Libben 1998; Siyanova-Chanturia 2015). Matsuno (2017) held that formulaic sequences are processed both holistically and analytically.

The current dissertation aimed to provide novel evidence for this debate. Specifically, Study II attempted to find out whether Chinese collocations are processed holistically or analytically by assessing the parafoveal processing of collocations. Two eye-tracking experiments were conducted using the boundary paradigm (Rayner 1975). An invisible boundary was put in the middle of a collocation. The previews of the nouns in collocations were manipulated in Experiment 2 and 3. Experiment 2 used a non-word consisting of two characters to replace the noun in a collocation in the dissimilar preview condition. Experiment 3 replaced the last character of the noun with another character. The current study found robust preview benefits for word $n+1$, due to shorter reading times for word $n+1$ in identical compared to dissimilar preview condition, in line with the previous studies (see

Cutter et al. 2015 for a review).

We observed the parafoveal-on-foveal (PoF) effect (the facilitation of the parafoveal processing of word *n+1* on the currently fixated word *n*) in both Experiment 2 and 3. This finding indicates that when word *n* is being processed, word *n+1* is accessed and processed. This finding stands in contrast with the E-Z Reader model (Pollatsek et al. 2006; Reichle 2011; Reichle et al. 2003; Reichle et al. 1998) which claims that lexical processing is serial, that is, the parafoveal processing of word *n+1* will not start until the identification of word *n* is finished. In contrast, the present finding supports the SWIFT model (Engbert & Kliegl 2011; Engbert et al. 2002; Engbert et al. 2005) suggests that a gradient of attention is distributed over a number of words within the perceptual span and the words are processed in parallel. Additionally, the PoF effect was observed in both early and late eye-movement measures, indicating that the parafoveal processing of word *n+1* facilitated the lexical recognition and the later processing of word *n*. This finding shows that the foveal and parafoveal processing occurs in parallel, which provides novel evidence supporting the component processing of collocations.

Further, the current study observed the effect of collocation strength with shorter reading times for strong compared to weak collocations, in line with the previous studies (Li et al. 2021; Sonbul 2015). As reviewed in Section 2.4.3, the MCU hypothesis (Zang 2019) proposes that formulaic sequences including collocations are stored and accessed as individual lexical units and the activation of the first constituent word of a MCU will lead to the activation of the whole unit, and thus facilitate the parafoveal processing of the other constituent. Similarly, the Lexical Representation Hypothesis (Swinney & Cutler 1979) suggests that idioms are represented as long words. When the first constituent of an idiom is accessed, the idiom and its constituents will be simultaneously activated and processed. According to the MCU Hypothesis (Zang 2019) and the Lexical Representation Hypothesis (Swinney & Cutler 1979), collocations may have multi-word unit representational status, that is, the first constituent of the collocations may activate the processing of the whole collocation, thus leading to the early extraction of information from word $n+1$ (the second constituent of the collocation). In Experiment 2, the main effect of collocation strength was found in word $n+1$, which shows the processing advantage of the nouns in strong collocations over weak collocations. This finding provides strong evidence for the collocation being processed as a multi-word unit. Additionally, this finding suggests that collocations are processed holistically as well, in line with the findings of English spaced compounds (Cutter et al. 2014) and idioms (e.g., Yu et al. 2016; Zang 2019).

Overall, the present findings shed light on the representation of Chinese collocations. This study provides novel evidence that Chinese collocations are processed both holistically and analytically. The present findings suggest that the processing of Chinese collocations is an integration of both holistic and analytical processing, in line with Matsuno (2017). Matsuno (2017) put forward the parallel language processing model. According to this model, collocations are processed in parallel. Specifically, when the first constituent word is activated, its related information will be retrieved. After the collocate of this word is activated, the whole collocation will be produced and the meaning of the collocations will be retrieved.

7.2.3 Linguistic factors influencing collocational processing

Study III aimed to find out how the three factors (contextual predictability, association strength and collocation strength) influnence the processing of Chinese collocations in natural reading using two eye-tracking experiments (Experiment 4 and 5). In Experiment 4, strong and weak collocations were embedded in either a predictable or netural context. In Experiment 5, strongly and weakly-associated collocations were embedded in either a predictable or netural context. The following sections will discuss the findings in detail.

Contextual predictability

The effects of contextual constraint were observed in both Experiment 4 and 5, due to shorter reading times, fewer fixations and higher skipping rates for collocations in predictable than neutral contexts, in line with the previous researches (e.g., Frisson et al. 2005; Li et al. 2021; Rayner 2009; Rayner & Well 1996). The present findings provide clear evidence showing that Chinese readers are sensitive to the effect of contextual predictability. The effect of contextual predictability was observed in both the early and later eye movement measures, indicating that contextual predictability facilitated the word recognition in the early stage and the integration of the collocation with the sentence context in the later stage.

The effect of contextual predictability can be accounted for using the lexical priming theory (Hoey 2005). As mentioned in Section 2.4.1, there are priming relationships between the constituent words of collocations. Due to the priming relationships, once a constituent word is encountered, the other one will be primed (activated), which makes collocations predictable. A large number of studies have shown that highly predictable words are processed faster compared than less predictable ones (see Staub 2015 for a review). This dissertation provides evidence that the effect of contextual constraint facilitates the processing of phrases as well. In other words, contextual predictability is a robust variable which can influence the processing of various units.

Collocation strength

The effect of collocation strength (defined using phrasal frequency and MI scores) was found in Experiment 4, due to faster reading for strong collocations compared to weak collocations. Both early measures (FPRT) and late measures (TRT and FC) showed the effect of collocation strength. This finding indicated that collocation strength influenced both the word recognition and the processing integration. Crucially, there was no interaction between contextual predictability and collocation strength, indicating that the effects of collocation frequency were independent of contextual effects. These findings provide further evidence showing that collocation strength is a vital factor influencing the processing of collocations, in line with the previous research (Li et al 2021; McDonald & Shillcock 2003a, b).

According to the usage-based theory (Bybee 1998, 2006; Goldberg 2006; Tomasello 2003), phrasal frequency facilitates the processing of words and phrases (Bod et al. 2003; Bybee & Hopper 2001; Ellis 2002b, 2008b; Hoey 2005; Robinson & Ellis 2008). Frequent exposure to formulaic sequences will lead them to be lexicalized and represented as single units (Zang et al. 2021). MI indicates how often the words co-occur in corpus. It is a measure of "the strength of association between two words" (Clear 1993:279-282). As noted in Section 2.4.1, the priming association between two words (Hoey 2005) facilitates the processing of collocations.

Collocation strength is defined using a combination of phrasal frequency and MI scores which are the statistical information of collocations (McDonaldn & Shillcock 2003a, b). The present findings indicate that Chinese readers took advantage of the statistical information to process collocations during reading. Therefore, we conclude that Chinese readers may store the statistical information in the mental lexicon, in line with McDonald & Shillcock (2003a, b).

Association strength

Experiment 5 examined the role of association strength in the processing of Chinese collocations during reading. The results showed that strongly associated collocations are processed more quickly compared to weakly-associated ones, due to less TRT and fewer FC. Crucially, FFD showed an interaction between association strength and contextual predictability, indicating that association strength was not independent of contextual predictability. This finding is against Luka & Petten (2014).

Collocations are defined as *semantically* related word combinations by Firth (1968). According the lexical priming theory (Hoey 2005), there is a priming association between constituent words in collocations. Constituent words predict each other due to the priming relationship. The predictability is determined by the strength of the association between constituent words. One type of measures of the strength of the association is association strength. However, the present finding suggests that association strength is part of contextual constraint.

In short, this dissertation provides evidence demonstrating that collocation strength and contextual predictability play a similar and important role in the processing of Chinese collocations compared to English collocations during reading.

7.3 The processing model for Chinese verb-noun collocations

Inspired by the models of Li et al. (2009), Li & Pollatsek (2020) and Matsuno (2017), we propose a Chinese verb-noun collocation processing (CVCP) model accounting for the processing of Chinese verb-noun collocations during reading (see Figure 7.1).

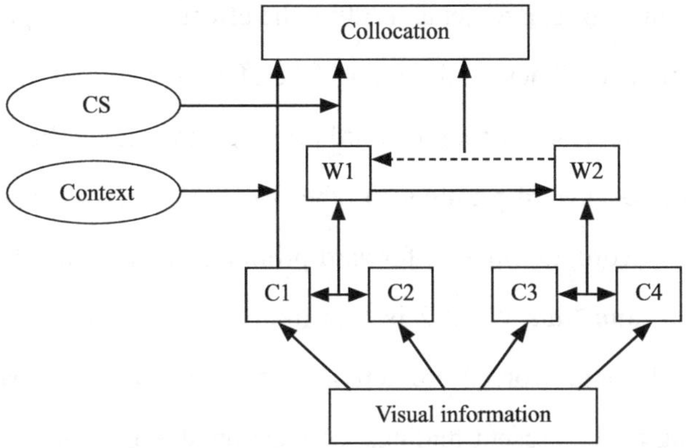

Figure 7.1 A processing model for Chinese *verb-noun* collocations

Note: C=character, W= word, CS = collocation strength.

The CVCP model assumes that the input of visual information of characters leads to the activation of characters. The characters in the perceptual span are processed in parallel, and word segmentation and word identification simultaneously, following Li et al. (2009) and Li & Pollatsek (2020). The identified character activates its related (graphemic, associative, syntactic and collocational) characters, due to priming effects between them (Planck & Sereno 1991), resulting in the activation of words. In the current model, Character 1 is related to Character 2, and thus they activate each other, so do Character 3 and 4. The activation of Character 1 and 2 leads to the production of Word 1. Similarly, when Character 3 and 4 are activated, Word 2 is produced. Based on the spreading activation model (Collins & Loftus 1975) and the lexical priming theory (Hoey 2005), the activation of a word will spread to other related words. The current model assumes that the activation of Word 1 leads Word 2 to be activated. According to the findings of Frisson et al. (2005), the effect of forward priming is larger than that of backward priming. Therefore, the current model uses solid line to represent strong forward priming and a dotted line to show the weaker backward priming. In other words, Word 1 is more likely to activate Word 2, which is forward priming. The backward priming is weaker, and thus Word 2 is less likely to prime Word 1. When both Word 1 and Word 2 are activated, the collocation is produced. According to the present findings, collocation strength and contextual predictability facilitate the processing of Chinese collocations. Thus, the current model includes these two factors. We assume that a character may directly activate the whole collocation in a highly predictable context. In addition, one constituent word of a collocation may activate the collocation as well if the collocation is a strong collocation (a collocation with high phrasal frequency and MI scores).

The CVCP model assumes that at the character level, the processing is analytical. At the word level, when Word 1 and Word 2 activate each other, the processing is analytical as well. When a collocation is directly activated by Word 1 or Character 1, it is a holistic processing. The current model accounts for the integration of analytical and holistic processing of Chinese collocations during reading. Additionally, the current model takes the effects of contextual predictability and collocation strength into consideration.

7.4 Conclusion

This chapter reviewed the present findings and discussed them based on the three research topics. Specifically, we discussed the processing advantage of Chinese collocations, the holistic and analytical processing of collocations during reading and the linguistic factors influencing the collocational processing. Based on the present findings, we proposed a model to describe the processing of Chinese collocations during reading.

Chapter 8 Conclusion

8.1 Major findings

This dissertation explored the processing of Chinese collocations during reading. Specifically, the study focuses on three questions: (1) Do Chinese collocations enjoy processing advantages over control novel phrases in reading? (2) Are Chinese collocations processed holistically or analytically? (3) How do collocation strength, contextual predictability and association strength influence the processing of Chinese collocations in reading? To answer these questions, this study conducted five eye-tracking experiments in which Chinese four-character verb-noun collocations were used as research materials. Main findings related to the three questions are briefly summarized as follows.

Firstly, the present findings provide strong evidence that Chinese collocations enjoy processing advantages over novel phrases, due to shorter reading times and higher skipping rates and fewer fixations for collocations, which is in line with the previous studies in English collocations (e.g., Durrant & Doherty 2010; Frisson et al. 2005; McDonald & Shillcock 2003a, b; Sonbul 2015; Vilkaite 2016). The processing advantage may be due to the frequent use of collocations in language. Thus, the findings support the usage-based theory (Bybee 2006) and exemplar-based (Bod 1998, 2006; Pierrehumbert 2001) theories.

Secondly, the present findings provide further evidence for the debate about whether or not formulaic sequences are processed holistically. Experiment 2 and 3 manipulated the previews of the nouns in collocations using the boundary paradigm. Robust preview effects of word *n+1* were found in the two experiments. Additionally, the PoF effects were observed as well. The findings indicate that Chinese collocations are processed both holistically and analytically. The findings provide evidence supporting the MCU Hypothesis (Zang 2019) and the Lexical Representation Hypothesis (Swinney & Cutler 1979).

Thirdly, the effect of contextual predictability which has been found in word processing (see Staub 2015 for a review) is also observed in the current study. The results show that collocations are read faster in predictable than neutral context. The findings provide novel evidence that collocation strength (defined using a combination of phrasal frequency and MI scores) facilitates the processing of collocations in reading. Moreover, the effect of collocation strength is independent of contextual effects, in consistent with the previous research in English collocations (Li et al. 2021). The effects of collocation strength and contextual predictability appear in both early lexical identification and later integration. It was found that the effect of association strength only emerged in late eye movement measures and it was influenced by the contextual effect.

The findings support the lexical priming theory (Hoey 2005, 2012). Due to the priming relationships between word pairs, one of them activates (or primes) the other (Hoey 2005, 2012). In other words, the priming relationships make collocations predictable, which results in the faster processing of collocations. The findings also support the spreading activation models (Collins & Loftus 1975) which suggest that the activation of a word will spread to other words related to the activated word. Hence, when one constituent word of a collocation is activated, its collocate will be activated as well.

8.2 Implications

The dissertation has examined three key research questions about the processing of Chinese collocations. The present findings contribute to the understanding of the processing mechanisms of Chinese collocations in natural reading. These findings have important theoretical and practical implications.

8.2.1 Theoretical implications

The present findings contribute to the study of Chinese multi-word sequences which mainly focused on idioms (e.g., Yu et al. 2016; Zang, 2019, 2021). It was found that idioms are processed faster than novel phrases (Zang 2019). The processing advantage of Chinese collocations is also found in the present study. The findings suggest that collocation and idioms are multi-constituent units which are lexicalized and stored as single lexical representations based on the multi-constituent unit hypothesis (Zang 2019). Previous studies have been taking the word as the basic processing unit in Chinese sentence reading (e.g., Rayner et al. 2007; Wang et al. 2010; Yan et al. 2010; Yang & McConkie

1999). The present findings sit alongside evidence from other studies imply that multi-constituent units are also processing units in Chinese reading. Moreover, the present findings provide further evidence for the advantage of formulaic language and the sensitivity of eye movements to frequency of usage at a phrasal level. Such findings may influence the development of the reading models. As introduced in Chapter 3, the current models of eye movement control in reading focus on word frequency. The present findings and other evidence from previous research (Conklin & Schmitt 2008, 2012; Li et al. 2021; Siyanova-Chanturia et al. 2011; Vilkaite 2016; Yu et al. 2016; Zang 2019) suggest that it is necessary to add mechanisms that are sensitive to frequency of multi-word phrases to the current Chinese models of eye movement control.

The fact that Chinese collocations are processed quantitatively differently from novel language has major implications for linguistic theory. It appears that the occurrence of a psychological event, a word or a phrase, leaves a trace in one's memory, which facilitates its further usage. Through recurrence, even highly complex events can become routinized, and as a result, be carried out with less effort. The results outlined above suggest that due to their frequency of occurrence, collocations become automatized to such an extent that they become represented in the mental lexicon.

The CVCP model proposed in this dissertation may shed light on the future research in the processing of Chinese collocations. To the best of our knowledge, the CVCP model is the first model to account for the processing of Chinese collocations during reading. This model may help us better understand the processing mechanism of Chinese collocations.

The results of the whole study have important implications for theories of language learning (Abbot-Smith & Tomasello 2006; Bannard & Mathews 2008). Words have traditionally been viewed as primary units of language acquisition in first and second language learning. The empirical finding shows that units above the word level may also serve as units of representation and processing in language.

More generally, the results reviewed in the current article can be taken to support a number of usage-based (Langacker 1987; Goldberg 1995, 2006; Bybee 1998; Tomasello 2003) and exemplar-based (Bod 1998, 2006; Pierrehumbert 2001) approaches to language acquisition, processing and use. According to the proponents of these theories, frequency effects are present in smaller (morphemes, words), as well as larger units (compounds, compositional phrases, idioms), and, thus, all linguistic materials should be represented and processed in a similar way. As Bod (2006) argues, the allocation of representations to linguistic exemplars is accomplished purely on the basis of statistics (i.e. the frequency of occurrence), and, thus, language should be viewed not as a set of specific grammar rules (and neither as two distinct and disjointed entities—the lexicon and grammar), but as a statistical accumulation of linguistic experiences that changes every time a particular word, phrase, or sentence is encountered (Bod 2006; also see Arnon and Snider 2010; Siyanova-Chanturia et al. 2011b).

8.2.2 Practical implications

The present findings have some implications for Chinese as a second language (CSL) acquisition. The proper use of English collocations is a prerequisite to be a proficient L2 learner (e.g., Cowie 1998; Granger & Bestgen 2014; Wray 2002). Chinese collocations are processed faster than novel phrases, indicating the holistic presentation in mental lexicon. Thus, the proper use of Chinese collocations will reduce L2 learners' processing load and help them speak naturally and fluently like native speakers. The acquisition of Chinese collocations will be vital for CSL learners to increase the knowledge of Chinese collocations and develop the awareness of collocations.

The current study provides evidence showing that the eye-tracking paradigm is a proper tool to study the processing of multi-word sequences during reading. The present findings demonstrate that eye movements are sensitive to factors affecting the processing of collocations during reading. The factors include phrasal frequency, collocation strength and association strength. In addition, the eye-tracking technology can be used to assess the parafoveal processing of collocations. With regards to the interest areas, the current study chose the phrase-final word and whole phrase, which is helpful for capturing the macro and micro pictures of collocation processing. In short, the use of eye movements helps us better understand the processing mechanism of collocations. Methodologically, the current study provides reference for future research on multi-word processing.

8.3 Limitations and suggestions for future studies

8.3.1 Limitations

The dissertation only focused on three crucial linguistic factors influencing the processing of Chinese collocations. Other factors such as semantic transparency are also valuable. For instance, previous studies have explored semantic transparency and found that it facilitated the processing of English collocations (Frisson et al. 2008; Gyllstad & Wolter 2016). To fully understand the processing of Chinese collocations in isolation and reading, we need to focus on other factors as well.

In Experiment 2 and 3, the boundary was placed in the middle of the collocation. This design manipulated the preview of the noun in the collocation. The finding may be different if the boundary is located before the whole collocation, that is, the whole collocation is put in the parafoveal region. This design will explore the parafoveal processing of collocations, which will better reveal whether or not collocations are processed holistically.

Although eye movements are widely regarded as the optimal method to study reading and can be used to infer the underlying cognitive processes, they do not provide a direct measure of neural activity. Many research findings have also come from EEG studies examining event-related potential (ERP) correlates of word recognition, but this dissertation fails to explore the processing of Chinese collocations from a neuro-psychological perspective without using the ERP technique.

8.3.2 Suggestions for future studies

This dissertation has shed light on several important issues. However, there is still much scope for further research. The future studies may assess other factors influencing the processing of Chinese collocations, like age of acquisition and semantic transparency which will help us have a better understanding about the influencing factors. It is also valuable to explore the processing of Chinese collocations by children, which can improve our knowledge about the processing and acquisition of collocations of children. The further studies may focus on other types of Chinese collocations such as adjective-noun collocations and noun-noun collocations which are frequently used in Chinese as well. This will enable us to capture a whole picture of the processing of Chinese collocations.

The future study may improve the research method. Although the ERP technique can be used to research collocations from a neuro-psychological perspective, it has some limitations as well. A major limitation is that sentences are presented word-by-word in ERP studies, which is not natural reading. A proper way to solve the problem is to combine eye movements and ERPs. This approach records ERPs that occur during specific fixations on words which captures the activity in the brain as it occurs in real-time during natural reading. The method has proven to be effective in reading research. Hopefully, this method will be used for future studies on Chinese collocations.

Appendices

Appendix 1: Materials for Experiment 1

Set	Condition	Sentences	Questions
1	1	为了训练记忆力老师常要求学生**背诵课文**和默写句子。	学生不用背书吗?
1	2	为了训练记忆力老师常要求学生**背诵生词**和默写句子。	学生不用背书吗?
1	3	我隔壁的小朋友林小伟每天都会**背诵课文**和默写句子。	林小伟从不背书吗?
1	4	我隔壁的小朋友林小伟每天都会**背诵生词**和默写句子。	林小伟从不背书吗?
2	1	游泳馆配备了柜子让游客**存放物品**安全便捷。	NA
2	2	游泳馆配备了柜子让游客**存放鞋子**非常方便。	NA
2	3	陈明丽他们将在那个房间**存放物品**然后离开。	NA
2	4	陈明丽他们将在那个房间**存放鞋子**然后离开。	NA
3	1	学生有疑惑时应主动**请教老师**帮忙解答。	NA
3	2	学生有疑惑时应主动**请教同学**帮忙解答。	NA
3	3	吴敏一直很胆小不敢**请教老师**只好自己想。	NA
3	4	吴敏一直很胆小不敢**请教同学**只好自己想。	NA
4	1	老韩想承包一片荒山来**种植树木**但他的家人反对。	老韩想种小麦吗?
4	2	老韩想承包一片荒山来**种植橘子**但他的家人反对。	老韩想种小麦吗?
4	3	刘立军如果想要在这里**种植树木**必须要得到批准。	刘立军想种玉米吗?

（续表）

Set	Condition	Sentences	Questions
4	4	刘立军如果想要在这里**种植橘子**必须要得到批准。	刘立军想种玉米吗？
5	1	有时需要居委会出面**调解纠纷**使大家和平共处。	NA
5	2	有时需要居委会出面**调解争斗**使大家和平共处。	NA
5	3	小明要是能够帮你们**调解纠纷**早就出手帮忙了。	NA
5	4	小明要是能够帮你们**调解争斗**早就出手帮忙了。	NA
6	1	编辑退回稿子希望他进一步**修改文章**并尽快提交。	他的稿子不需要修改了吗？
6	2	编辑退回稿子希望他进一步**修改结尾**并尽快提交。	他的稿子不需要修改了吗？
6	3	吴小丽的老师为了帮助她们**修改文章**很晚才回家。	吴小丽的老师很早回家了吗？
6	4	吴小丽的老师为了帮助她们**修改结尾**很晚才回家。	吴小丽的老师很早回家了吗？
7	1	该俱乐部只为会员**提供服务**并不对外开放。	NA
7	2	该俱乐部只为会员**提供号码**并不对外公布。	NA
7	3	王琳希望这里可以**提供服务**而且是免费的。	NA
7	4	王琳希望这里可以**提供号码**帮她联系家人。	NA
8	1	笼中鸟总是**向往自由**期待在天空飞翔。	NA
8	2	笼中鸟总是**向往好运**期待在天空飞翔。	NA
8	3	李萍萍同学**向往自由**希望独自去远方。	NA
8	4	李萍萍同学**向往好运**希望找个好工作。	NA
9	1	军人的职责是**保卫祖国**抵御入侵。	NA
9	2	军人的职责是**保卫校园**抵御入侵。	NA
9	3	小东长大后要**保卫祖国**奉献青春。	NA

（续表）

Set	Condition	Sentences	Questions
9	4	小东长大后要**保卫校园**奉献青春。	NA
10	1	我邀请女儿的同学过来一起给她**庆祝生日**热闹一下。	NA
10	2	我邀请女儿的同学过来一起给她**庆祝出生**热闹一下。	NA
10	3	陈雪期待这个周末能和闺蜜一起**庆祝生日**开心地玩。	NA
10	4	陈雪期待这个周末能和闺蜜一起**庆祝出生**开心地玩。	NA
11	1	婆媳住在一起久了会**产生矛盾**使家庭不和睦。	NA
11	2	婆媳住在一起久了会**产生负担**使家庭不和睦。	NA
11	3	这件事情使他和林君**产生矛盾**不再做朋友了。	NA
11	4	这件事情使他和林君**产生负担**不再做朋友了	NA
12	1	由于招工困难公司只好在招聘时**降低标准**录用员工。	现在难招工吗？
12	2	由于招工困难公司只好在招聘时**降低资格**录用员工。	现在难招工吗？
12	3	李明华现在只能想尽办法进一步**降低标准**收购产品。	李明华在收购产品吗？
12	4	李明华现在只能想尽办法进一步**降低资格**招收人员。	李明华在收购产品吗？
13	1	政府应谨防行业巨头**垄断市场**操纵价格。	NA
13	2	政府应谨防行业巨头**垄断中国**影响发展。	NA
13	3	政府应明令禁止他们**垄断市场**控制经济。	NA
13	4	政府应明令禁止他们**垄断中国**控制经济。	NA
14	1	恶婆婆故意在他们夫妻间**挑拨是非**使他们感情破裂。	NA

（续表）

Set	Condition	Sentences	Questions
14	2	恶婆婆故意在他们夫妻间**挑拨恩怨**使他们感情破裂。	NA
14	3	小莉因为嫉妒她的朋友就**挑拨是非**损害别人的名誉。	NA
14	4	小莉因为嫉妒她的朋友就**挑拨恩怨**损害别人的名誉。	NA
15	1	异国求学的学生在中秋节格外**想念家乡**是正常的。	NA
15	2	异国求学的学生在中秋节格外**想念爱人**是正常的。	NA
15	3	许多年之后小王依旧难忘当初**想念家乡**时的痛苦。	NA
15	4	许多年之后小王依旧难忘当初**想念爱人**时的痛苦。	NA
16	1	离婚后他和前妻彻底**断绝关系**不再联系了。	NA
16	2	离婚后他和前妻彻底**断绝电话**不再联系了。	NA
16	3	陈娜娜已经和董小伟**断绝关系**成了陌路人。	NA
16	4	陈娜娜已经和董小伟**断绝电话**成了陌路人。	NA
17	1	前面危险路段经常**发生事故**要小心驾驶。	NA
17	2	前面危险路段经常**发生坏事**要小心驾驶。	NA
17	3	听别人说这里曾经**发生事故**他赶紧走了。	NA
17	4	听别人说这里曾经**发生坏事**他赶紧走了。	NA
18	1	在深山中他用大砍刀为我们**开辟道路**探查方向。	NA
18	2	在深山中他用大砍刀为我们**开辟领域**探查方向。	NA
18	3	在研讨会上他的理论为我们**开辟道路**指明方向。	NA
18	4	在研讨会上他的理论为我们**开辟领域**指明方向。	NA
19	1	从不同的角度**看待事物**会有不同的结果。	NA

（续表）

Set	Condition	Sentences	Questions
19	2	从不同的角度**看待提议**会有不同的结果。	NA
19	3	对于我该如何**看待事物**爸爸给了些建议。	NA
19	4	对于我该如何**看待提议**爸爸给了些建议。	NA
20	1	教授鼓励年轻人勇敢**追求梦想**成就未来。	NA
20	2	教授鼓励年轻人勇敢**追求惊喜**发现不同。	NA
20	3	李明和他的朋友为了**追求梦想**离开了家。	NA
20	4	李明和他的朋友为了**追求惊喜**离开了家。	NA
21	1	为有需要的人**提供帮助**是企业的社会责任。	NA
21	2	为有需要的人**提供爸爸**是福利机构的责任。	NA
21	3	哥哥希望我们**提供帮助**让他能渡过这一关。	NA
21	4	哥哥希望我们**提供爸爸**新的家庭住址信息。	NA
22	1	中国队在不利局面下及时**调整状态**赢得了比赛。	中国队输掉了比赛吗？
22	2	中国队在不利局面下及时**调整攻击**赢得了比赛。	中国队输掉了比赛吗？
22	3	幸运的是李文斌他们及时**调整状态**打败了敌人。	李文斌被敌人打败了吗？
22	4	幸运的是李文斌他们及时**调整攻击**打败了敌人。	李文斌被敌人打败了吗？
23	1	有些企业为了快速发展从国外**引进技术**提升竞争力。	NA
23	2	有些企业为了快速发展从国外**引进成员**提升竞争力。	NA
23	3	陈华经理正在和外方代表商谈**引进技术**等相关事宜。	NA
23	4	陈华经理正在和外方代表商谈**引进成员**等相关事宜。	NA

（续表）

Set	Condition	Sentences	Questions
24	1	他的遗嘱中写道让他的儿子**继承财产**并接管公司。	NA
24	2	他的遗嘱中写道让他的儿子**继承沙发**并搬出去住。	NA
24	3	王华最近在考虑到底让谁来**继承财产**会比较合适。	NA
24	4	王华最近在考虑到底让谁来**继承沙发**会比较合适。	NA
25	1	家政工作包括做饭**打扫房间**和洗衣服。	家政工作包括洗衣服吗?
25	2	家政工作包括做饭**打扫外面**和洗衣服。	家政工作包括洗衣服吗?
25	3	孙丽丽一起床就会**打扫房间**和洗衣服。	孙丽丽会洗衣服吗?
25	4	孙丽丽一起床就会**打扫外面**和洗衣服。	孙丽丽会洗衣服吗?
26	1	魏爷爷爱看老照片**回想过去**感慨青春。	NA
26	2	魏爷爷爱看老照片**回想名字**怀恋友人。	NA
26	3	老曹喝过酒后喜欢**回想过去**感叹时光。	NA
26	4	老曹喝过酒后喜欢**回想名字**怀恋友人。	NA
27	1	据说古人通过观星象**预测天气**安排农事。	NA
27	2	据说古人通过观星象**预测对手**占卜吉凶。	NA
27	3	林忠伟希望自己能够**预测天气**安排出行。	NA
27	4	林忠伟希望自己能够**预测对手**做好防备。	NA
28	1	热心肠的小林经常**帮助朋友**解决各种问题。	NA
28	2	热心肠的小林经常**帮助先生**解决各种问题。	NA
28	3	李美玉曾在火车站**帮助朋友**购票和拿行李。	NA

（续表）

Set	Condition	Sentences	Questions
28	4	李美玉曾在火车站**帮助先生**购票和拿行李。	NA
29	1	卧底在潜伏时要避免**暴露身份**以免自己被抓。	NA
29	2	卧底在潜伏时要避免**暴露老板**以免他们被抓。	NA
29	3	王东他们知道绝不能**暴露身份**以免影响工作。	NA
29	4	王东他们知道绝不能**暴露老板**以免影响工作。	NA
30	1	圣诞节朋友之间**交换礼物**是一个习俗。	NA
30	2	圣诞节朋友之间**交换任务**是一个习俗。	NA
30	3	小娜和小丽决定**交换礼物**做好朋友了。	NA
30	4	小娜和小丽决定**交换任务**做好朋友了。	NA
31	1	陈丽欣然地**接受邀请**并出席了这个典礼。	陈丽出席了典礼吗？
31	2	陈丽欣然地**接受提醒**并修改了这个错误。	陈丽修改了错误吗？
31	3	王乐乐最终**接受邀请**并参加了这个会议。	王乐乐参加了这个会议吗？
31	4	王乐乐最终**接受提醒**并修改了这个错误。	王乐乐修改了错误吗？
32	1	人生短暂请**珍惜时光**好好生活。	NA
32	2	人生短暂请**珍惜角色**把握机会。	NA
32	3	希望小妹能**珍惜时光**好好学习。	NA
32	4	希望小妹能**珍惜角色**好好演戏。	NA
33	1	他通过不断努力在事业上**取得成功**获得认可。	他获得认可了吗？
33	2	他通过不断努力在事业上**取得不同**获得认可。	他获得认可了吗？
33	3	赵军在朋友的帮助下终于**取得成功**获得认可。	赵军得到了朋友的帮助吗？

（续表）

Set	Condition	Sentences	Questions
33	4	赵军在朋友的帮助下终于**取得不同**获得认可。	赵军得到了朋友的帮助吗？
34	1	人们总是在犹豫中**丧失机会**接着又很后悔。	NA
34	2	人们总是在犹豫中**丧失生活**不敢往前迈步。	NA
34	3	教练提醒吴伟不要**丧失机会**否则就会输的。	NA
34	4	教练提醒吴伟不要**丧失生活**否则就会输的。	NA

Appendix 2: Materials for Experiment 2

Set	Condition	Sentences	Questions
1	1	林萍萍说在线上**办理手续**可以有优惠。	NA
1	2	林萍萍说在线上**办理天康**可以有优惠。	NA
1	3	林萍萍说在线上**办理事务**可以有优惠。	NA
1	4	林萍萍说在线上**办理非术**可以有优惠。	NA
2	1	小梅只能自己**承担责任**没人帮得了她。	NA
2	2	小梅只能自己**承担或全**没人帮得了她。	NA
2	3	小梅只能自己**承担后果**没人帮得了她。	NA
2	4	小梅只能自己**承担肉单**没人帮得了她。	NA
3	1	董莉莉决定和父亲**断绝关系**独自生活。	董莉莉和父亲关系好吗？
3	2	董莉莉决定和父亲**断绝年况**独自生活。	董莉莉和父亲关系好吗？
3	3	董莉莉决定和父亲**断绝来往**独自生活。	董莉莉和父亲关系好吗？
3	4	董莉莉决定和父亲**断绝步实**独自生活。	董莉莉和父亲关系好吗？
4	1	事情发生后他们立刻**封锁消息**减低影响。	NA

（续表）

Set	Condition	Sentences	Questions
4	2	事情发生后他们立刻**封锁班旁**减低影响。	NA
4	3	事情发生后他们立刻**封锁现场**减低影响。	NA
4	4	事情发生后他们立刻**封锁国年**减低影响。	NA
5	1	他们承诺尽快**公布结果**并给出解决办法。	NA
5	2	他们承诺尽快**公布俩明**并给出解决办法。	NA
5	3	他们承诺尽快**公布信息**并给出解决办法。	NA
5	4	他们承诺尽快**公布相值**并给出解决办法。	NA
6	1	李小伟正在**思考问题**不想被打扰。	NA
6	2	李小伟正在**思考在懂**不想被打扰。	NA
6	3	李小伟正在**思考人生**不想被打扰。	NA
6	4	李小伟正在**思考厂去**不想被打扰。	NA
7	1	王书记明天会来**听取意见**并回答询问。	NA
7	2	王书记明天会来**听取感气**并回答询问。	NA
7	3	王书记明天会来**听取报告**并回答询问。	NA
7	4	王书记明天会来**听取严身**并回答询问。	NA
8	1	这个东西会**污染环境**危害健康。	NA
8	2	这个东西会**污染些舞**危害健康。	NA
8	3	这个东西会**污染水源**危害健康。	NA
8	4	这个东西会**污染水源**危害健康。	NA
9	1	他现在终于可以**享受生活**不再拼命工作了。	他现在还要拼命工作吗？
9	2	他现在终于可以**享受正送**不再拼命工作了。	他现在还要拼命工作吗？
9	3	他现在终于可以**享受时光**不再拼命工作了。	他现在还要拼命工作吗？
9	4	他现在终于可以**享受每动**不再拼命工作了。	他现在还要拼命工作吗？

（续表）

Set	Condition	Sentences	Questions
10	1	爸爸让我帮他**招呼客人**他去买酒去了。	妈妈去买酒了吗?
10	2	爸爸让我帮他**招呼持又**他去买酒去了。	妈妈去买酒了吗?
10	3	爸爸让我帮他**招呼朋友**他去买酒去了。	妈妈去买酒了吗?
10	4	爸爸让我帮他**招呼味历**他去买酒去了。	妈妈去买酒了吗?
11	1	李锐让我一定要**珍惜生命**好好活着。	NA
11	2	李锐让我一定要**珍惜兄玩**好好活着。	NA
11	3	李锐让我一定要**珍惜时光**好好活着。	NA
11	4	李锐让我一定要**珍惜私吃**好好活着。	NA
12	1	没想到李峰能够**战胜困难**赢得比赛。	李峰赢得比赛了吗?
12	2	没想到李峰能够**战胜何恶**赢得比赛。	李峰赢得比赛了吗?
12	3	没想到李峰能够**战胜失败**赢得比赛。	李峰赢得比赛了吗?
12	4	没想到李峰能够**战胜发事**赢得比赛。	李峰赢得比赛了吗?
13	1	最后还是小东**发挥作用**解决了问题。	NA
13	2	最后还是小东**发挥词号**解决了问题。	NA
13	3	最后还是小东**发挥想象**解决了问题。	NA
13	4	最后还是小东**发挥搞章**解决了问题。	NA
14	1	张强说他会**完成任务**尽快归队的。	张强暂时离开队伍了吗?
14	2	张强说他会**完成因可**尽快归队的。	张强暂时离开队伍了吗?

（续表）

Set	Condition	Sentences	Questions
14	3	张强说他会**完成使命**尽快归队的。	张强暂时离开队伍了吗？
14	4	张强说他会**完成空事**尽快归队的。	张强暂时离开队伍了吗？
15	1	董俊由于无法**忍受痛苦**选择了放弃化疗。	董俊还在化疗吗？
15	2	董俊由于无法**忍受喜者**选择了放弃化疗。	董俊还在化疗吗？
15	3	董俊由于无法**忍受折磨**选择了放弃化疗。	董俊还在化疗吗？
15	4	董俊由于无法**忍受位赞**选择了放弃化疗。	董俊还在化疗吗？
16	1	刘经理在**培养人才**上面花费了不少精力。	NA
16	2	刘经理在**培养了已**上面花费了不少精力。	NA
16	3	刘经理在**培养兴趣**上面花费了不少精力。	NA
16	4	刘经理在**培养早增**上面花费了不少精力。	NA
17	1	李锐最近**消耗能量**比较多要好好补补才行。	李锐需要补一补吗？
17	2	李锐最近**消耗哥超**比较多要好好补补才行。	李锐需要补一补吗？
17	3	李锐最近**消耗精力**比较多要好好补补才行。	李锐需要补一补吗？
17	4	李锐最近**消耗需几**比较多要好好补补才行。	李锐需要补一补吗？
18	1	王梅每个周末都会**观看电影**或去逛街。	NA
18	2	王梅每个周末都会**观看东靠**或去逛街。	NA
18	3	王梅每个周末都会**观看节目**或去逛街。	NA
18	4	王梅每个周末都会**观看头议**或去逛街。	NA

（续表）

Set	Condition	Sentences	Questions
19	1	为了在夏季**灌溉农田**他买了新的水泵。	他买了新的水泵吗？
19	2	为了在夏季**灌溉宇史**他买了新的水泵。	他买了新的水泵吗？
19	3	为了在夏季**灌溉土地**他买了新的水泵。	他买了新的水泵吗？
19	4	为了在夏季**灌溉凡划**他买了新的水泵。	他买了新的水泵吗？
20	1	我国早已**颁布法令**禁止封建迷信活动。	NA
20	2	我国早已**颁布图击**禁止封建迷信活动。	NA
20	3	我国早已**颁布法律**禁止封建迷信活动。	NA
20	4	我国早已**颁布图击**禁止封建迷信活动。	NA
21	1	林书华决定**保留意见**不作评论。	NA
21	2	林书华决定**保留群片**不作评论。	NA
21	3	林书华决定**保留权利**暂不追究。	NA
21	4	林书华决定**保留回助**暂不追究。	NA
22	1	吴小丽希望在这里**获得知识**增长智慧。	NA
22	2	吴小丽希望在这里**获得幸作**增长智慧。	NA
22	3	吴小丽希望在这里**获得安慰**得到鼓励。	NA
22	4	吴小丽希望在这里**获得件聪**得到鼓励。	NA
23	1	他们公司在**建造房屋**时发生了意外。	NA
23	2	他们公司在**建造知统**时发生了意外。	NA
23	3	他们公司在**建造大厦**时发生了意外。	NA
23	4	他们公司在**建造个惑**时发生了意外。	NA
24	1	周小平因为**违反规定**被单位处罚了。	周小平被处罚了吗？

（续表）

Set	Condition	Sentences	Questions
24	2	周小平因为**违反和拉**被单位处罚了。	周小平被处罚了吗？
24	3	周小平因为**违反纪律**被单位处罚了。	周小平被处罚了吗？
24	4	周小平因为**违反刚说**被单位处罚了。	周小平被处罚了吗？
25	1	人们用语言来**传递信息**促进交流。	NA
25	2	人们用语言来**传递面脑**促进交流。	NA
25	3	人们用语言来**传递文化**促进交流。	NA
25	4	人们用语言来**传递牙太**促进交流。	NA
26	1	朱鹏将负责**接待客人**和安排活动。	NA
26	2	朱鹏将负责**接待怎丁**和安排活动。	NA
26	3	朱鹏将负责**接待领导**和安排活动。	NA
26	4	朱鹏将负责**接待第而**和安排活动。	NA
27	1	小朋友们要**开动脑筋**好好答题。	NA
27	2	小朋友们要**开动剧策**好好答题。	NA
27	3	小朋友们要**开动火车**去旅行了。	NA
27	4	小朋友们要**开动父长**去旅行了。	NA
28	1	小俊希望在这个活动中**释放压力**放松心情。	NA
28	2	小俊希望在这个活动中**释放当入**放松心情。	NA
28	3	小俊希望在这个活动中**释放热情**收获快乐。	NA
28	4	小俊希望在这个活动中**释放桌随**收获快乐。	NA
29	1	老师希望李娜能**树立榜样**并发挥带头作用。	NA
29	2	老师希望李娜能**树立旗部**并发挥带头作用。	NA
29	3	老师希望李娜能**树立理想**并为之努力奋斗。	NA
29	4	老师希望李娜能**树立蛋照**并为之努力奋斗。	NA

（续表）

Set	Condition	Sentences	Questions
30	1	爸爸让我们认真**吸取教训**不再犯错。	NA
30	2	爸爸让我们认真**吸取清业**不再犯错。	NA
30	3	爸爸让我们认真**吸取经验**改进工作。	NA
30	4	爸爸让我们认真**吸取实病**改进工作。	NA
31	1	李明为了**争取胜利**付出了不少代价。	NA
31	2	李明为了**争取药体**付出了不少代价。	NA
31	3	李明为了**争取成功**付出了不少代价。	NA
31	4	李明为了**争取名平**付出了不少代价。	NA
32	1	小李突然**转移话题**聊起了买房子的事。	NA
32	2	小李突然**转移周暴**聊起了买房子的事。	NA
32	3	小李突然**转移目标**盯上了隔壁的女孩。	NA
32	4	小李突然**转移半冒**盯上了隔壁的女孩。	NA

Appendix 3: Substitute Characters for Experiment 2

T1	NOS	Freq	S1	NOS	Freq	T2	NOS	Freq	S2	NOS	Freq
法	8	3.78	图	8	3.58	令	5	3.60	击	5	3.63
法	8	3.78	变	8	3.77	律	9	3.48	济	9	3.00
手	4	3.79	天	4	3.79	续	11	3.70	康	11	3.30
事	8	3.80	非	8	3.77	务	5	3.62	术	5	3.56
意	13	3.80	群	13	3.41	见	4	3.79	片	4	3.69
权	6	3.55	回	6	3.79	利	7	3.72	助	7	3.69
责	8	3.59	或	8	3.75	任	6	3.76	全	6	3.78
后	6	3.79	肉	6	3.46	果	8	3.79	单	8	3.72
信	9	3.79	面	9	3.79	息	10	3.72	脑	10	3.65
文	4	3.57	牙	4	3.38	化	4	3.61	太	4	3.79

（续表）

T1	NOS	Freq	S1	NOS	Freq	T2	NOS	Freq	S2	NOS	Freq
关	6	3.79	年	6	3.78	系	7	3.75	况	7	3.66
来	7	3.80	步	7	3.61	往	8	3.63	实	8	3.79
作	7	3.79	词	7	3.46	用	5	3.79	号	5	3.67
想	13	3.80	搞	13	3.70	象	11	3.68	章	11	3.23
消	10	3.71	班	10	3.56	息	10	3.72	旁	10	3.39
现	8	3.80	国	8	3.71	场	6	3.76	年	6	3.78
结	9	3.77	俩	9	3.55	果	8	3.79	明	8	3.79
信	9	3.79	相	9	3.79	息	10	3.72	值	10	3.56
电	5	3.76	东	5	3.78	影	15	3.65	靠	15	3.59
节	5	3.63	头	5	3.78	目	5	3.71	议	5	3.63
农	6	2.95	宇	6	2.80	田	5	2.80	史	5	3.41
土	3	3.32	凡	3	3.03	地	6	3.79	划	6	3.60
知	8	3.80	幸	8	3.66	识	7	3.73	作	7	3.79
安	6	3.77	件	6	3.76	慰	15	3.00	聪	15	3.43
房	8	3.71	知	8	3.80	屋	9	3.45	统	9	3.52
大	3	3.80	个	3	3.80	厦	12	2.41	惑	12	3.10
客	9	3.63	怎	9	3.79	人	2	3.80	丁	2	3.14
领	11	3.51	第	11	3.78	导	6	3.49	而	6	3.79
脑	10	3.65	剧	10	3.43	筋	12	2.77	策	12	3.17
火	4	3.67	父	4	3.64	车	4	3.74	长	4	3.77
人	2	3.80	了	2	3.80	才	3	3.79	已	3	3.79
兴	6	3.74	早	6	3.75	趣	15	3.63	增	15	3.17
痛	12	3.56	喜	12	3.78	苦	8	3.53	者	8	3.77
折	7	3.35	位	7	3.75	磨	16	3.27	赞	16	3.25
压	6	3.48	当	6	3.79	力	2	3.78	入	2	3.73

（续表）

T1	NOS	Freq	S1	NOS	Freq	T2	NOS	Freq	S2	NOS	Freq
热	10	3.60	桌	10	3.31	情	11	3.79	随	11	3.68
榜	14	2.65	旗	14	2.76	样	10	3.80	部	10	3.76
理	11	3.78	蛋	11	3.65	想	13	3.80	照	13	3.71
问	6	3.79	在	6	3.80	题	15	3.78	懂	15	3.53
人	2	3.80	厂	2	2.97	生	5	3.80	去	5	3.80
意	13	3.80	感	13	3.79	见	4	3.79	气	4	3.76
报	7	3.70	严	7	3.54	告	7	3.79	身	7	3.78
任	6	3.76	因	6	3.79	务	5	3.62	可	5	3.80
使	8	3.69	空	8	3.66	命	8	3.72	事	8	3.80
规	8	3.50	和	8	3.79	定	8	3.79	拉	8	3.66
纪	6	3.49	刚	6	3.76	律	9	3.48	说	9	3.80
环	8	3.36	些	8	3.79	境	14	3.40	舞	14	3.46
水	4	3.71	反	4	3.69	源	13	3.29	腿	13	3.37
教	11	3.66	清	11	3.74	训	5	3.35	业	5	3.64
经	8	3.79	实	8	3.79	验	10	3.51	病	10	3.60
生	5	3.80	正	5	3.79	活	9	3.78	送	9	3.70
时	7	3.80	每	7	3.76	光	6	3.70	动	6	3.78
能	10	3.80	哥	10	3.57	量	12	3.64	超	12	3.58
精	14	3.65	需	14	3.78	力	2	3.78	几	2	3.77
困	7	3.48	何	7	3.77	难	10	3.77	恶	10	3.62
失	5	3.76	发	5	3.79	败	8	3.45	事	8	3.80
客	9	3.63	持	9	3.70	人	2	3.80	又	2	3.78
朋	8	3.75	味	8	3.65	友	4	3.77	历	4	3.55
生	5	3.80	兄	5	3.55	命	8	3.72	玩	8	3.74
时	7	3.80	私	7	3.53	光	6	3.70	吃	6	3.74

（续表）

T1	NOS	Freq	S1	NOS	Freq	T2	NOS	Freq	S2	NOS	Freq
胜	9	3.40	药	9	3.50	利	7	3.72	体	7	3.74
成	6	3.79	名	6	3.78	功	5	3.58	平	5	3.68
话	8	3.79	周	8	3.70	题	15	3.78	暴	15	3.44
目	5	3.71	半	5	3.64	标	9	3.55	冒	9	3.50

Appendix 4: Materials for Experiment 3

Set	Condition	Sentences	Questions
1	1	我们每个人都应该**保护环境**爱护家园。	NA
1	2	我们每个人都应该**保护环舞**爱护家园。	NA
1	3	我们每个人都应该**保护自然**爱护家园。	NA
1	4	我们每个人都应该**保护自筋**爱护家园。	NA
2	1	我估计让王芳芳**承认错误**比较困难。	NA
2	2	我估计让王芳芳**承认错标**比较困难。	NA
2	3	我估计让王芳芳**承认事实**比较困难。	NA
2	4	我估计让王芳芳**承认事往**比较困难。	NA
3	1	王教授今天会**出席会议**并发表讲话。	NA
3	2	王教授今天会**出席会目**并发表讲话。	NA
3	3	王教授今天会**出席活动**并发表讲话。	NA
3	4	王教授今天会**出席活光**并发表讲话。	NA
4	1	他最近一直在**打听消息**以了解事情的进展。	NA
4	2	他最近一直在**打听消样**以了解事情的进展。	NA
4	3	他最近一直在**打听情况**以了解事情的进展。	NA
4	4	他最近一直在**打听情弄**以了解事情的进展。	NA
5	1	爸爸希望我能**改正错误**做个好孩子。	爸爸希望我做个好孩子吗？

（续表）

Set	Condition	Sentences	Questions
5	2	爸爸希望我能**改正错活**做个好孩子。	爸爸希望我做个好孩子吗？
5	3	爸爸希望我能**改正缺点**做个好孩子。	爸爸希望我做个好孩子吗？
5	4	爸爸希望我能**改正缺屋**做个好孩子。	爸爸希望我做个好孩子吗？
6	1	目前哥哥已经**恢复健康**顺利出院。	现在哥哥还在住院吗？
6	2	目前哥哥已经**恢复健情**顺利出院。	现在哥哥还在住院吗？
6	3	目前哥哥已经**恢复身体**顺利出院。	现在哥哥还在住院吗？
6	4	目前哥哥已经**恢复身告**顺利出院。	现在哥哥还在住院吗？
7	1	书记要求我们在**汇报工作**时要实事求是。	NA
7	2	书记要求我们在**汇报工来**时要实事求是。	NA
7	3	书记要求我们在**汇报成绩**时要实事求是。	NA
7	4	书记要求我们在**汇报成折**时要实事求是。	NA
8	1	吴波想让我给他**提供帮助**让他完成实验。	吴波有实验吗？
8	2	吴波想让我给他**提供帮识**让他完成实验。	吴波有实验吗？
8	3	吴波想让我给他**提供材料**让他完成实验。	吴波有实验吗？
8	4	吴波想让我给他**提供材验**让他完成实验。	吴波有实验吗？
9	1	王经理为了**扩大规模**开了新店。	王经理开了新店吗？

（续表）

Set	Condition	Sentences	Questions
9	2	王经理为了**扩大规嘗**开了新店。	王经理开了新店吗？
9	3	王经理为了**扩大影响**开了新店。	王经理开了新店吗？
9	4	王经理为了**扩大影持**开了新店。	王经理开了新店吗？
10	1	没想到陈斌因为**缺乏自信**放弃了比赛。	陈斌比赛赢了吗？
10	2	没想到陈斌因为**缺乏自面**放弃了比赛。	陈斌比赛赢了吗？
10	3	没想到陈斌因为**缺乏勇气**放弃了比赛。	陈斌比赛赢了吗？
10	4	没想到陈斌因为**缺乏勇历**放弃了比赛。	陈斌比赛赢了吗？
11	1	刘家栋想要**实现梦想**为社会服务。	NA
11	2	刘家栋想要**实现梦源**为社会服务。	NA
11	3	刘家栋想要**实现价值**为社会服务。	NA
11	4	刘家栋想要**实现价旁**为社会服务。	NA
12	1	周末小华会去**拍摄照片**或打羽毛球。	NA
12	2	周末小华会去**拍摄照友**或打羽毛球。	NA
12	3	周末小华会去**拍摄风景**或打羽毛球。	NA
12	4	周末小华会去**拍摄风厦**或打羽毛球。	NA
13	1	我们公司将要**引进技术**促进发展。	NA
13	2	我们公司将要**引进技写**促进发展。	NA
13	3	我们公司将要**引进文化**促进发展。	NA
13	4	我们公司将要**引进文车**促进发展。	NA
14	1	大家希望陈军能**发表文章**评论高考改革。	NA

（续表）

Set	Condition	Sentences	Questions
14	2	大家希望陈军能**发表文续**评论高考改革。	NA
14	3	大家希望陈军能**发表演说**评论高考改革。	NA
14	4	大家希望陈军能**发表演送**评论高考改革。	NA
15	1	所有人都很清楚**保卫祖国**是我们的责任。	NA
15	2	所有人都很清楚**保卫祖苦**是我们的责任。	NA
15	3	所有人都很清楚**保卫安全**是我们的责任。	NA
15	4	所有人都很清楚**保卫安任**是我们的责任。	NA
16	1	李明叮嘱父亲要**预防疾病**保持健康。	NA
16	2	李明叮嘱父亲要**预防疾脑**保持健康。	NA
16	3	李明叮嘱父亲要**预防感冒**保持健康。	NA
16	4	李明叮嘱父亲要**预防感帮**保持健康。	NA
17	1	陈经理喝过酒后喜欢**怀念过去**感叹时光。	陈经理从不喝酒吗？
17	2	陈经理喝过酒后喜欢**怀念过用**感叹时光。	陈经理从不喝酒吗？
17	3	陈经理喝过酒后喜欢**怀念童年**感叹时光。	陈经理从不喝酒吗？
17	4	陈经理喝过酒后喜欢**怀念童地**感叹时光。	陈经理从不喝酒吗？
18	1	他们希望能重新**选举总统**改变现状。	NA
18	2	他们希望能重新**选举总养**改变现状。	NA
18	3	他们希望能重新**选举干部**改变现状。	NA
18	4	他们希望能重新**选举干换**改变现状。	NA
19	1	林聪他们为了**消灭敌人**想尽了办法。	NA
19	2	林聪他们为了**消灭敌十**想尽了办法。	NA
19	3	林聪他们为了**消灭害虫**想尽了办法。	NA
19	4	林聪他们为了**消灭害导**想尽了办法。	NA

（续表）

Set	Condition	Sentences	Questions
20	1	现在钟敏不得不**承受压力**继续前行。	NA
20	2	现在钟敏不得不**承受压又**继续前行。	NA
20	3	现在钟敏不得不**承受打击**继续前行。	NA
20	4	现在钟敏不得不**承受打本**继续前行。	NA
21	1	谁也没料到这里会**爆发战争**变得混乱不堪。	这里很混乱吗？
21	2	谁也没料到这里会**爆发战早**变得混乱不堪。	这里很混乱吗？
21	3	谁也没料到这里会**爆发革命**变得混乱不堪。	这里很混乱吗？
21	4	谁也没料到这里会**爆发革定**变得混乱不堪。	这里很混乱吗？
22	1	李国华在**继承遗产**后变得不一样了。	NA
22	2	李国华在**继承遗多**后变得不一样了。	NA
22	3	李国华在**继承事业**后变得不一样了。	NA
22	4	李国华在**继承事功**后变得不一样了。	NA
23	1	政府将尽快**落实政策**促进中小企业的发展。	NA
23	2	政府将尽快**落实政量**促进中小企业的发展。	NA
23	3	政府将尽快**落实计划**促进中小企业的发展。	NA
23	4	政府将尽快**落实计场**促进中小企业的发展。	NA
24	1	在这个活动中我们**回顾历史**展望未来。	NA
24	2	在这个活动中我们**回顾历生**展望未来。	NA
24	3	在这个活动中我们**回顾往事**展望未来。	NA
24	4	在这个活动中我们**回顾往明**展望未来。	NA
25	1	萍萍正在帮别人**解答问题**没空接电话。	萍萍现在正忙吗？

（续表）

Set	Condition	Sentences	Questions
25	2	萍萍正在帮别人**解答问影**没空接电话。	萍萍现在正忙吗？
25	3	萍萍正在帮别人**解答疑惑**没空接电话。	萍萍现在正忙吗？
25	4	萍萍正在帮别人**解答疑超**没空接电话。	萍萍现在正忙吗？
26	1	林浩知道只有**克服困难**才能走到最后。	NA
26	2	林浩知道只有**克服困恶**才能走到最后。	NA
26	3	林浩知道只有**克服恐惧**才能走到最后。	NA
26	4	林浩知道只有**克服恐随**才能走到最后。	NA
27	1	遗憾的是她没能**挽救生命**创造奇迹。	她创造奇迹了吗？
27	2	遗憾的是她没能**挽救生玩**创造奇迹。	她创造奇迹了吗？
27	3	遗憾的是她没能**挽救病人**创造奇迹。	她创造奇迹了吗？
27	4	遗憾的是她没能**挽救病丁**创造奇迹。	她创造奇迹了吗？
28	1	我们大家都要**遵守法律**没有例外。	NA
28	2	我们大家都要**遵守法茶**没有例外。	NA
28	3	我们大家都要**遵守法则**没有例外。	NA
28	4	我们大家都要**遵守法有**没有例外。	NA
29	1	他们为了**举办活动**做了大量的准备工作。	NA
29	2	他们为了**举办活次**做了大量的准备工作。	NA
29	3	他们为了**举办晚会**做了大量的准备工作。	NA
29	4	他们为了**举办晚吃**做了大量的准备工作。	NA
30	1	我们希望进一步**发展经济**保障供给。	NA

（续表）

Set	Condition	Sentences	Questions
30	2	我们希望进一步**发展经突**保障供给。	NA
30	3	我们希望进一步**发展关系**加强合作。	NA
30	4	我们希望进一步**发展关身**加强合作。	NA
31	1	他们的责任是**维护和平**和促进发展。	NA
31	2	他们的责任是**维护和号**和促进发展。	NA
31	3	他们的责任是**维护安全**和促进发展。	NA
31	4	他们的责任是**维护安成**和促进发展。	NA
32	1	邓飞因为没有**执行任务**被开除了。	邓飞升职了吗？
32	2	邓飞因为没有**执行任训**被开除了。	邓飞升职了吗？
32	3	邓飞因为没有**执行命令**被开除了。	邓飞升职了吗？
32	4	邓飞因为没有**执行命可**被开除了。	邓飞升职了吗？

Appendix 5: Substitute Characters for Experiment 3

Target character	Number of strokes	Frequency	Substituted character	Number of strokes	Frequency
境	14	3.4038	舞	14	3.4571
然	12	3.7946	筋	12	2.7686
误	9	3.5421	标	9	3.5494
实	8	3.7889	往	8	3.6303
议	5	3.6316	目	5	3.7053
动	6	3.7813	光	6	3.6978
息	10	3.7163	样	10	3.795

（续表）

Target character	Number of strokes	Frequency	Substituted character	Number of strokes	Frequency
况	7	3.6584	弄	7	3.6857
误	9	3.5421	活	9	3.7784
点	9	3.795	屋	9	3.4479
康	11	3.3032	情	11	3.7908
体	7	3.7366	告	7	3.7922
作	7	3.7884	来	7	3.7953
绩	11	2.8549	折	7	3.3541
助	7	3.6884	识	7	3.7322
料	10	3.5626	验	10	3.5085
模	14	3.4358	誓	14	3.4126
响	9	3.5001	持	9	3.704
信	9	3.7859	面	9	3.7924
气	4	3.7577	历	4	3.5539
想	13	3.7953	源	13	3.2947
值	10	3.5583	旁	10	3.3854
片	4	3.6901	友	4	3.7668
景	12	3.3361	厦	12	2.4116
术	5	3.5583	写	5	3.6278
化	4	3.6114	车	4	3.7379
章	11	3.2297	续	11	3.6978
说	9	3.7954	送	9	3.7033
国	8	3.7149	苦	8	3.5302
全	6	3.7825	任	6	3.7611
病	10	3.6018	脑	10	3.649
冒	9	3.4953	帮	9	3.78

（续表）

Target character	Number of strokes	Frequency	Substituted character	Number of strokes	Frequency
去	5	3.7953	用	5	3.7939
年	6	3.7818	地	6	3.7932
统	9	3.5231	养	9	3.498
部	10	3.7606	换	10	3.619
人	2	3.7952	十	2	3.6208
虫	6	3.0903	导	6	3.4898
力	2	3.7788	又	2	3.7782
击	5	3.626	本	5	3.7782
争	6	3.5402	早	6	3.7536
命	8	3.7183	定	8	3.7937
产	6	3.5244	多	6	3.7949
业	5	3.6381	功	5	3.5835
策	12	3.1676	量	12	3.6445
划	6	3.6012	场	6	3.7555
史	5	3.4071	生	5	3.795
事	8	3.795	明	8	3.7925
题	15	3.7751	影	15	3.6547
惑	12	3.0993	超	12	3.5835
难	10	3.7735	恶	10	3.6189
惧	11	3.1255	随	11	3.6782
命	8	3.7183	玩	8	3.7439
人	2	3.7952	丁	2	3.1427
律	9	3.4832	茶	9	3.0241
则	6	3.5723	有	6	3.7954
动	6	3.7813	次	6	3.7912

（续表）

Target character	Number of strokes	Frequency	Substituted character	Number of strokes	Frequency
会	6	3.7953	吃	6	3.7398
济	9	3	突	9	3.5491
系	7	3.754	身	7	3.7789
平	5	3.6788	号	5	3.6696
全	6	3.7825	成	6	3.7906
务	5	3.616	训	5	3.3537
令	5	3.5957	可	5	3.7951

Appendix 6: Materials for Experiment 4

Set	Condition	Sentences	Questions
1	1	运动会上班长动员我们积极**参加活动**为班级争光。	NA
1	2	运动会上班长动员我们积极**参加比赛**为班级争光。	NA
1	3	张小亮希望自己能通过经常**参加活动**来丰富经历。	NA
1	4	张小亮希望自己能通过经常**参加比赛**来丰富经历。	NA
2	1	内心脆弱的她因为无法**承受压力**彻底崩溃了。	她很坚强吗？
2	2	内心脆弱的她因为无法**承受痛苦**彻底崩溃了。	她很坚强吗？
2	3	和那些人的聊天让李瑞**承受压力**变得很烦躁。	李瑞喜欢和那些人聊天吗？
2	4	和那些人的聊天让李瑞**承受痛苦**变得很烦躁。	李瑞喜欢和那些人聊天吗？

（续表）

Set	Condition	Sentences	Questions
3	1	离婚后他和前妻彻底**断绝关系**不再联系了。	他离婚了吗？
3	2	离婚后他和前妻彻底**断绝来往**不再联系了。	他离婚了吗？
3	3	陈娜娜已经和董小伟**断绝关系**成了陌路人。	陈娜娜和董小伟是好朋友吗？
3	4	陈娜娜已经和董小伟**断绝来往**成了陌路人。	陈娜娜和董小伟是好朋友吗？
4	1	美国航天局明年将向金星**发射火箭**执行探测任务。	美国明年将探测金星吗？
4	2	美国航天局明年将向金星**发射卫星**执行探测任务。	美国明年将探测金星吗？
4	3	朝鲜近些年曾多次在东海**发射火箭**但都没有成功。	朝鲜的卫星发射成功了吗？
4	4	朝鲜近些年曾多次在东海**发射卫星**但都没有成功。	朝鲜的卫星发射成功了吗？
5	1	前面危险路段经常**发生事故**要小心驾驶。	NA
5	2	前面危险路段经常**发生意外**要小心驾驶。	NA
5	3	陈国华说他在这里**发生事故**失去了双腿。	NA
5	4	陈国华说他在这里**发生意外**失去了双腿。	NA
6	1	听轻音乐能**放松心情**减轻压力。	听轻音乐能让人放松吗？
6	2	听轻音乐能**放松警惕**减轻压力。	听轻音乐能让人放松吗？
6	3	陈斌希望我**放松心情**好好休息。	陈斌想让我去运动吗？

（续表）

Set	Condition	Sentences	Questions
6	4	陈斌希望我**放松警惕**好好休息。	陈斌想让我去运动吗？
7	1	当建筑工程质量不**符合要求**时应返工重做。	NA
7	2	当建筑工程质量不**符合条件**时应返工重做。	NA
7	3	我们都认为李晓冰**符合要求**能担任小组长。	NA
7	4	我们都认为李晓冰**符合条件**能担任小组长	NA
8	1	苹果公司投入大量资金用于**开发产品**吸引顾客。	NA
8	2	苹果公司投入大量资金用于**开发资源**吸引顾客。	NA
8	3	据说他们公司打算未来两年**开发产品**积累资产。	NA
8	4	据说他们公司打算未来两年**开发资源**积累资产。	NA
9	1	在深山中他用大砍刀为我们**开辟道路**探查方向。	NA
9	2	在深山中他用大砍刀为我们**开辟路线**探查方向。	NA
9	3	在研讨会上他的理论为我们**开辟道路**指明方向。	NA
9	4	在研讨会上他的理论为我们**开辟路线**指明方向。	NA
10	1	从不同的角度**看待问题**会有不同的结果。	NA
10	2	从不同的角度**看待事物**会有不同的结果。	NA
10	3	对于我该如何**看待问题**爸爸给了些建议。	NA
10	4	对于我该如何**看待事物**爸爸给了些建议。	NA
11	1	一些企业因效益好想要进一步**扩大规模**做大做强。	NA
11	2	一些企业因效益好想要进一步**扩大生产**做大做强。	NA
11	3	现在林经理他们正在讨论是否**扩大规模**加快发展。	NA
11	4	现在林经理他们正在讨论是否**扩大生产**加快发展。	NA

（续表）

Set	Condition	Sentences	Questions
12	1	有些展馆禁止**拍摄照片**和触碰展品。	所有展馆都可以拍照片吗？
12	2	有些展馆禁止**拍摄电影**和触碰展品。	所有展馆都可以拍电影吗？
12	3	现在章俊正在**拍摄照片**不要去打扰。	章俊正在画画吗？
12	4	现在章俊正在**拍摄电影**不要去打扰。	章俊正在画画吗？
13	1	教授鼓励年轻人勇敢**追求梦想**成就未来。	NA
13	2	教授鼓励年轻人勇敢**追求理想**成就未来。	NA
13	3	李明和他的朋友为了**追求梦想**离开了家。	NA
13	4	李明和他的朋友为了**追求理想**离开了家。	NA
14	1	一个演讲者如果对自己**缺乏自信**肯定讲不好。	NA
14	2	一个演讲者如果对自己**缺乏信心**肯定讲不好。	NA
14	3	王敏并不知道她的儿子**缺乏自信**不敢去比赛。	NA
14	4	王敏并不知道她的儿子**缺乏信心**不敢去比赛。	NA
15	1	年轻人应该为了**实现梦想**去努力一把。	NA
15	2	年轻人应该为了**实现目标**去努力一把。	NA
15	3	我哥哥周峰为了**实现梦想**在北京打拼。	NA
15	4	我哥哥周峰为了**实现理想**在北京打拼。	NA
16	1	老师应从自身做起为学生**树立榜样**起到表率作用。	NA
16	2	老师应从自身做起为学生**树立形象**起到表率作用。	NA
16	3	我们希望李桦能够给大家**树立榜样**认真完成作业。	NA
16	4	我们希望李桦能够给大家**树立形象**认真完成作业。	NA

（续表）

Set	Condition	Sentences	Questions
17	1	为有需要的人**提供帮助**是企业的社会责任。	NA
17	2	为有需要的人**提供资金**是企业的社会责任。	NA
17	3	他不希望我们**提供帮助**他想自己解决困难。	NA
17	4	他不希望我们**提供资金**他想自己解决困难。	NA
18	1	中国队在不利局面下及时**调整状态**从低谷中奋起。	NA
18	2	中国队在不利局面下及时**调整时间**提前开始训练。	NA
18	3	行动开始前指挥官一定要**调整状态**适应任务环境。	NA
18	4	行动开始前指挥官一定要**调整时间**适应任务环境。	NA
19	1	警察在总统大选期间负责**维持秩序**保护安全。	NA
19	2	警察在总统大选期间负责**维持和平**保护安全。	NA
19	3	美国总统决定再次派士兵**维持秩序**稳定社会。	NA
19	4	美国总统决定再次派士兵**维持和平**稳定社会。	NA
20	1	有些企业为了快速发展从国外**引进技术**提升竞争力。	NA
20	2	有些企业为了快速发展从国外**引进人才**提升竞争力。	NA
20	3	陈华经理正在和外方代表商谈**引进技术**等相关事宜。	NA
20	4	陈华经理正在和外方代表商谈**引进人才**等相关事宜。	NA
21	1	这位富豪死后将由他的儿子来**继承财产**并接管公司。	NA
21	2	这位富豪死后将由他的儿子来**继承事业**担任董事长。	NA

（续表）

Set	Condition	Sentences	Questions
21	3	王国华最近在考虑到底让谁来**继承财产**会比较合适。	NA
21	4	王国华最近在考虑到底让谁来**继承事业**会比较合适。	NA
22	1	为了训练记忆力老师常要求学生**背诵课文**默写生字。	学生要写生字吗？
22	2	为了训练记忆力老师常要求学生**背诵诗歌**默写生字。	学生要写生字吗？
22	3	对于刚入学的小学生来说每天要**背诵课文**难度很大。	小学生要背课文吗？
22	4	对于刚入学的小学生来说每天要**背诵诗歌**难度很大。	小学生要背诗歌吗？
23	1	老师讲完课之后给学生**布置作业**巩固知识点。	NA
23	2	老师讲完课之后给学生**布置任务**巩固知识点。	NA
23	3	该系统会自动地在课后**布置作业**并完成批改。	NA
23	4	该系统会自动地在课后**布置任务**并进行检查。	NA
24	1	手机在隧道中不仅能**接收信号**而且信号强。	手机在隧道中有信号吗？
24	2	手机在隧道中不仅能**接收信息**而且速度快。	手机在隧道中能收到信息吗？
24	3	在这个偏远的小村庄**接收信号**非常不容易。	小村庄很容易收到信号吗？
24	4	在这个偏远的小村庄**接收信息**非常不容易。	小村庄很容易收到信息吗？
25	1	王栋辞职后自己**创办公司**当老板了。	王栋当老板了吗？
25	2	王栋辞职后自己**创办学校**当校长了。	王栋当校长了吗？

（续表）

Set	Condition	Sentences	Questions
25	3	据说刘冰林后来**创办公司**做外贸了。	刘冰林做飞行员了吗？
25	4	据说刘冰林后来**创办学校**做教育了。	刘冰林做生意了吗？
26	1	游泳馆配备了柜子让游客**存放物品**安全便捷。	NA
26	2	游泳馆配备了柜子让游客**存放东西**安全便捷。	NA
26	3	陈明丽他们将在那个房间**存放物品**然后离开。	NA
26	4	陈明丽他们将在那个房间**存放东西**然后离开。	NA
27	1	在练习钢琴时老师会及时给她**指出错误**让她改正。	NA
27	2	在练习钢琴时老师会及时给她**指出缺点**让她改正。	NA
27	3	陈乐乐非常希望吴敏能够给她**纠正错误**帮她过关。	NA
27	4	陈乐乐非常希望吴敏能够给她**纠正缺点**帮她过关。	NA
28	1	春节期间不少人去剧院**观看电影**放松心情。	NA
28	2	春节期间不少人去剧院**观看节目**放松心情。	NA
28	3	李莉打算下午和同事去**观看电影**打发时间。	NA
28	4	李莉打算下午和同事去**观看节目**打发时间。	NA
29	1	这位司机曾因酒后**驾驶汽车**受过行政处罚。	NA
29	2	这位司机曾因酒后**驾驶车辆**受过行政处罚。	NA
29	3	为了尽快回去小李**驾驶汽车**很早就出发了。	NA
29	4	为了尽快回去小李**驾驶车辆**很早就出发了。	NA
30	1	殖民者来到岛上后疯狂地**掠夺资源**杀害土著。	NA
30	2	殖民者来到岛上后疯狂地**掠夺财富**杀害土著。	NA
30	3	历史上有很多国家曾为了**掠夺资源**发动战争。	NA

（续表）

Set	Condition	Sentences	Questions
30	4	历史上有很多国家曾为了**掠夺财富**发动战争。	NA
31	1	学生有疑惑时应主动**请教老师**获得解答。	NA
31	2	学生有疑惑时应主动**请教问题**获得解答。	NA
31	3	吴敏一直很胆小不敢**请教老师**寻求建议。	NA
31	4	吴敏一直很胆小不敢**请教问题**寻求建议。	NA
32	1	老韩想承包一片荒山来**种植树木**但他的家人反对。	老韩的家人支持他吗？
32	2	老韩想承包一片荒山来**种植庄稼**但他的家人反对。	老韩的家人支持他吗？
32	3	刘立军如果想要在这里**种植树木**必须要得到批准。	刘立军种树要得到批准吗？
32	4	刘立军如果想要在这里**种植庄稼**必须要得到批准。	刘立军种庄稼要得到批准吗？
33	1	人们总是在犹豫中**丧失机会**接着又很后悔。	NA
33	2	人们总是在犹豫中**丧失自信**不敢往前迈步。	NA
33	3	教练提醒吴伟不要**丧失机会**否则就会输的。	NA
33	4	教练提醒吴伟不要**丧失自信**否则就会输的。	NA
34	1	该车队的任务是给被困地区**输送物资**和转移人员。	NA
34	2	该车队的任务是给被困地区**输送原料**和转移人员。	NA
34	3	他正在思考怎样才能更快地**输送物资**以帮助灾民。	NA
34	4	他正在思考怎样才能更快地**输送原料**以帮助灾民。	NA
35	1	有时需要居委会出面**调解矛盾**使大家和平共处。	NA

（续表）

Set	Condition	Sentences	Questions
35	2	有时需要居委会出面**调解关系**使大家和平共处。	NA
35	3	小明要是能够帮你们**调解矛盾**早就出手帮忙了。	NA
35	4	小明要是能够帮你们**调解关系**早就出手帮忙了。	NA
36	1	社区领导每逢过年过节都会**慰问老人**和看望孤儿。	NA
36	2	社区领导每逢过年过节都会**慰问病人**和看望孤儿。	NA
36	3	我们区的陈小华书记昨天去**慰问老人**后感触良多。	NA
36	4	我们区的陈小华书记昨天去**慰问病人**后感触良多。	NA
37	1	编辑退回稿子希望他进一步**修改文章**并尽快提交。	他投稿了吗？
37	2	编辑退回稿子希望他进一步**修改作文**并尽快提交。	他投稿了吗？
37	3	高三的老师为了帮助同学们**修改文章**很晚才回家。	高三的老师很忙吗？
37	4	高三的老师为了帮助同学们**修改作文**很晚才回家。	高三的老师很忙吗？
38	1	小军识字后可以自己**阅读书籍**不让妈妈读了。	小军识字了吗？
38	2	小军识字后可以自己**阅读文章**不让妈妈读了。	小军识字了吗？
38	3	刘琴经常和儿子一起**阅读书籍**或者听听音乐。	刘琴和女儿一起听音乐吗？
38	4	刘琴经常和儿子一起**阅读文章**或者听听音乐。	刘琴和女儿一起听音乐吗？

Appendix 7: Materials for Experiment 5

Set	Condition	Sentences	Questions
1	1	政府禁止滥砍滥伐有助于**保护自然**维系平衡。	NA
1	2	政府禁止滥砍滥伐有助于**保护生命**维系平衡。	NA
1	3	该市将通过出台高压政策**保护自然**打击犯罪。	NA
1	4	该市将通过出台高压政策**保护生命**打击犯罪。	NA
2	1	卧底在潜伏时要避免**暴露身份**被特务们抓住。	NA
2	2	卧底在潜伏时要避免**暴露缺点**被人抓住把柄。	NA
2	3	王大强不想在公司里**暴露身份**引起老板怀疑。	NA
2	4	王大强不想在公司里**暴露缺点**引起老板怀疑。	NA
3	1	婆媳住在一起久了会**产生矛盾**使家庭不和睦。	婆媳不会有矛盾吗?
3	2	婆媳住在一起久了会**产生想法**使家庭不和睦。	婆媳不会有矛盾吗?
3	3	这件事情使他和林君**产生矛盾**不再做朋友了。	他和林君一直是朋友吗?
3	4	这件事情使他和林君**产生想法**不再做朋友了。	他和林君一直是朋友吗?
4	1	刘华强和朋友决定共同出资**成立公司**做外贸了。	刘华强做老师了吗?
4	2	刘华强和朋友决定共同出资**成立小组**研发产品。	刘华强一个人研发产品吗?
4	3	据说冯明伟已经在他的老家**成立公司**当老板了。	冯明伟当老板了吗?
4	4	据说冯明伟已经在他的老家**成立小组**做销售了。	冯明伟做销售了吗?
5	1	和家人在一起让我**感到幸福**非常开心。	NA
5	2	和家人在一起让我**感到满足**非常开心。	NA
5	3	她一个人生活时会**感到幸福**不会孤独。	NA

（续表）

Set	Condition	Sentences	Questions
5	4	她一个人生活时会**感到满足**不会孤独。	NA
6	1	考试前父母都会**鼓励孩子**增强他们的信心。	NA
6	2	考试前父母都会**鼓励同学**增强他们的信心。	NA
6	3	我们要记住经常**鼓励孩子**让他们更加自信。	NA
6	4	我们要记住经常**鼓励同学**让他们更加自信。	NA
7	1	由于招工困难公司只好在招聘时**降低标准**录用员工。	招工容易吗？
7	2	由于招工困难公司只好在招聘时**降低要求**录用员工。	招工容易吗？
7	3	现在许多纺织品公司会想尽办法**降低标准**减少成本。	纺织品公司想减少成本吗？
7	4	现在许多纺织品公司会想尽办法**降低要求**减少成本。	纺织品公司想减少成本吗？
8	1	圣诞节朋友之间**交换礼物**是一个习俗。	NA
8	2	圣诞节朋友之间**交换物品**是一个习俗。	NA
8	3	小娜和小丽决定**交换礼物**做好朋友了。	NA
8	4	小娜和小丽决定**交换物品**做好朋友了。	NA
9	1	陈丽欣然地**接受邀请**出席了这个典礼。	陈丽出席典礼了吗？
9	2	陈丽欣然地**接受礼物**并原谅了男朋友。	陈丽原谅男友了吗？
9	3	王乐乐最终**接受邀请**参加了这个会议。	王乐乐参加会议了吗？
9	4	王乐乐最终**接受礼物**并与小惠和好了。	王乐乐收到礼物了吗？
10	1	中国女排和巴西女排将**进行比赛**争夺冠亚军。	NA
10	2	中国女排和巴西女排将**进行计划**争夺冠亚军。	NA

（续表）

Set	Condition	Sentences	Questions
10	3	这次是李国强和王俊峰**进行比赛**争夺第一名。	NA
10	4	这次是李国强和王俊峰**进行计划**争夺第一名。	NA
11	1	经历了风雨后他更懂得**珍惜生活**和关爱家人了。	NA
11	2	经历了风雨后他更懂得**珍惜时光**和关爱家人了。	NA
11	3	我们希望小妹以后能够**珍惜生活**和快乐地成长。	NA
11	4	我们希望小妹以后能够**珍惜时光**和快乐地成长。	NA
12	1	美国驻华大使应邀**出席大会**并发表讲话。	NA
12	2	美国驻华大使应邀**出席活动**并发表讲话。	NA
12	3	据说王炳国可能会**出席大会**并发表演讲。	NA
12	4	据说王炳国可能会**出席活动**并发表演讲。	NA
13	1	政府应谨防行业巨头**垄断市场**操纵价格。	NA
13	2	政府应谨防行业巨头**垄断资源**操纵价格。	NA
13	3	政府应明令禁止他们**垄断市场**控制经济。	NA
13	4	政府应明令禁止他们**垄断资源**控制经济。	NA
14	1	防护服可以阻止病毒**侵入人体**破坏免疫系统。	防护服不能阻挡病毒吗？
14	2	防护服可以阻止病毒**侵入身体**破坏免疫系统。	防护服不能阻挡病毒吗？
14	3	崔铭教授说这种东西**侵入人体**后会大量繁殖。	这种东西会繁殖吗？
14	4	崔铭教授说这种东西**侵入身体**后会大量繁殖。	这种东西会繁殖吗？
15	1	他通过不断努力在事业上**取得成功**获得认可。	NA
15	2	他通过不断努力在事业上**取得进步**获得认可。	NA
15	3	赵军在朋友的帮助下终于**取得成功**获得认可。	NA
15	4	赵军在朋友的帮助下终于**取得进步**获得认可。	NA

（续表）

Set	Condition	Sentences	Questions
16	1	吸毒使大脑千疮百孔严重**损伤神经**造成精神障碍。	NA
16	2	吸毒使大脑千疮百孔严重**损伤身体**造成严重后果。	NA
16	3	去年发生的事情使朱小平**损伤神经**留下了后遗症。	NA
16	4	去年发生的事情使朱小平**损伤身体**留下了后遗症。	NA
17	1	小何总是能超额**完成工作**并且保障质量。	NA
17	2	小何总是能超额**完成作业**并且保障质量。	NA
17	3	谢小东打算下午**完成工作**后去看场电影。	NA
17	4	谢小东打算下午**完成作业**后去看场电影。	NA
18	1	异国求学的学生在中秋节格外**想念家乡**是正常的。	NA
18	2	异国求学的学生在中秋节格外**想念亲人**是正常的。	NA
18	3	许多年之后小王依旧难忘当初**想念家乡**时的痛苦。	NA
18	4	许多年之后小王依旧难忘当初**想念亲人**时的痛苦。	NA
19	1	申请贷款的话需要到银行**办理手续**并提供担保。	NA
19	2	申请贷款的话需要到银行**办理业务**并提供担保。	NA
19	3	林萍萍说如果我们在线上**办理手续**可以有优惠。	NA
19	4	林萍萍说如果我们在线上**办理业务**可以有优惠。	NA
20	1	连长正在考虑用什么战术**打败敌人**赢得胜利。	连长想赢得胜利吗？
20	2	连长正在考虑用什么战术**打败对手**赢得胜利。	连长想赢得胜利吗？

（续表）

Set	Condition	Sentences	Questions
20	3	年轻的赵勇希望自己能够**打败敌人**为国争光。	赵勇想为国争光吗？
20	4	年轻的赵勇希望自己能够**打败对手**为国争光。	赵勇想为国争光吗？
21	1	家政工作包括做饭**打扫卫生**和洗衣服。	NA
21	2	家政工作包括做饭**打扫房间**和洗衣服。	NA
21	3	孙丽丽一起床就会**打扫卫生**收拾房间。	NA
21	4	孙丽丽一起床就会**打扫房间**整理床铺。	NA
22	1	为避免这事传出去引起恐慌政府**封锁消息**控制舆论。	NA
22	2	为避免这事传出去引起恐慌政府**封锁道路**不让出城。	NA
22	3	吴玉琳他们都怀疑最近有人故意**封锁消息**制造混乱。	NA
22	4	吴玉琳他们都怀疑最近有人故意**封锁道路**制造混乱。	NA
23	1	魏爷爷爱看老照片**回想过去**感慨青春。	魏爷爷有老照片吗？
23	2	魏爷爷爱看老照片**回想往事**感慨青春。	魏爷爷有老照片吗？
23	3	老曹喝过酒后喜欢**回想过去**感叹时光。	老曹从不喝酒吗？
23	4	老曹喝过酒后喜欢**回想往事**感叹时光。	老曹从不喝酒吗？
24	1	地产公司买下地皮**建造房屋**再高价售出。	NA
24	2	地产公司买下地皮**建造大厦**再高价售出。	NA
24	3	现在各个地方都在**建造房屋**发展房地产。	NA
24	4	现在各个地方都在**建造大厦**发展房地产。	NA

（续表）

Set	Condition	Sentences	Questions
25	1	我邀请女儿的同学过来一起给她**庆祝生日**热闹一下。	女儿一个人过生日吗？
25	2	我邀请女儿的同学过来一起给她**庆祝胜利**热闹一下。	女儿一个人庆祝吗？
25	3	陈雪期待这个周末能和闺蜜一起**庆祝生日**开心地玩。	陈雪一个人过生日吗？
25	4	陈雪期待这个周末能和闺蜜一起**庆祝胜利**开心地玩。	陈雪一个人庆祝吗？
26	1	该俱乐部只为会员**提供服务**并不对外开放。	NA
26	2	该俱乐部只为会员**提供帮助**并不对外开放。	NA
26	3	王琳希望这里可以**提供服务**而且是免费的。	NA
26	4	王琳希望这里可以**提供帮助**把她送回家去。	NA
27	1	情报部门要尽力**搜集资料**以查找恐怖分子。	NA
27	2	情报部门要尽力**搜集证据**来证实这个消息。	NA
27	3	小华现在要拼命**搜集资料**来完成这篇论文。	NA
27	4	小华现在要拼命**搜集证据**证明自己的清白。	NA
28	1	联合国派遣部队前往战乱地区**维护和平**保护平民。	NA
28	2	联合国派遣部队前往战乱地区**维护秩序**保护平民。	NA
28	3	游客们希望当地政府能够共同**维护和平**保障安全。	NA
28	4	游客们希望当地政府能够共同**维护秩序**保障安全。	NA
29	1	笼中鸟总是**向往自由**期待在天空飞翔。	NA
29	2	笼中鸟总是**向往未来**期待在天空飞翔。	NA
29	3	现在的人们**向往自由**都追求诗和远方。	NA

（续表）

Set	Condition	Sentences	Questions
29	4	现在的人们**向往未来**都追求诗和远方。	NA
30	1	据说古人通过观星象**预测未来**和占卜吉凶。	NA
30	2	据说古人通过观星象**预测天气**和占卜吉凶。	NA
30	3	林忠伟一直希望能够**预测未来**并掌握命运。	NA
30	4	林忠伟一直希望能够**预测天气**和占卜运势。	NA
31	1	只要我们团结在一起就一定能**战胜困难**继续前行。	NA
31	2	只要我们团结在一起就一定能**战胜敌人**继续前行。	NA
31	3	几乎所有人都没想到李峰能够**战胜困难**赢得比赛。	NA
31	4	几乎所有人都没想到李峰能够**战胜敌人**赢得胜利。	NA
32	1	为避免聊天时冷场及时**转移话题**非常重要。	NA
32	2	为避免聊天时冷场及时**转移目标**非常重要。	NA
32	3	王峰和他的领导交往时**转移话题**比较谨慎。	NA
32	4	王峰和他的领导交往时**转移目标**比较谨慎。	NA
33	1	对于是否支持工会罢工他还没有**表明态度**给予答复。	他反对罢工吗?
33	2	对于是否支持工会罢工他还没有**表明立场**给予答复。	他反对罢工吗?
33	3	在这种情况下刘仲军不得不立刻**表明态度**以求自保。	刘仲军表态了吗?
33	4	在这种情况下刘仲军不得不立刻**表明立场**以求自保。	刘仲军表态了吗?
34	1	这次考试题目的难度已经**超出想象**高得离谱了。	这次考试题目很简单吗?

（续表）

Set	Condition	Sentences	Questions
34	2	这次考试题目的难度已经**超出范围**高得离谱了。	这次考试题目很简单吗？
34	3	没想到这次客户的要求会**超出想象**真让人无语。	客户的要求很合理吗？
34	4	没想到这次客户的要求会**超出范围**真让人无语。	客户的要求很合理吗？
35	1	军人的职责是**保卫祖国**抵御入侵。	NA
35	2	军人的职责是**保卫国家**抵御入侵。	NA
35	3	小东长大后要**保卫祖国**奉献青春。	NA
35	4	小东长大后要**保卫国家**奉献青春。	NA
36	1	为测量世界屋脊的海拔他们要**攀登高峰**挑战极限。	他们要挑战极限吗？
36	2	为测量世界屋脊的海拔他们要**攀登山峰**挑战极限。	他们要挑战极限吗？
36	3	最近越来越多的成功人士想去**攀登高峰**挑战自己。	他们要挑战自己吗？
36	4	最近越来越多的成功人士想去**攀登山峰**挑战自己。	他们要挑战自己吗？

References

ABBOT-SMITH K, TOMASELLO M, 2006. Exemplar-learning and schematization in a usage-based account of syntactic acquisition[J]. The linguistic review, 23: 275-290.

ANGELE B, RAYNER K, 2011. Parafoveal processing of word n+2 during reading: Do the preceding words matter?[J]. Journal of experimental psychology: human perception and performance, 37: 1210-1220.

ANGELE B, SLATTERY T J, YANG J, et al., 2008. Parafoveal processing in reading: manipulating n+1 and n+2 previews simultaneously[J]. Visual cognition, 16: 697-707.

ARNON I, COHEN PRIVA U, 2013. More than words: the effect of multi-word frequency and constituency on phonetic duration[J]. Language and speech, 56 (3) : 349-371.

ARNON I, SNIDER N, 2010. More than words: frequency effects for multi-word phrases[J]. Journal of memory and language, 62: 67-82.

ASHBY J, RAYNER K, CLIFTON J R, 2005. Eye movements of highly skilled and average readers: differential effects of frequency and predictability[J]. Quarterly journal of experimental psychology, 58A: 1065-1086.

BAAYEN R H, 2008. Analyzing linguistic data: a practical introduction to statistics using R[M]. Cambridge: Cambridge University Press.

BAAYEN R H, DAVIDSON D J, BATES D M, 2008. Mixed-effects modeling with crossed random effects for subjects and items[J]. Journal of memory and language, 59: 390-412.

BADECKER W, 2001. Lexical composition and the production of compounds: evidence from errors in naming[J]. Language and cognitive processes, 16(4) : 337-366.

BAHNS J, 1993. Lexical collocations: a contrastive view[J]. English language teaching journal, 47(1): 56-63.

BAI X, YAN G, LIVERSEDGE S P, et al., 2008. Reading spaced and unspaced Chinese text: evidence from eye movements[J]. Journal of experimental psychology: human perception and performance, 34(5) : 1277-1287.

BALOTA D A, CHUMBLEY J I, 1984. Are lexical decisions a good measure of lexical access? The role of word frequency in the neglected decision stage[J]. Journal of experimental psychology: human perception and performance, 10: 340-357.

BALOTA D A, CORTESE M J, SERGENT-MARSHALL S D, et al., 2004. Visual word recognition of single-syllable words[J]. Journal of experimental psychology: general, 133: 283-316.

BALOTA D A, POLLATSEK A, RAYNER K, 1985. The interaction of contextual constraints and parafoveal visual information in reading[J]. Cognitive psychology, 17(3) : 364-390.

BARFIELD A, GYLLSTAD H, 2009. Researching collocations in another language: multiple perspectives[M]. Basingstoke: Palgrave Macmillan.

BARSALOU L W, 2008. Grounded cognition[J]. Annual review of psychology, 59: 617-645.

BARTSCH S, 2004. Structural and functional properties of collocations in English: a corpus study of lexical and pragmatic constraints on lexical co-occurrence[M]. Tübingen: Narr.

BANNARD C, MATTHEWS D, 2008. Stored word sequences in language learning: the effect of familiarity on children's repetition of four-word combinations[J]. Psychological science, 19: 241-248.

BATES D, MAECHLER M, BOLKER B, 2012. lme4: Linear mixed-effects models using S4 classes: R Package Version 0.999999-0[EB/OL].[2023-6-23]. http://CRAN.R-project.org/package=lme4.

BENSON M, 1989b. The structure of the collocational dictionary[J]. International journal of lexicography, 2(1) : 1-14.

BENSON M, BENSON E, ILSON R, 1997. The BBI dictionary of English word combinations[M]. Amsterdam: John Benjamins.

BIBER D, JOHANSSON S, LEECH G, et al., 1999. Longman grammar of spoken and written English[M]. Harlow, England: Longman.

BINDER K, POLLATSEK A, RAYNER K, 1999. Extraction of information to the left of the fixated word in reading[J]. Journal of experimental psychology: human perception and performance, 25: 1162-1172.

BOD R, 1998. Beyond grammar: an experience-based theory of language[M]. Stanford, CA: Center for the Study of Language and Information Publications.

BOD R, 2006. Exemplar-based syntax: how to get productivity from exemplars[J]. The linguistic review, 23: 291-320.

BOD R, HAY J, JANNEDY S, 2003. Probabilistic linguistics[M]. Cambridge, MA: MIT Press.

BROOKS B A, IMPELMAN D M K, LUM J T, 1981. Backward and forward masking associated with saccadic eye movements[J]. Perception and psychophysics, 30: 62-70.

BROWN R, 1973. A first language[M]. London: Allen & Unwin.

BRYSBAERT M, DUYCK W, 2010. Is it time to leave behind the revised hierarchical model of bilingual language processing after fifteen years of service?[J]. Bilingualism: language and cognition, 13: 359-371.

BRYSBAERT M, BUCHMEIER M, CONRAD M, et al., 2011. The word frequency effect: a review of recent developments and implications for the choice of frequency estimates in German[J]. Experimental psychology, 58(5) : 412-424.

BURNAGE G, DUNLOP D. Encoding the British national corpus[C] // AARTS J, DE HAAN P, OOSTDIJK N, 1992. English language corpora: design, analysis, exploitation. Amsterdam: Rodopi: 79-95.

BYBEE J, BECKNER C. Usage-based theory[C] // HEINE B, NARROW H, 2009. The Oxford handbook of linguistic analysis. Oxford: Oxford University Press: 1-30.

BYBEE J, MCCLELLAND J L, 2005. Alternatives to the combinatorial paradigm of linguistic theory based on domain general principles of human cognition[J]. The linguistic review, 22: 381-410.

BYBEE J, SCHEIBMAN J, 1999. The effect of usage on degrees of constituency: the reduction of don’t in English[J]. Linguistics, 37(4) : 575-596.

BYBEE J, 2001. Phonology and language use[M]. Cambridge: Cambridge University Press.

BYBEE J, 2006. From usage to grammar: the mind's response to repetition[J]. Language, 82: 711-733.

BYBEE J, 1998. The mergent lexicon[J]. Chicago Linguistic Society, 34: 421-435.

CACCIARI C, TABOSSI P, 1988. The comprehension of idioms[J]. Journal of memory and language, 27(6) : 668-683.

CAI Q, BRYSBAERT M, 2010. Subtlex-ch: Chinese word and character frequencies based on film subtitles[J]. Plos one, 5(6) : e10729.

CALVO M G, MESEGUER E, 2002. Eye movements and processing stages in reading: relative contributions of visual, lexical, and contextual factors[J]. The Spanish journal of psychology, 5: 66-77.

CAMBLIN C C, GORDON P C, SWAAB T Y, 2007. The interplay of discourse congruence and lexical association during sentence processing: evidence from ERPs and eye tracking[J]. Journal of memory and language, 56(1) : 103-128.

CAMPBELL E W, WURTZ R H, 1979. Saccadic omission: Why we do not see a gray-out during a saccadic eye movement?[J]. Vision research, 18: 1297-1303.

CARPENTER P A, JUST M A. What your eyes do while your mind is reading[C] // RAYNER K, 1983. Eye movements in reading: perceptual and language processes. San Diego, CA: Academic Press: 275-307.

CARROL G, CONKLIN K, 2014. Eye-tracking multi-word units: some methodological questions[J]. Journal of eye movement research, 7: 1-11.

CARROL G, CONKLIN K, 2015. Cross language priming extends to formulaic units: evidence from eye-tracking suggests that this idea "has legs" [J]. Bilingualism: language and cognition, 20(2): 299-317.

CARROL G, CONKLIN K, 2019. Is all formulaic language created equal? unpacking the processing advantage for different types of formulaic sequences[J]. Language and speech, 63(1) : 95-122.

CARROL G, CONKLIN K, GYLLSTAD H, 2016. Found in translation[J]. Studies in second language acquisition, 38(03) : 403-443.

CARROLL P, SLOWIACZEK M, 1986. Constraints on semantic priming in reading: a fixation time analysis[J]. Memory and cognition, 14(6) : 509-522.

CHEKALUK E, LLEWELLYN K R, 1990. Visual stimulus input, saccadic suppression, and detection of information from the postsaccadic scene[J]. Perception and psychophysics, 48: 135-142.

CHEN H-C, SONG H, LAU W Y, et al. Developmental characteristics of eye movements in reading Chinese[C] // MCBRIDE-CHANG C, CHEN H-C, 2003. Reading development in Chinese children. Westport, CT: Praeger: 157-169.

CHEN H-C, TANG C K, 1998. The effective visual field in Chinese[J]. Reading and writing, 10: 245-254.

CHRISTIANSEN M, CHATER N, 1999. Toward a connectionist model of recursion in human linguistic performance[J]. Cognitive science, 23: 157-205.

CHURCH K, HANKS P, 1990. Word association norms, mutual information, and lexicography[J]. Computational linguistics, 16: 22-29.

CIEŚLICKA A, 2006. Literal salience in on-line processing of idiomatic expressions by second language learners[J]. Second language research, 22(2) : 115-144.

CLARK R, 1974. Performing without competence[J]. Journal of child language, 1: 1-10.

CLEAR J. From Firth Principles: computational tools for the study of collocation[C] // BAKER M, FRANCIS G, TOGNINI-BONELLI E, 1993. Text and technology. Amsterdam: John Benjamins: 271-292.

COLE R A, PERFETTI C A, 1980. Listening for mispronunciations in a children's story: the use of context by children and adults[J]. Journal of verbal learning and verbal behavior, 19(3) : 297-315.

COLLINS A, LOFTUS E, 1975. A spreading-activation theory of semantic processing[J]. Psychological review, 82(6) : 407-428.

CONKLIN K, PELLICER-SÁNCHEZ A, 2016. Using eye-tracking in applied linguistics and second language acquisition research[J]. Second language research, 32(3) : 453-467.

CONKLIN K, SCHMITT N, 2008. Formulaic sequences: Are they processed more quickly than nonformulaic language by native and nonnative speakers?[J]. Applied linguistics, 29: 72-89.

CONKLIN K, SCHMITT N, 2012. The processing of formulaic language[J]. Annual review of applied linguistics, 32: 45-61.

COWAN D G, 2015. Investigating the effectiveness of involvement load in acquisition and retention of ESL learners' collocational knowledge[D]. Australia: The University of Queensland.

COWIE A P, 1981. The treatment of collocations and idioms in learners' dictionaries[J]. Applied linguistics, 2: 223-235.

COWIE A P. Stable and creative aspects of vocabulary use in R[C] // CARTER R, MCCARTHY M, 1988. Vocabulary and language teaching. London: Routledge: 126-139.

COWIE A P. Multiword units in newspaper language[C] // GRANGER S, 1991. Perspectives on the English lexicon: a tribute to Jaquez van Roey. Louvain-la-Neuve: Institut de Linguistiques: 101-116.

COWIE A P. Phraseology[C] // ASHER R E, 1994. The encyclopedia of language and linguistics. Oxford, UK: Pergamon: 3168-3171.

COWIE A P, 1998. Phraseology: theory, analysis, and applications[M]. Oxford: Oxford University Press.

CROFT W, 2001. Radical construction grammar: syntactic theory in typological perspective[M]. Oxford: Oxford University Press.

CROFT W, CRUISE A, 2004. Cognitive linguistics[M]. Cambridge: Cambridge University Press.

CRUTTENDEN A, 1981. Item-learning and system-learning[J]. Journal of psycholinguistic research, 10: 79-88.

CUTTER M G, DRIEGHE D, LIVERSEDGE S P, 2014. Preview benefit in English spaced compounds[J]. Journal of experimental psychology: learning, memory, and cognition, 40: 1778-1786.

DAHLMANN I, ADOLPHS S. Pauses as an indicator of psycholinguistically valid multi-word expressions (MWEs) [C] // GREGOIRE N, EVERT S, KIM S N, 2007. Proceedings of the ACL workshop on a broader perspective on multiword expressions. Prague: Association of Computational Linguistics: 49-56.

DECHERT H. How a story is done in a second language[C] // FAERCH C, KASPER G, 1983. Strategies in interlanguage communication. New York: Longman: 175-

195.

DRIEGHE D, RAYNER K, POLLATSEK A, 2005. Eye movements and word skipping during reading revisited[J]. Journal of experimental psychology: human perception and performance, 31(5) : 954-959.

DEUTSCH A, FROST R, PELEG S, et al., 2003. Early morphological effects in reading: evidence from parafoveal preview benefit in Hebrew[J]. Psychonomic bulletin & review, 10: 415-422.

DEUTSCH A, FROST R, POLLATSEK A, et al., 2005. Morphological parafoveal preview benefit effects in reading: evidence from Hebrew[J]. Language and cognitive processes, 20: 341-371.

DUÑABEITIA J A, PEREA M, CARREIRAS M, 2007. The role of the frequency of constituents in compound words: evidence from Basque and Spanish[J]. Psychonomic bulletin & review, 14: 1171-1176.

DURRANT P, DOHERTY A, 2010. Are high-frequency collocations psychologically real? investigating the thesis of collocational priming[J]. Corpus linguistics and linguistic theory, 6: 125-155.

DURRANT P, 2009. Investigating the viability of a collocation list for students of English for academic purposes[J]. English for specific purposes, 28(3) : 157-169.

DURRANT P, SCHMITT N, 2009. To what extent do native and non-native writers make use of collocations?[J]. International review of applied linguistics, 47: 157-177.

DUYCK W, VAN ASSCHE E, DRIEGHE D, et al., 2007. Visual word recognition by bilinguals in a sentence context: evidence for nonselective lexical access[J]. Journal of experimental psychology: learning, memory, and cognition, 33: 663-679.

EHRLICH S F, RAYNER K, 1981. Contextual effects on word perception and eye movements during reading[J]. Journal of verbal learning and verbal behavior, 20: 641-655.

EL-BIALY R, GAGN´E C L, SPALDING T L, 2013. Processing of English compounds is sensitive to the constituents' semantic transparency[J]. Mental lexicon, 8: 75-95.

ELLIS N, 2002. Frequency effects in language processing[J]. Studies in second language acquisition 24(2): 143-188.

ELLIS N C, 2012. Formulaic language and second language acquisition: Zipf and the phrasal teddy bear[J]. Annual review of applied linguistics, 32: 17-44.

ELLIS N C. Frequency-based accounts of second language acquisition[C] // GASS S, MACKEY A, 2014. The Routledge handbook of second language acquisition. London: Routledge: 193-210.

ELLIS N C, FREY E, JALKANEN I. The psycholinguistic reality of collocation and semantic prosody (1): lexical access[C] // RÖMER U, SCHULZE R, 2009. Exploring the lexis-grammar interface. Amsterdam: John Benjamins: 89-114.

ELLIS N C, SIMPSON-VLACH R, MAYNARD C, 2008. Formulaic language in native and second language speakers: psycholinguistics, corpus linguistics, and TESOL[J]. Tesol quarterly, 42: 375-396.

ELMAN J L, 1990. Finding structure in time[J]. Cognitive science, 14: 179-211.

ENGBERT R, LONGTIN A, KLIEGL R, 2002. A dynamical model of saccade generation in reading based on spatially distributed lexical processing[J]. Vision research, 42: 621-636.

ENGBERT R, NUTHMANN A, RICHTER E, et al., 2005. SWIFT: a dynamical model of saccade generation during reading[J]. Psychological review, 112: 777-813.

ERMAN B, WARREN B, 2000. The idiom principle and the open choice principle[J]. Text, 20(1): 29-62.

EVERT S. Corpora and collocations[C] // LÜDELING A, KYTÖ M, 2008. Corpus linguistics: an international handbook. Berlin, Germany: Walter de Gruyter: 223-233.

FEDERMEIER K D, KUTAS M, 1999. A rose by any other name: long-term memory structure and sentence processing[J]. Journal of memory and language, 41(4) : 469-495.

FEDERMEIER K D, WLOTKO E W, DE OCHOA-DEWALD E, et al., 2007. Multiple effects of sentential constraint on word processing[J]. Brain research, 1146: 75-84.

FILLMORE C. On fluency[C] // FILLMORE C, KEMPLER D, WANG W, 1979.

Individual differences in language ability and language behavior. New York: Academic Press: 85-101.

FINDLAY J M, WALKER R, 1999. A model of saccade generation based on parallel processing and competitive inhibition[J]. Behavioural and brain sciences, 22(4) : 661-674.

FIRTH J R. A synopsis of linguistic theory, 1930-1955[C] // PALMER F R, 1968. Selected papers of J. R. FIRTH. Bloomington: Indiana University Press: 168-205.

FISCHLER I, BLOOM P, 1979. Automatic and attentional processes in the effects of sentence contexts on word recognition[J]. Journal of verbal learning and verbal behavior, 18: 1-20.

FIRTH J R, 1957. Papers in linguistics 1934-1951[M]. London: Oxford University Press.

FORSTER K I, 1981. Priming and the effects of sentence and lexical contexts on naming time: evidence for autonomous lexical processing[J]. Quarterly journal of experimental psychology, 33A: 465-495.

FRENCK-MESTRE C, PRINCE P, 1997. Second language autonomy[J]. Journal of memory and language, 37(4) : 481-501.

FRISSON S, NISWANDER-KLEMENT E, POLLATSEK A, 2008. The role of semantic transparency in the processing of English compound words[J]. British journal of psychology, 99: 87-107.

FRISSON S, RAYNER K, PICKERING M J, 2005. Effects of contextual predictability and transitional probability on eye movements during reading[J]. Journal of experimental psychology: learning, memory, and cognition, 31(5) : 862-877.

RAYNER K, PICKERING M J, 2005. Effects of contextual predictability and transitional probability on eye movements during reading[J]. Journal of experimental psychology: learning, memory, and cognition, 31(5) : 862-877.

GABLASOVA D, BREZINA V, MCENERY T, 2017. Collocations in corpus-based language learning research: identifying, comparing, and interpreting the evidence[J]. Language learning, 67(S1) : 155-179.

GEYKEN A. The DWDS corpus: a reference corpus for the German language of the twentieth century[C] // FELLBAUM C, 2007. Idioms and collocations: corpus-based linguistic and lexicographic studies. London: Continuum: 212-234.

GOLDBERG A, 1995. Constructions: a construction grammar approach to argument structure[M]. Chicago: The University of Chicago Press.

GOLDBERG A E, 2006. Constructions at work: the nature of generalization in language[M]. Oxford: Oxford University Press.

GOLDMAN A, DE VIGNEMONT F, 2009. Is social cognition embodied?[J]. Trends in cognitive sciences, 13(4) : 154-159.

GRANGER S, BESTGEN Y, 2014. The use of collocations by intermediate vs. advanced non-native writers: a bigram-based study[J]. International review of applied linguistics in language teaching, 52: 229-252.

GREENBAUM S, 1974. Some verb-intensifier collocations in American and British English[J]. American speech, 49(1, 2) : 79-89.

GREGORY M, RAYMOND W D, BELL A, et al., 1999. The effects of collocational strength and contextual predictability in lexical production[J]. Chicago linguistic society, 35: 151-166.

GRIES S T, ELLIS N C, 2015. Statistical measures for usage-based linguistics[J]. Language learning, 65: 228-255.

GU B, MIAO X, 1995. A study on the comprehension of Chinese idioms (in Chinese)[J]. Acta psychological sinica, 27: 15-19.

GYLLSTAD H, WOLTER B, 2016. Collocational processing in light of the phraseological continuum model: Does semantic transparency matter?[J]. Language learning, 66 (2): 296-323.

HAKUTA K, 1974. Prefabricated patterns and the emergence of structure in second language acquisition[J]. Language learning, 24: 287-297.

HALLIDAY M A K. Lexis as a linguistic level[C] // BAZELL C E, CATFORD J C, HALLIDAY M A K, 1966. In memory of J. R. Firth. London: Longman: 148-162.

HALLIDAY M A K,1976. System and function in language[M]. Oxford: Oxford University Press.

HALLIDAY M A K, HASAN R, 1976. Cohesion in English[M]. London: Longman.

HAUSMANN F J, 1984. Wortschatzlernen ist kollokationslernen. Zum lehren und lernen französischer wortwendungen[J]. Praxis des neusprachlichen unterrichts,

31(4): 395-406.

HENDERSON J M, FERREIRA F, 1990. Effects of foveal processing difficulty on the perceptual span in reading: implications for attention and eye movement control[J]. Journal of experimental psychology: learning, memory, and cognition, 16: 417-429.

HICKEY T, 1993. Identifying formulas in first language acquisition[J]. Journal of child language, 20(1): 27-41.

HILL J. Revising priorities: from grammatical failure to collocational success[C] // LEWIS M, 2000. Teaching collocation: further developments in the lexical approach. Hove: Language Teaching Publications: 47-69.

HILL J, LEWIS M, 1997. LTP dictionary of selected collocations[M]. Hove: Language Teaching Publications.

HOEY M, 1991. Patterns of lexis in text[M]. Oxford: Oxford University Press.

HOEY M. A world beyond collocation: new perspectives on vocabulary teaching[C] // LEWIS M, 2000. Teaching collocation: further developments in the lexical approach. Hove: Language Teaching Publications: 224-245.

HOEY M, 2005. Lexical priming: a new theory of words and language[M]. New York: Routledge.

HOEY M, 2012. Lexical priming: in the encyclopedia of applied linguistics[M]. Oxford: Blackwell Publishing.

HOHENSTEIN S, KLIEGL R, 2014. Semantic preview benefit during reading[J]. Journal of experimental psychology: learning, memory, and cognition, 40:166-190.

HOHENSTEIN S, LAUBROCK J, KLIEGL R, 2010. Semantic preview benefit in eye movements during reading: a parafoveal fast-priming study[J]. Journal of experimental psychology: learning, memory, and cognition, 36: 1150-1170.

HOOSAIN R. Psychological reality of the word in Chinese[C] // CHEN H-C, TZENG O J L, 1992. Language processing in Chinese. Boston: Elsevier: 111-130.

HOWARTH P, 1998. Phraseology and second language proficiency[J]. Applied linguistics, 19: 24-44.

HUNSTON S, 2002. Corpora in applied linguistics[M]. Cambridge: Cambridge

University Press.
HUTCHISON K, 2003. Is semantic priming due to association strength or feature overlap? a microanalytic review[J]. Psychonomic bulletin & review, 10(4): 785-813.
HYÖNÄ J, BERTRAM R, POLLATSEK A, 2004. Are long compound words identified serially via their constituents? evidence from an eye-movement contingent display change study[J]. Memory and cognition, 32: 523-532.
HYÖNÄ J, OLSON R K, 1995. Eye fixation patterns among dyslexic and normal readers: effects of word length and word frequency[J]. Journal of experimental psychology: learning, memory, and cognition 21: 1430-1440.
INHOFF A W, LIU W. The perceptual span during the reading of Chinese text[C] // CHEN H-C, 1997. The cognitive processing of Chinese and related Asian languages. Hong Kong: The Chinese University Press: 31-41.
INHOFF A W, LIU W, 1998. The perceptual span and oculomotor activity during the reading of Chinese sentences[J]. Journal of experimental psychology: human perception and performance, 24: 20-34.
INHOFF A W, RAYNER K, 1986. Parafoveal word processing during fixations in reading: effects of word frequency[J]. Perception and psychophysics, 40: 431-439.
INHOFF A W, RADACH R, EITER B M, et al., 2003. Distinct subsystems for the parafoveal processing of spatial and linguistic information during eye movements in reading[J]. Quarterly journal of experimental psychology, 56A: 803-827.
INHOFF A W, START M, LIU W, et al., 1998. Eye-movement contingent display changes are not compromised by flicker and phosphor persistence[J]. Psychonomic bulletin & review, 5: 101-106.
JANSSEN N, BARBER H, 2012. Phrase frequency effects in language production[J]. Plos one, 7(3): e33202.
JANSSEN N, CARAMAZZA A, 2011. Lexical selection in multi-word production[J]. Frontiers in language sciences, 2: 81.
JIANG S, JIANG X, SIYANOVA-CHANTURIA A, 2020. The processing of multiword expressions in children and adults: an eye-tracking study of

Chinese[J]. Applied psycholinguistics, 41(4): 901-931.
JIANG N, NEKRASOVA T M, 2007. The processing of formulaic sequences by second language speakers[J]. The modern language journal, 91(3):433-445.
JONES S, SINCLAIR J, 1974. English lexical collocations: a study in computational linguistics[J]. Cahiers de lexicologie, 24(1): 15-61.
JOSEPH H S S L, LIVERSEDGE S P, BLYTHE H I, et al., 2009. Word length and landing position effects during reading in children and adults[J]. Vision research, 49(16): 2078-2086.
JUHASZ B J. The influence of semantic transparency on eye movements during English compound word recognition[C] // VON GOMPEL R G, MURRAY W, FISCHER M, 2007. Eye movements: a window on mind and brain. Boston: Elsevier: 373-389.
JUHASZ B J, POLLATSEK A, HYÖNÄ J, et al., 2009. Parafoveal processing within and between words[J]. Quarterly journal of experimental psychology, 62: 1356-1376.
JUHASZ B J, STARR M, INHOFF A W, et al., 2003. The effects of morphology on the processing of compound words: evidence from naming, lexical decisions, and eye fixations[J]. British journal of psychology, 94: 223-244.
JUHASZ B J, YAP M J, DICKE J, et al., 2011. Tangible words are recognized faster: the grounding of meaning in sensory and perceptual systems[J]. Quarterly journal of experimental psychology, 64(9): 1683-1691.
JURAFSKY D, 1996. A probabilistic model of lexical and syntactic disambiguation[J]. Cognitive science, 20(2): 137-194.
JUST M A, CARPENTER P A, 1980. A theory of reading: from eye fixations to comprehension[J]. Psychological review, 87: 329-354.
KAMBE G, 2004. Parafoveal processing of prefixed words during eye fixations in reading: evidence against morphological influences on parafoveal preprocessing[J]. Perception & psychophysics, 66: 279-292.
KEMMER S, BARLOW M. Introduction: a usage-based conception of language[C] // BARLOW M, KEMMER S, 2000. Usage based models of language. Stanford: Center for the Study of Language and Information Publications: vii-xxviii.

KENNEDY A, PYNTE J, 2005. Parafoveal-on-foveal effects in normal reading[J]. Vision research, 45: 153-168.

KIM S H, KIM J H, 2012. Frequency effects in L2 multiword unit processing: evidence from self-paced reading[J]. Tesol quarterly, 46: 831-841.

KJELLMER G. Aspects of English collocations[C] // MEIJS W, 1987. Corpus linguistics and beyond: proceedings of the seventh international conference on English language research on computerized corpora. Amsterdam: Rodopi: 133-140.

KJELLMER G. A mint of phrases[C] // AIJMER K, ALTENBERG B, 1991. English corpus linguistics. London: Longman: 111-127.

KLIEGL R, ENGBERT R. SWIFT explorations[C] // HYÖNÄ J, RADACH R, DEUBEL H, 2003. The mind's eye: cognitive and applied aspects of eye movement research. Oxford: Elsevier: 391-411.

KLIEGL R, RISSE S, LAUBROCK J, 2007. Preview benefit and parafoveal-on-foveal effects from word n+2[J]. Journal of experimental psychology: human perception and performance, 33: 1250-1255.

KOLERS P A, DUCHNICKY R L, FERGUSON D C, 1981. Eye movement measurement of readability of CRT displays[J]. Human factors, 23: 517-527.

KONG L, ZHANG J X, ZHANG Y, 2016. Are Chinese correlative conjunctions psychologically real? an investigation of the combination frequency effect[J]. Psychological reports, 119: 106-123.

KRASHEN S, SCARCELLA R, 1978. On routines and patterns in second language acquisition and performance[J]. Language learning, 28: 283-300.

KUTAS M, HILLYARD S A, 1980. Reading senseless sentences: brain potentials reflect semantic incongruity[J]. Science, 207: 203-205.

KUTAS M, HILLYARD S A, 1983. Event-related brain potentials to grammatical errors and semantic anomalies[J]. Memory and cognition, 11(5): 539-550.

KUTAS M, HILLYARD S A, 1984. Brain potentials during reading reflect word expectancy and semantic association[J]. Nature, 307(5947): 161-163.

KUPERMAN V, BERTRAM R, BAAYEN R H, 2008. Morphological dynamics in compound processing[J]. Language and cognitive processes, 23: 1089-1132.

KUPERMAN V, SCHREUDER R, BERTRAM R, 2009. Reading polymorphemic Dutch compounds: toward a multiple route model of lexical processing[J]. Journal of experimental psychology, 35: 876-895.

LANGACKER R, 1987. Foundations of cognitive grammar (Vol.1) [M]. Stanford: Stanford University Press.

LANGACKER R W. A dynamic usage-based model[C] // BARLOW M, KEMMER S, 2000. Usage based models of language. Stanford: Center for the Study of Language and Information Publications: 1-64.

LAVIGNE F, VITU F, D'YDEWALLE G, 2000. The influence of semantic context on initial landing sites in words[J]. Acta psychologica, 104: 191-214.

LENTH R, 2017. Emeans: estimated marginal means, aka least-squares means. R package version 0.9.1[EB/OL]. [2023-09-08]. https://CRAN.R-project.org/package=emmeans.

LEWIS M, 1997. Implementing the lexical approach: putting theory into practice[M]. Hove: Language Teaching Publications.

LEWIS M, 2000. Teaching collocation: further developments in the lexical approach[M]. Hove: Language Teaching Publications.

LEWIS M. There is nothing as practical as a good theory[C] // LEWIS M, 2000. Teaching collocation: further developments in the lexical approach. Hove: Language Teaching Publications: 155-185.

Lexicon of common words in contemporary Chinese research team, 2008. Lexicon of common words in contemporary Chinese[M]. Beijing: The Commercial Press.

LIBBEN G, 1998. Semantic transparency in the processing of compounds: consequences for representation, processing, and impairment[J]. Brain and language, 61: 30-44.

LIBBEN M, TITONE D, 2008. The multi-determined nature of idiomatic expressions[J]. Memory and cognition, 36: 1103-1131.

LIEVEN E V M, PINE J M, BARNES H D, 1992. Individual differences in early vocabulary development: redefining the referential-expressive distinction[J]. Journal of child language, 19: 287-310.

LI H, PATERSON K B, WARRINGTON K L, et al., 2022. Insights into the processing of collocations during l2 English reading: evidence from eye movements[J]. Front. Psychol, 13:1-8.

LI H, WARRINGTON K L, PAGAN A, et al., 2021. Independent effects of collocation strength and contextual predictability on eye movements during reading[J]. Language, cognition, and neuroscience 36(8): 1001-1009.

LI X, POLLATSEK A, 2020. An integrated model of word processing and eye-movement control during Chinese reading[J]. Psychological review, 127(6): 1139-1162.

LIU C P, 1999. An analysis of collocational errors in EFL writings. Proceedings of the eighth international symposium on English teaching[M]. Taipei: Crane.

LIU I M, YEH J S, WANG L H, et al., 1974. Effects of arranging Chinese words as units on reading efficiency[J]. Chinese journal of psychology, 16: 25-32.

LI X, GU J, LIU P, et al., 2013. The advantage of word-based processing in Chinese reading: evidence from eye movements[J]. Journal of experimental psychology: learning, memory, and cognition, 39: 879-889.

LI X, POLLATSEK A, 2020. An integrated model of word processing and eye-movement control during Chinese reading[J]. Psychological review, 127(6): 1139-1162.

LI X, RAYNER K, CAVE K R, 2009. On the segmentation of Chinese words during reading[J]. Cognitive psychology, 58: 525-552.

LI X, ZANG C, LIVERSEDGE S P, et al. The role of words in Chinese reading[C] // POLLATSEK A, TREIMAN R, 2015. The Oxford handbook of reading. New York: Oxford University Press: 232-244.

LIU P P, LI J, LIN N, et al., 2013. Do Chinese readers follow the standard rules for word segmentation during reading? [J]. Plos one, 8: e55440.

LIVERSEDGE S P, FINDLAY J M, 2000. Saccadic eye movements and cognition[J]. Trends in cognitive science, 4: 6-14.

LIVERSEDGE S P, HYÖNÄ J, RAYNER K, 2013. Eye movements during Chinese reading[J]. Journal of research in reading, 36: S1-S3.

LIVERSEDGE S P, DRIEGHE D, LI X, et al., 2016. Universality in eye movements and reading: a trilingual investigation[J]. Cognition, 147: 1-20.

LIVERSEDGE S P, PATERSON K B, PICKERING M J. Eye movements and measures of reading time[C] // UNDERWOOD G, 1998. Eye guidance in reading and scene perception. Oxford: Elsevier: 55-75.

LUCAS M, 2000. Semantic priming without association: a meta-analytic review[J]. Psychonomic bulletin & review, 7: 618-630.

LUKA B J, VAN PETTEN C, 2014. Prospective and retrospective semantic processing: prediction, time, and relationship strength in event-related potentials[J]. Brain and language, 135: 115-129.

LUKATELA G, GLIGORIJEVIĆ B, KOSTIĆ A, et al., 1980. Representation of inflected nouns in the internal lexicon[J]. Memory and cognition, 8(5): 415-423.

LYONS J, 1968. Introduction to theoretical linguistics[M]. Cambridge: Cambridge University Press.

MACWHINNEY B. Emergenist approaches to language[C] // BYBEE J, HOPPER P, 2001. Frequency and the emergence of linguistic structure. Amsterdam: John Benjamins: 449-470.

MA G, LI X, RAYNER K, 2015. Readers extract character frequency information from nonfixated-target word at long pretarget fixations during Chinese reading[J]. Journal of experimental psychology: human perception and performance, 41: 1409-1419.

MANNING C, SCHÜTZE H, 1999. Foundations of statistical natural language processing[M]. Cambridge, MA: MIT Press.

MATIN E, 1974. Saccadic suppression: a review[J]. Psychological bulletin, 81: 899-917.

MATLOCK T, HEREDIA R. Understanding phrasal verbs in monolinguals and bilinguals[C] // HEREDIA R, ALTARRIBA J, 2002. Bilingual sentence processing. Amsterdam: Elsevier Press: 251-274.

MATSUNO K, 2017. Processing collocations: Do native speakers and second language learners simultaneously access prefabricated patterns and each single word? [J]. Journal of the European second language association, 1(1): 61-72.

MCCLELLAND J M, O'REGAN J K, 1981. Expectations increase the benefit derived from parafoveal visual information in reading words aloud[J]. Journal of

experimental psychology: human perception and performance, 7: 634-644.
MCCONKIE G W, RAYNER K, 1975. The span of the effective stimulus during a fixation in reading[J]. Perception and psychophysics, 17: 578-586.
MCDONALD J, 2006. Beyond the critical period: processing-based explanations for poor grammaticality judgment performance by late second language learners[J]. Journal of memory and language, 55: 381-401.
MCDONALD S A, SHILLCOCK R C, 2003a. Eye movements reveal the on-line computation of lexical probabilities during reading[J]. Psychological science, 14(6): 648-652.
MCDONALD S A, SHILLCOCK R C, 2003b. Low-level predictive inference in reading: the influence of transitional probabilities on eye movements[J]. Vision research, 43(16): 1735-1751.
MCENERY T, WILSON A, 2001. Corpus linguistics: an introduction[M]. 2nd ed. Edinburgh: Edinburgh University Press.
MCNAMARA T P, 2004. Semantic priming: perspectives from memory and word recognition[M]. New York: Psychology Press.
MEYER D E, SCHVANEVELDT R W, 1971. Facilitation in recognizing pairs of words: evidence of a dependence between retrieval operations[J]. Journal of experimental psychology, 90 (2): 227-234.
MIELLET S, O'DONNELL P J, SERENO S C, 2009. Parafoveal magnification: visual acuity does not modulate the perceptual span in reading[J]. Psychological science, 20: 721-728.
MIELLET S, SPARROW L, 2004. Phonological codes are assembled before word fixation: evidence from boundary paradigm in sentence reading[J]. Brain and language, 90: 299-310.
MILLAR N, 2011. The processing of malformed formulaic language[J]. Applied linguistics, 32(2): 129-148.
MOON R, 1998. Fixed expressions and idioms in English[M]. Oxford: Oxford University Press.
MONDINI S C, LUZZATTI P, SALETTA N, et al., 2005. Mental representation of prepositional compounds: evidence from Italian a grammatical patients[J]. Brain

and language, 94: 178-187.

MORRISON R E, INHOFF A W, 1981. Visual factors and eye movements in reading[J]. Visible language, 15: 129-146.

MORTON J, 1969. The interaction of information in word recognition[J]. Psychological review, 76: 165-178.

NAGY W, SCOTT J A. Vocabulary processes[C] // KAMIL M L, MOSENTHAL P, PEARSON P D, 2000. Handbook of reading research (Vol. 3). Mahwah, NJ: Erlbaum: 269-284.

NATION I S P, 2001. Learning vocabulary in another language[M]. Cambridge: Cambridge University Press.

NATION I S P, 2013. Learning vocabulary in another language[M]. 2nd ed. Cambridge: Cambridge University Press.

NATTINGER J R, DECARRICO J S, 1992. Lexical phrases and language teaching[M]. Oxford: Oxford University Press.

NELSON K, 1973. Structure and strategy in learning to talk[J]. Monographs of the society for research in child development, 149: 1-2.

NESSELHAUF N, 2003. The use of collocations by advanced learners of English and some implications for teaching[J]. Applied linguistics, 24: 2.

NESSELHAUF N, 2005. Collocations in a learner corpus[M]. Amsterdam: John Benjamins.

NEWCOMBE P I, CAMPBELL C, SIAKALUK P D, et al., 2012. Effects of emotional and sensorimotor knowledge in semantic processing of concrete and abstract nouns[J]. Frontiers in human neuroscience, 6: 275.

OPPENHEIM N. The importance of recurrent sequences for non-native speaker fluency and cognition[C] // RIGGENBACH H, 2000. Perspectives on fluency. Ann Arbor: University of Michigan Press: 220-240.

O'REGAN J K. The convenient viewing position hypothesis[C] // FISHER D F, MONTY R A, SENDERS J W, 1981. Eye movements: cognition and visual perception. Hillsdale, NJ: Erlbaum: 289-298.

PACE-SIGGE M, 2013. The concept of lexical priming in the context of language use[J]. International computer archive of modern and medieval English journal,

37: 149-174.

PARTINGTON A, 1998. Patterns and meanings: using corpora for English language research and teaching[M]. Amsterdam: John Benjamins.

PATERSON K, LIVERSEDGE S, UNDERWOOD G, 1999. The influence of focus operators on syntactic processing of short relative clause sentences[J]. The quarterly journal of experimental psychology, 52A: 717-737.

PAWLEY A, SYDER F. Two puzzles for linguistic theory nativelike selection and nativelike fluency[C] // RICHARDS J, SCHMIDT R, 1983. Language and communication. London: Longman: 191-225.

PENG D L, DING G S, WANG C M, et al., 1999. The processing of Chinese reversible words: the role of morphemes in lexical access[J]. Acta psychologica, 31(1): 36-46.

PETERS A M, 1977. Language learning strategies: Does the whole equal the sum of the parts? [J]. Language, 53: 560-573.

PETERS A M, 1983. Units of language acquisition[M]. Cambridge: Cambridge University Press.

PICKERING M J, FRISSON S, MCELREE B, et al. Eye movements and semantic composition[C] // CARRERIRAS M, CLIFTON C, 2004. The on-line study of sentence comprehension: eyetracking, ERPs and beyond. New York: Psychology Press: 33-50.

PIERREHUMBERT J. Exemplar dynamics: word frequency, lenition and contrast[C] // BYBEE J, HOPPER P, 2001. Frequency and the emergence of linguistic structure. Amsterdam: John Benjamins: 137-157.

PINE J M, LIEVEN E V M, 1993. Reanalysing rote-learned phrases: individual differences in the transition to multi-word speech[J]. Journal of child language, 20: 551-571.

PINKER S, 1999. Words and rules: the ingredients of language[M]. New York: Harper-Collins.

PLANCK M, SERENO J A, 1991. Graphemic, associative, and syntactic priming effects at a brief stimulus onset asynchrony in lexical decision and naming[J]. Journal of experimental psychology: learning, memory, and cognition, 17(3):

459-477.

POLLATSEK A, BOLOZKY S, WELL A D, et al., 1981. Asymmetries in the perceptual span for Israeli readers[J]. Brain and language, 14: 174-180.

POLLATSEK A, HYÖNÄ J, BERTRAM R, 2000. The role of morphological constituents in reading Finnish compound words[J]. Journal of experimental psychology: human perception and performance, 26: 820-833.

POLLATSEK A, LESCH M, MORRIS R K, et al., 1992. Phonological codes are used in integrating information across saccades in word identification and reading[J]. Journal of experimental psychology: human perception and performance, 18: 148-162.

POLLATSEK A, REICHLE E D, RAYNER K, 2006. Tests of the E-Z Reader model: exploring the interface between cognition and eye-movement control[J]. Cognitive psychology, 52: 1-52.

POWELL M J D, 2009. The BOBYQA algorithm for bound constrained optimization without derivatives[R]. Cambridge: Report No. DAMTP 2009/NA06, Centre for Mathematical Sciences, University of Cambridge.

R CORE TEAM, 2015. R: a language and environment for statistical computing[M/OL]. Vienna: R foundation for statistical computing. [2023-09-08]. http://www.R-project.org.

RADACH R, KEMPE V. An individual analysis of initial fixation positions in reading[C] // D'YDEWALLE G, VAN RENSBERGEN J, 1993. Perception and cognition: advances in eye movement research. Amsterdam: North-Holland: 213-226.

RADACH R, INHOFF A W, GLOVER L, et al., 2013. Contextual constraint and n+2 preview effects in reading[J]. Quarterly journal of experimental psychology, 66: 619-633.

RAUPACH M. Formulae in second language speech production[C] // DECHERT H W, MOLE D, RAUPAHC M, 1984. Second language productions. Tübingen, Germany: Gunter Narr Verlag: 114-137.

RAYNER K, 1975. The perceptual span and peripheral cues during reading[J]. Cognitive psychology, 7: 65-81.

RAYNER K. Foveal and parafoveal cues in reading[C] // REQUIN J, 1978. Attention and performance VII. Hillsdale, NJ: Erlbaum: 149-162.

RAYNER K, 1998. Eye movements in reading and information processing 20 years of research[J]. Psychological bulletin, 124: 372-422.

RAYNER K, 2009. Eye movements and attention in reading, scene perception, and visual search[J]. Quarterly journal of experimental psychology, 62(8): 1457-1506.

RAYNER K, ASHBY J, POLLATSEK A, et al., 2004. The effects of frequency and predictability on eye fixations in reading: implications for the E-Z Reader model[J]. Journal of experimental psychology: human perception and performance, 30: 720-732.

RAYNER K, BALOTA D A, POLLATSEK A, 1986. Against parafoveal semantic preprocessing during eye fixations in reading[J]. Canadian journal of psychology, 40: 473-483.

RAYNER K, BERTERA J H, 1979. Reading without a fovea[J]. Science, 206: 468-469.

RAYNER K, DUFFY S A, 1986. Lexical complexity and fixation times in reading: effects of word frequency, verb complexity, and lexical ambiguity[J]. Memory and cognition, 14: 191-201.

RAYNER K, DUFFY S A. On-line comprehension processes and eye movements in reading[C] // DANEMAN M, MACKINNON G E, WALLER T G, 1988. Reading research: advances in theory and practice. New York: Academic Press: 13-66.

RAYNER K, FISCHER M H, 1996. Mindless reading revisited: eye movements during reading and scanning are different[J]. Perception and psychophysics, 58: 734-747.

RAYNER K, JUHASZ B J, 2004. Eye movements in reading: old questions and new directions[J]. European journal of cognitive psychology, 16: 340-352.

RAYNER K, JUHASZ B J, BROWN S J, 2007. Do readers obtain preview benefit from word n+2? a test of serial attention shift versus distributed lexical processing models of eye movement control in reading[J]. Journal of experimental

psychology: human perception and performance, 33: 230-245.
RAYNER K, LI X, POLLATSEK A, 2007. Extending the E-Z Reader model of eye movement control to Chinese readers[J]. Cognitive science, 31: 1021-1033.
RAYNER K, MCCONKIE G W, 1976. What guides a reader's eye movements[J]. Vision research, 16: 829-837.
RAYNER K, POLLATSEK A, 1989. The psychology of reading[M]. Englewood Cliffs, NJ: Prentice Hall.
RAYNER K, REICHLE E D, STROUD M J, et al., 2006. The effect of word frequency, word predictability, and font difficulty on the eye movements of young and older readers[J]. Psychology and aging, 21: 448-465.
RAYNER K, SERENO S, MORRIS R, et al., 1989. Eye movements and on-line language comprehension processes[J]. Language and cognitive processes, 4: 21-50.
RAYNER K, SLATTERY T J, DRIEGHE D, et al., 2011. Eye movements and word skipping during reading: effects of word length and predictability[J]. Journal of experimental psychology: human perception and performance 37(2): 514-528.
RAYNER K, WARREN T, JUHASZ B J, et al., 2004. The effects of plausibility on eye movements in reading[J]. Journal of experimental psychology: learning, memory, and cognition, 30: 1290-1301.
RAYNER K, WELL A D, 1996. Effects of contextual constraint on eye movements in reading: a further examination[J]. Psychonomic bulletin & review, 3: 504-509.
RAYNER K, WELL A D, POLLATSEK A, et al., 1982. The availability of useful information to the right of fixation in reading[J]. Perception and psychophysics, 31: 537-550.
RAYNER K, WHITE S J, KAMBE G, et al. On the processing of meaning from parafoveal vision during eye fixations in reading[C] // HYÖNÄ J, RADACH R, DEUBEL H, 2003. The mind's eye: cognitive and applied aspects of eye movement research. Amsterdam: Elsevier Science: 213-234.
REICHLE E D, POLLATSEK A, RAYNER K, 2006. E-Z Reader: a cognitive-control, serial-attention model of eye-movement behavior during reading[J]. Cognitive systems research, 7: 4-22.

REICHLE E D, DRIEGHE D, 2013. Using E-Z Reader to examine skipping during reading[J]. Journal of experimental psychology: learning, memory, and cognition, 39: 1311-1320.

REICHLE E D, POLLATSEK A, FISHER D L, et al., 1998. Toward a model of eye movement control in reading[J]. Psychological review, 105: 125-157.

REICHLE E D, POLLATSEK A, RAYNER K, 2012. Using E-Z Reader to simulate eye movements in nonreading tasks: a unified framework for understanding the eyemind link[J]. Psychological review, 119: 155-185.

REILLY R G, RADACH R, 2006. Some empirical tests of an interactive activation model of eye movement control in reading[J]. Journal of cognitive systems research, 7: 34-55.

REICHLE E D, RAYNER K, POLLATSEK A, 1999. Eye movement control in reading: accounting for initial fixation locations and refixations within the E-Z Reader model[J]. Vision research, 39: 4403-4411.

REICHLE E D, RAYNER K, POLLATSEK A, 2003. The E-Z Reader model of eye movement control in reading: comparisons to other models[J]. Behavioral and brain sciences, 26: 445-526.

RISSE S, KLIEGL R, 2011. Adult age differences in the perceptual span during reading[J]. Psychology and aging, 26: 451-460.

RISSE S, KLIEGL R, 2012. Evidence for delayed parafoveal-on-foveal effects from word n+2 in reading[J]. Journal of experimental psychology: human perception and performance, 38: 1026-1042.

ROBERTS L, SIYANOVA-CHANTURIA A, 2013. Using eye-tracking to investigate topics in L2 acquisition and L2 processing[J]. Studies in second language acquisition, 35: 213-235.

ROBINSON P, ELLIS N C, 2008. A handbook of cognitive linguistics and second language acquisition[M]. London: Routledge.

RUMELHART D, MCCLELLAND J. On learning the past tenses of English verbs[C] // UMELHART D, MCCLELLAND J, 1986. Parallel distributed processing: explorations in the microstructure of cognition. Cambridge, MA: MIT Press: 216-271.

SCHAD D J, ENGBERT R, 2012. The zoom lens of attention: simulating shuffled versus normal text reading using the SWIFT model[J]. Visual cognition, 20: 391-421.

SCHMITT N, UNDERWOOD G. Exploring the processing of formulaic sequences through a self-paced reading task[C] // SCHMITT N, 2004. Formulaic sequences: acquisition, processing, and use. Philadelphia: John Benjamins: 173-189.

SCHOONBAERT S, DUYCK W, BRYSBAERT M, et al., 2009. Semantic and translation priming from a first language to a second and back: making sense of the findings[J]. Memory and cognition, 37: 569-586.

SCHOTTER E R, ANGELE B, RAYNER K, 2012. Parafoveal processing in reading[J]. Attention, perception, and psychophysics, 74(1): 5-35.

SCHOTTER E R, JIA A, 2016. Semantic and plausibility preview benefit effects in English: evidence from eye movements[J]. Journal experimental psychology: learning, memory, and cognition, 42: 1839-1866.

SCHOTTER E R, LEINENGER M, 2016. Reversed preview benefit effects: Forced fixations emphasize the importance of parafoveal vision for efficient reading[J]. Journal experimental psychology: human perception and performance, 42: 2039-2067.

SINCLAIR J, 1991. Corpus, concordance and collocation[M]. Oxford: Oxford University Press.

SINCLAIR J, JONES S, DALEY R, 2004. English collocation studies: the Office of Scientific and Technical Information report[M]. London: Continuum.

SIYANOVA A, SCHMITT N, 2008. L2 learner production and processing of collocation: a multi-study perspective[J]. Canadian modern language review, 64: 429-458.

SIYANOVA-CHANTURIA A, 2015. On the "holistic" nature of formulaic language[J]. Corpus linguistics and linguistic theory, 11(2): 285-301.

SIYANOVA-CHANTURIA A, CONKLIN K, CAFFARRA S, et al., 2017. Representation and processing of multi-word expressions in the brain[J]. Brain and language, 175: 111-122.

SIYANOVA-CHANTURIA A, CONKLIN K, SCHMITT N, 2011. Adding more fuel to the fire: an eye-tracking study of idiom processing by native and non-native speakers[J]. Second language research, 27(2): 251-272.

SIYANOVA-CHANTURIA A, CONKLIN K, VAN HEUVEN W J B, 2011. Seeing a phrase "time and again" matters: the role of phrasal frequency in the processing of multiword sequences[J]. Journal of experimental psychology: learning, memory, and cognition, 37: 776-784.

SIYANOVA-CHANTURIA A, MARTINEZ R, 2015. The idiom principle revisited[J]. Applied linguistics, 36: 549-569.

SCHMITT N, 1998. Quantifying word association responses: What is native-like? [J]. System, 26: 389-401.

SCHMITT N, 2008. Instructed second language vocabulary learning[J]. Language teaching research, 12(3): 329-363.

SONBUL S, 2015. Fatal mistake, awful mistake, or extreme mistake? frequency effects on off-line/on-line collocational processing[J]. Bilingualism: Language and cognition, 18(3): 419-437.

SOSA A V, MACFARLANE J, 2002. Evidence for frequency-based constituents in the mental lexicon: collocations involving the word of[J]. Brain and language, 83: 227-236.

SPRENGER S, LEVELT W, KEMPEN G, 2006. Lexical access during the production of idiomatic phrases[J]. Journal of memory and language, 54: 161-184.

STANOVICH K E, WEST R F, 1983. On priming by sentence context[J]. Journal of experimental psychology: general, 112: 1-136.

STARR M S, RAYNER K, 2001. Eye movements during reading: some current controversies[J]. Trends in cognitive sciences, 5: 156-163.

STAUB A, 2015. The effect of lexical predictability on eye movements in reading: critical review and theoretical interpretation[J]. Language and linguistics compass, 9(8): 311-327.

STUBBS M, 1995. Collocations and semantic profiles: on the cause of the trouble with quantitative studies[J]. Functions of language, 2: 23-55.

STUBBS M, 2001. Words and phrases: corpus studies of lexical semantics[M]. Oxford: Blackwell Publishing.

SUN F, FENG D. Eye movements in reading Chinese and English text[C] // WANG J, INHOFF A W, CHEN H-C, 1999. Reading Chinese script: a cognitive analysis. Mahwah, NJ: Erlbaum: 189-206.

SWINNEY D A, CUTLER A, 1979. The access and processing of idiomatic expressions[J]. Journal of verbal learning and verbal behavior, 18: 523-534.

TABOSSI P, FANARI R, WOLF K, 2009. Why are idioms recognized fast?[J]. Memory and cognition, 37: 529-540.

TAFT M, FORSTER K I, 1975. Lexical storage and retrieval of prefixed words[J]. Journal of verbal learning and verbal behavior, 14(6): 638-647.

TAFT M, FORSTER K I, 1976. Lexical storage and retrieval of polymorphemic and polysyllabic words[J]. Journal of verbal learning and verbal behavior, 15(6): 607-620.

TESNIERE L, 1959. Elements de la syntaxe structurale[M]. Paris: Klincksieck.

TITONE D A, CONNINE C M, 1999. On the compositional and noncompositional nature of idiomatic expressions[J]. Journal of pragmatics, 31(12): 1655-1674.

TOGNINI-BONELLI E, 2001. Corpus linguistics at work: studies in corpus linguistics (Vol. 6) [M]. Amsterdam: John Benjamins.

TOMASELLO M, 2003. Constructing a language: a usage-based theory of language acquisition[M]. Cambridge, MA: Harvard University Press.

TOMASELLO M, 2005. Constructing a language: a usage-based theory of language acquisition[M]. Cambridge, MA: Harvard University Press.

TOMASELLO M, BROOKS P J. Early syntactic development: a construction grammar approach[C] // BARRETT M, 1999. The development of language. Hove, UK: Psychology Press: 161-190.

TOWNSEND D J, BEVER T G, 2001. Sentence comprehension: the integration of habits and rules[M]. Cambridge, MA: MIT Press.

TAYLOR W, 1953. “Cloze” procedure: a new tool for measuring readability[J]. Journalism quarterly, 30: 415-433.

TREMBLAY A, BAAYEN H. Holistic processing of regular four-word sequences: a behavioural and ERP study of the effects of structure, frequency, and probability on immediate free recall[C] // WOOD D, 2010. Perspectives on formulaic

language: acquisition and communication. London: Continuum: 151-173.
TREMBLAY A, DERWING B, LIBBEN G, et al., 2011. Processing advantages of lexical bundles: evidence from self-paced reading and sentence recall tasks[J]. Language learning, 61: 569-613.
TREMBLAY A, TUCKER B V, 2011. The effects of N-gram probabilistic measures on the recognition and production of four-word sequences[J]. The mental lexicon, 6(2): 302-324.
ULLMAN M T, 2001. The neural basis of lexicon and grammar in first and second language: the declarative/procedural model[J]. Bilingualism: Language and cognition, 4: 105-122.
UNDERWOOD G, SCHMITT N, GALPIN A. The eyes have it: an eye-movement study into the processing of formulaic sequences[C] // SCHMITT N, 2004. Formulaic sequences. Amsterdam: John Benjamins: 153-172.
UTTAL W R, SMITH E, 1968. Recognition of alphabetic characters during voluntary eye movements[J]. Perception and psychophysics, 3: 257-264.
VAN LANCKER SIDTIS D. Two-track mind: formulaic and novel language support a dual-process model[C] // FAUST M, 2012. The handbook of the neuropsychology of language. Chichester, UK: Wiley-Blackwell: 342-367.
VENABLES W N, RIPLEY B D, 2002. Modern applied statistics with S[M]. 4th ed. New York: Springer-Verlag.
VESPIGNANI F, CANAL P, MOLINARO N, et al., 2009. Predictive mechanisms in idiom comprehension[J]. Journal of cognitive neuroscience, 22(8): 1682-1700.
VILKAITE L, 2016. Are non-adjacent collocations processed faster?[J]. Journal of experimental psychology: learning, memory, and cognition 42(10): 1632-1642.
VILKAITĖ L, SCHMITT N, 2017. Reading collocations in an L2: Do collocation processing benefits extend to non-adjacent collocations?[J]. Applied linguistics, 40: 329-354.
VITU F, 1991. The influence of parafoveal preprocessing and linguistic context on the optimal landing position effect[J]. Perception and psychophysics, 50: 58-75.
VITU F, O'REGAN J K, INHOFF A W, et al., 1995. Mindless reading: Eye movement characteristics are similar in scanning letter strings and reading texts[J].

Perception and psychophysics, 57: 352-364.
WANG H C, POMPLUN M, CHEN M, et al., 2010. Estimating the effect of word predictability on eye movements in Chinese reading using latent semantic analysis and transitional probability[J]. The quarterly journal of experimental psychology, 63 (7): 1374-1386.
WANG X L, ZHENG W, ZHAO L X, et al., 2019. The role of context in processing Chinese three-character verb-object metaphors: an event-related potential study[J]. Psychological reports, 122(4): 1327-1348.
WANNER L, 2004. Towards automatic fine-grained semantic classification of verb-noun collocations[J]. Natural language engineering, 10(2): 95-143.
WEINERT R, 1995. The role of formulaic language in second language acquisition: a review[J]. Applied linguistics, 16: 180-205.
WHITE S J, BERTRAM R, HYÖNÄ J, 2008. Semantic processing of previews within compound words[J]. Journal of experimental psychology: learning, memory, and cognition, 34: 988-993.
WHITFORD V, TITONE D, 2014. Second-language experience modulates eye movements during first-and second-language sentence reading: evidence from a gaze-contingent moving window paradigm[J]. Journal of experimental psychology: learning, memory, and cognition, 41: 1118-1129.
WOLTER B, GYLLSTAD H, 2011. Collocational links in the L2 mental lexicon and the influence of L1 intralexical knowledge[J]. Applied linguistics, 32: 430-449.
WOLTER B, GYLLSTAD H, 2013. Frequency of input and L2 collocational processing[J]. Studies in second language acquisition, 35: 451-482.
WOLTER B, YAMASHITA J, 2015. Processing collocations in a second language: a case of first language activation? [J]. Applied psycholinguistics, 36: 1193-1221.
WRAY A, 1999. Formulaic language in learners and native speakers[J]. Language teaching, 32(4): 213-231.
WRAY A, 2002. Formulaic language and the lexicon[M]. Cambridge: Cambridge University Press.
WRAY A, 2008. Formulaic language: pushing the boundaries[M]. Oxford: Oxford University Press.

WRAY A, PERKINS M R, 2000. The functions of formulaic language: an integrated model[J]. Language and communication, 20: 1-28.

YAMASHITA J, JIANG N, 2010. L1 influence on the acquisition of L2 collocations: Japanese ESL users and EFL learners acquiring English collocations[J]. Teaching English to speakers of other languages quarterly, 44: 647-668.

YAN M, KLIEGL R, RICHTER E, et al., 2010. Flexible saccade target selection in Chinese reading[J]. The quarterly journal of experimental psychology, 63: 705-725.

YAN M, RICHTER E M, SHU H, et al., 2009. Readers of Chinese extract semantic information from parafoveal words[J]. Psychonomic bulletin & review,16: 561-566.

YAN G, TIAN H, BAI X, et al., 2006. The effect of word and character frequency on the eye movements of Chinese readers[J]. British journal of psychology, 97: 259-268.

YAN M, ZHOU W, SHU H, et al., 2015. Perceptual span depends on font size during the reading of Chinese sentences[J]. Journal of experimental psychology: learning, memory, and cognition, 41(1), 209-219.

YANG H M, MCCONKIE G W. Reading Chinese: some basic eye-movement characteristic[C] // WANG J, INHOFF A W, CHEN H-C, 1999. Reading Chinese script: a cognitive analysis. Mahwah, NJ: Erlbaum Associates: 207-222.

YANG J, WANG S, TONG X, et al., 2012. Semantic and plausibility effects on preview benefit during eye fixations in Chinese reading[J]. Reading and writing, 25: 1031-1052.

YANG J, RAYNER K, LI N, et al., 2012. Is preview benefit from word n+2 a common effect in reading Chinese? evidence from eye movements[J]. Reading and writing, 25: 1079-1091.

YANG J, WANG S, XU Y, et al., 2009. Do Chinese readers obtain preview benefit from word n+2? evidence from eye movements[J]. Journal of experimental psychology: human perception and performance, 35: 1192-1204.

YASSAMI S, 2011. Curious collocations: congruent and non-congruent collocations[M]. Köln: Lambert Academic Publishing.

YI W, LU S, MA G, 2017. Frequency, contingency and online processing of multiword sequences: an eye-tracking study[J]. Second language research, 33: 519-549.

YU L, CUTTER M G, YAN G, et al., 2016. Word n+2 preview effects in three-character Chinese idioms and phrases[J]. Language, cognition and neuroscience, 31: 1130-1149.

ZANG C, 2019. New perspectives on serialism and parallelism in oculomotor control during reading: the multi-constituent unit hypothesis[J]. Vision, 3(50): 1-13.

ZANG C, LIVERSEDGE S P, BAI X, et al. Eye movements during Chinese reading[C] // LIVERSEDGE S P, GILCHRIST I, EVERLING S, 2011. The Oxford handbook of eye movements. Oxford: Oxford University Press: 961-978.

ZANG C, FU Y, BAI X, et al., 2021. The parafoveal processing of Chinese three-character idioms in reading[J]. Journal of memory and language, 119: 104-243.

ZHANG B, PENG D. Decomposed storage in the Chinese lexicon[C] // CHEN H-C, TZENG O J L, 1992. Language processing in Chinese (Vol. 90). Amsterdam: North-Holland: 131-149.

ZHANG J, SHI Y, 2009. The production mechanism of Chinese idioms (in Chinese)[J]. Acta psychologica sinica, 41: 659-667.

ZHANG Y S, 2013. Xiandai hanyu (modern Chinese) [M]. Beijing: China Renmin University Press.

李守纪，2016. 美国留学生词语搭配的偏误分析及其对词语教学的启示[J]，汉语教学研究—美国中文教授学会学报，51(1): 62-78.

吕叔湘，1942. 中国文法要略[M]. 北京：商务印书馆.

吕行，施家炜，2016. 汉语搭配信息对词汇识别的影响[J]. 心理与行为研究，14: 453-458.

宋丹贵，李德高，2019. 汉语双字词常模特征跨词性对比研究[J]. 浙江大学学报（人文社会科学版），49(1): 120-128.

荀恩东，饶高琦，肖晓悦，等，2016. 大数据背景下BCC语料库的研制[J]. 语料库语言学，3(01): 93-109, 118.

余莉莉，2014. 中文熟语认知中的整体加工与成分加工研究[D]. 天津：天津师范大学.

王小潞，程和奔，2021. CFL 视角下的汉字加工神经机制[J]. 外语学刊，(6): 94-101.